T0074782

Artificial Intelligence in Radiation Oncology and Biomedical Physics

This pioneering book explores how machine learning and other AI techniques impact millions of cancer patients who benefit from ionizing radiation. It features contributions from global researchers and clinicians, focusing on the clinical applications of machine learning for medical physics.

AI and machine learning have attracted much recent attention and are being increasingly adopted in medicine, with many clinical components and commercial software including aspects of machine learning integration. General principles and important techniques in machine learning are introduced, followed by a discussion on clinical applications, particularly in radiomics, outcome prediction, registration and segmentation, treatment planning, quality assurance, image processing, and clinical decision-making. Finally, a futuristic look at the role of AI in radiation oncology is provided.

This book brings medical physicists and radiation oncologists up to date with the most novel applications of machine learning to medical physics. Practitioners will appreciate the insightful discussions and detailed descriptions in each chapter. Its emphasis on clinical applications reaches a wide audience within the medical physics profession.

Imaging in Medical Diagnosis and Therapy
Series Editors: Bruce R. Thomadsen and David W. Jordan

Beam's Eye View Imaging in Radiation Oncology
Ross I. Berbeco, Ph.D.

Principles and Practice of Image-Guided Radiation Therapy of Lung Cancer
Jing Cai, Joe Y. Chang, and Fang-Fang Yin

Radiochromic Film: Role and Applications in Radiation Dosimetry
Indra J. Das

Clinical 3D Dosimetry in Modern Radiation Therapy
Ben Mijnheer

Hybrid Imaging in Cardiovascular Medicine
Yi-Hwa Liu and Albert J. Sinusas

Observer Performance Methods for Diagnostic Imaging: Foundations, Modeling, and Applications with R-Based Examples
Dev P. Chakraborty

Ultrasound Imaging and Therapy
Aaron Fenster and James C. Lacefield

Dose, Benefit, and Risk in Medical Imaging
Lawrence T. Dauer, Bae P. Chu, and Pat B. Zanzonico

Big Data in Radiation Oncology
Jun Deng and Lei Xing

Monte Carlo Techniques in Radiation Therapy: Introduction, Source Modelling, and Patient Dose Calculations, Second Edition
Frank Verhaegen and Joao Seco

Monte Carlo Techniques in Radiation Therapy: Applications to Dosimetry, Imaging, and Preclinical Radiotherapy, Second Edition
Joao Seco and Frank Verhaegen

Introductory Biomedical Imaging: Principles and Practice from Microscopy to MRI
Bethe A. Scalettar and James R. Abney

Medical Image Synthesis: Methods and Clinical Applications
Xiaofeng Yang

Artificial Intelligence in Radiation Oncology and Biomedical Physics
Gilmer Valdes and Lei Xing

For more information about this series, please visit https://www.routledge.com/Imaging-in-Medical-Diagnosis-and-Therapy/book-series/CRCIMAINMED

Artificial Intelligence in Radiation Oncology and Biomedical Physics

Edited by
Gilmer Valdes and Lei Xing

CRC Press
Taylor & Francis Group
Boca Raton London New York

CRC Press is an imprint of the
Taylor & Francis Group, an **informa** business

First edition published 2023
by CRC Press
6000 Broken Sound Parkway NW, Suite 300, Boca Raton, FL 33487-2742

and by CRC Press
4 Park Square, Milton Park, Abingdon, Oxon, OX14 4RN

CRC Press is an imprint of Taylor & Francis Group, LLC

© 2023 selection and editorial matter, Gilmer Valdes and Lei Xing; individual chapters, the contributors

ISBN: 9780367538101 (hbk)
ISBN: 9780367556198 (pbk)
ISBN: 9781003094333 (ebk)

DOI: 10.1201/9781003094333

Typeset in Palatino
by codeMantra

To our parents:

Shoushi Xing and Shijing Gao

Gilberto and Mercedes

To our families:

Zhen Shao, Sarah Y. Xing, Samuel S. Xing

Emma and Shenia

Contents

Authors

Dr. Gilmer Valdes earned his PhD in medical physics from the University of California, Los Angeles, in 2013. He was a postdoctoral fellow with the University of California, San Francisco between 2013 and 2014 and a medical physics resident from 2014 to 2016 with the University of Pennsylvania. He is currently an associate professor with dual appointments in the Department of Radiation Oncology and the Department of Epidemiology and Biostatistics at the University of California, San Francisco. His main research focus is on the development of algorithms to satisfy special needs that machine learning applications have in medicine.

Dr. Lei Xing is the Jacob Haimson & Sarah S. Donaldson Professor and Director of Medical Physics Division of Radiation Oncology Department at Stanford University School of Medicine. He also holds affiliate faculty positions in the Department of Electrical Engineering, Biomedical Informatics, Bio-X, and Molecular Imaging Program at Stanford (MIPS). Dr. Xing earned his PhD in Physics from the Johns Hopkins University and his medical physics training at the University of Chicago. His research has been focused on artificial intelligence in medicine, medical imaging, treatment planning and dose optimization, medical imaging, imaging instrumentations, image-guided interventions, nanomedicine, and applications of molecular imaging in radiation oncology. He has made unique and significant contributions to each of the above areas. Dr. Xing is an author of more than 400 peer-reviewed publications, an inventor/co-inventor on many issued and pending patents, and a co-investigator or principal investigator of numerous NIH, DOD, NSF, RSNA, AAPM, Komen, ACS, and corporate grants. He is a fellow of AAPM (American Association of Physicists in Medicine) and AIMBE (American Institute for Medical and Biological Engineering).

Contributors

Sanjay Aneja
Department of Radiology and
    Biomedical Imaging
Yale University School of Medicine
New Haven, Connecticut

Arman Avesta
Department of Radiology and
    Biomedical Imaging
Yale University School of Medicine
New Haven, Connecticut

Carlos Cardenas
Department of Radiation Oncology
The University of Alabama at
    Birmingham
Birmingham, Alabama

Dante P. I. Capaldi
Department of Radiation Oncology
University of California
San Francisco, California

Maria F. Chan
Memorial Sloan Kettering Cancer
    Center
Basking Ridge, New Jersey

Rachel Choi
Department of Dermatology
Yale University School of Medicine
New Haven, Connecticut

Issam El Naqa
Machine Learning
Moffitt Cancer Centre
Tampa, Florida

Jiawei Fan
Department of Radiation Oncology
Fudan University Shanghai Cancer
    Center
Shanghai, China
and
Department of Oncology
Shanghai Medical College Fudan
    University
Shanghai, China
and
Shanghai Key Laboratory of
    Radiation Oncology
Shanghai, China

Weigang Hu
Department of Radiation Oncology
Fudan University Shanghai Cancer
    Center
Shanghai, China
and
Department of Oncology
Shanghai Medical College Fudan
    University
Shanghai, China
and
Shanghai Key Laboratory of
    Radiation Oncology
Shanghai, China

Charles Huang
Department of Radiation Oncology
Stanford University
Stanford, California

Bulat Ibragimov
University of Copenhagen
Copenhagen, Denmark

Xun Jia
Medical Artificial Intelligence and
    Automation (MAIA) Laboratory
Department of Radiation Oncology
University of Texas Southwestern
    Medical Center
Dallas, Texas

Steve Jiang
Medical Artificial Intelligence and
    Automation (MAIA) Laboratory
Department of Radiation Oncology
University of Texas Southwestern
    Medical Center
Dallas, Texas

Paul J. Keall
ACRF Image X Institute, Sydney
    School of Health Sciences
Faculty of Medicine and Health
The University of Sydney
Sydney, Australia

Nataliya Kovalchuk
Department of Radiation Oncology
Stanford University
Stanford, California

Tomi F. Nano
Department of Radiation Oncology
University of California
San Francisco, California

Dan Nguyen
Medical Artificial Intelligence and
    Automation (MAIA) Laboratory
Department of Radiation Oncology
University of Texas Southwestern
    Medical Center
Dallas, Texas

Yusuke Nomura
Department of Radiation Oncology
Stanford University
Stanford, California

Chenyang Shen
Medical Artificial Intelligence and
    Automation (MAIA) Laboratory
Department of Radiation Oncology
University of Texas Southwestern
    Medical Center
Dallas, Texas

Alon Witztum
Department of Radiation Oncology
and
Department of Epidemiology and
    Biostatistics
University of California
San Francisco, California

Daniel X. Yang
Department of Radiation Oncology
University of Texas Southwestern
    Medical Center
Dallas, Texas

Yong Yang
Department of Radiation Oncology
Stanford University
Stanford, California

1

AI Applications in Radiation Therapy and Medical Physics

Issam El Naqa

Machine Learning, Moffitt Cancer Centre

CONTENTS

1.1 Why Artificial Intelligence for Radiotherapy?

Radiotherapy practice represents a complex operational process, which uses heterogeneous amounts of data at every step of its workflow from the initial consultation to treatment planning, to quality assurance, and to delivery that aims to ensure that the patients have received the prescribed radiation treatment safely and accurately. These steps can vary and may involve several stages of

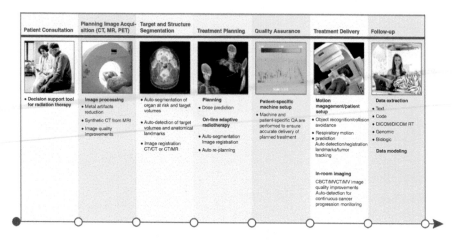

FIGURE 1.1
The schematics highlights the AI role in radiation oncology [2].

sophisticated human–machine interactions (HCIs) and decision making (DM) such as chart review, machine and patient quality assurances, tumour/organ contouring, treatment planning, image guidance, respiratory motion management, response modelling, and outcomes prediction. This experience grows with every newly treated patient creating a wealth of information. This is coupled with the error-averse nature of radiotherapy practice, which makes it an ideal candidate for leveraging artificial intelligence (AI) unique capabilities [1].

The potential application of AI along the workflow of radiotherapy is depicted in Figure 1.1 [2]. It is noted that AI can play a dual role in radiotherapy, which includes (1) automation of its processes and (2) predictive analytics for optimizing decision making.

1.1.1 Automation Applications of AI in Radiotherapy

This has been an area of tremendous growth and it includes many examples such as

- Auto-contouring (segmentation). The (auto)-segmentation of organs, tissues, and the targeted cancer is a major hindrance in terms of treatment planning efficiency. The availability of such AI tools can reduce this burden significantly and accelerate radiotherapy practice [3–24].

- Dose prediction is another important area where AI can improve the efficiency of radiotherapy and mitigate prior authorization delays by substituting complex physics calculations with direct predictive models of irradiation dose [25–27].

- Knowledge-based treatment planning [28–34] is an important application for mitigating common errors or mistakes level performance for disadvantaged settings with limited resources and can further provide expert input to under-served communities.

- Radiation physics (machine or patient) quality assurance (QA) to improve safe radiation administration [35–40].
- Motion management (respiratory or cardiac) during radiation delivery [41,42] to enhance tumour targeting and limit uninvolved tissue radiation exposure.
- *Predictive analytics in radiotherapy:*

As in the case of automation, this area is undergoing tremendous progress too with examples including

- Image guidance [43,44] to ensure that the treatment planning objectives of tumour targeting and normal tissue avoidance are maintained throughout the course.
- Response modelling of treatment outcomes such as tumour control or toxicities [45–52].
- Treatment adaptation to account for geometrical changes [53] or adapting prescription to improve outcomes [54,55].

Details about these and other AI applications in radiotherapy are reviewed in the literature [1,56] and sample examples are discussed in subsequent sections.

1.2 AI in Radiotherapy

Historically, AI applications in radiotherapy trace their origins to the mid-1990s by training artificial neural networks (ANNs) for automating treatment planning evaluation [57], beam orientation customization [58], or standardization (knowledge-based planning) [59], to name a few examples. Later applications in the mid-2000s focused on predicting normal tissue complications probability (NTCP) in different treatment sites [60–62].

As noted earlier, a key motivation for AI in radiotherapy is driven by its own nature, which involves a large set of processes spanning consultation to treatment with a large amount of information, human–machine interactions, optimization, and decision making. AI methods can offer two main characteristics that can aid radiotherapy practice:

1. Identifying data patterns and complex relationships among variables and processes.
2. The ability to generalize unseen experiences and perform quasi-auto nomously.

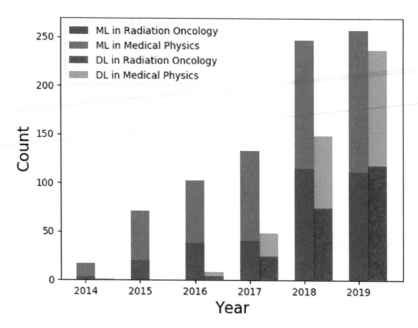

FIGURE 1.2
Frequency counts of published PubMed studies in radiotherapy/medical physics by ML/DL techniques [63].

This potential is highlighted in the exponential growth of AI applications in radiotherapy whether using conventional machine learning (ML) algorithms or more recent deep learning (DL) techniques, as summarized in Figure 1.2 [63].

1.3 Sample Applications of AI in Radiotherapy

As mentioned earlier, the application of AI in radiotherapy can be broadly categorized into automating processes or predictive analytics. Sample examples of each category will be presented in the following sections.

1.3.1 AI for Radiotherapy Automation

1.3.1.1 Autocontouring (Segmentation)

The premise of auto-contouring is that AI tools would allow significant saving of time given the laborious nature of this process. Although this was an active area for many years in radiotherapy using basic computer vision and image processing techniques [64–67], recent methods have focused more on DL technologies. For instance, Ibragimov and Xing presented an approach based on convolutional neural network (CNN) algorithms followed by Markov fields, with respect to head and neck cancer cases [68]. This task was extended by the Google deepMind group using 3D U-Net architectures that achieved performance similar to experts in delineating a wide range of head and neck organs-at-risk [69], as shown in Figure 1.3.

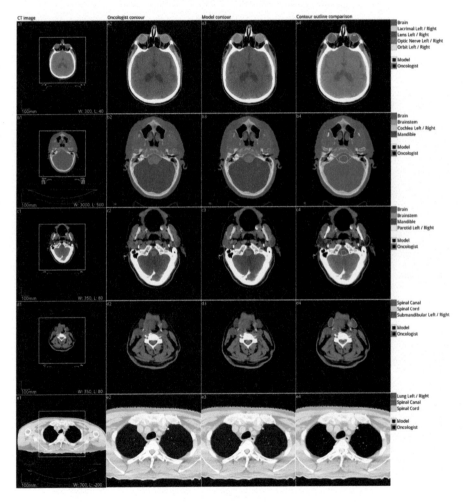

FIGURE 1.3
Sample results of U-Net segmentation of head and neck cancer compared to oncologist delineation of different OARs [69]. The approach achieved superior performance when compared with the other published results.

1.3.1.2 Knowledge-Based Planning

Knowledge-based RT planning (KBP) as a tool for improving planning quality and consistency among practitioners has achieved notable successes [70,71]. However, existing systems still require a human expert's definition of optimization constraints and priority weighing with explicit information about the field parameters [72,73]. New approaches based on DL seem to bypass this problem by direct prediction of the radiation dose. The potentials of these approaches have been demonstrated, for example, using 3D U-Net and DenseNet to predict 3D distributions in cancers of the prostate, head, and neck [74–76], an example is shown in Figure 1.4.

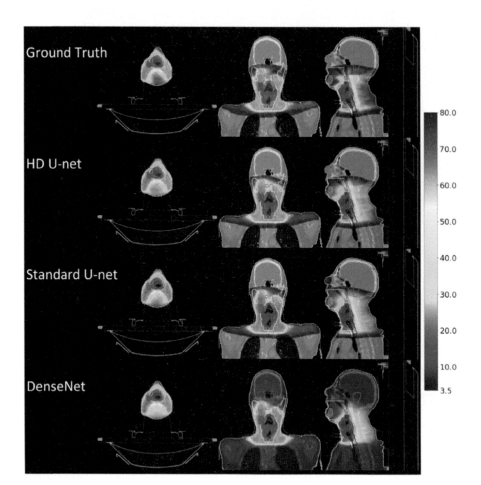

FIGURE 1.4
Example of 3D dose prediction using deep learning [76].

1.3.1.3 Quality Assurance and Error Detection

Quality assurance (QA) in radiotherapy is essential to ensure the safe delivery of treatment as prescribed. It typically follows the guidelines of national and international bodies (AAPM, ASTRO, ACR, ESTRO, and IAEA). For instance, the task group (TG) report TG-40 and its updated version TG-142 have provided a comprehensive QA program for institutional radiation oncology practice accounting for potential risks during the planning and delivery of high energy irradiation, harmonizing the treatment of patients, and accommodating new advances in technology. It is recognized that such errors are rare events with no well-defined characteristics, which would make the traditional two-class classification with ML intractable mathematically due to a large imbalance. Therefore, an alternative approach is to use a one-class classifier by recognizing that there is one class in the data (say, normal performance), while everything else is considered an outlier or anomaly. One approach to address this problem is by modelling the domain support, i.e., the region where the model is nonzero and outside it would be considered an anomaly (outlier). An example application is shown in Figure 1.5.

Using a support vector machine (SVM) formalism, the data are first mapped into a feature space using an appropriate kernel function (e.g., linear, polynomials and Gaussian functions) and then maximally separated from the origin using a proper hyperplane as shown in Figure 1.5. Using a dataset of lung cancer patients who received stereotactic body radiation therapy (SBRT) as part of their treatment, features related to monitor units (MUs), beam energies (MV), the number of beams, the number of fractions, in addition to the percentage lung volume receiving 20 Gy were extracted from the DICOM files and were used to train the QA-SVM detector. A combination of cases for testing were considered "safe" and assigned class label "+1", and a set of randomly simulated cases were considered "unsafe" by adding different levels of white Gaussian noise to the data [1]. The results indicated that a training accuracy on cross-validation of 84% could be attained and a testing

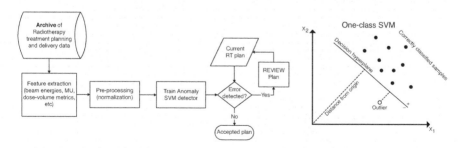

FIGURE 1.5
An error detection system for radiotherapy. (a) Application to RT planning. (b) SVM one-class formalism, where a hyperplane in the feature space $[x_1, x_2]$ separates correct samples (closed circles) from outliers (open circles) by maximizing the distance from the origin.

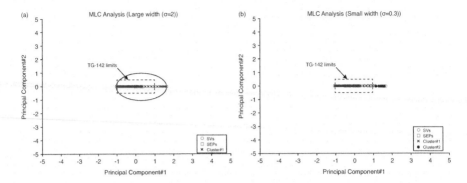

FIGURE 1.6
MLC shift analysis using SVDD clustering, principal components 1 and 2 correspond to LoC and transmission, respectively, with the dashed rectangle representing TG-142 limits. (a) Using a large Gaussian kernel width ($\sigma=2$), it is noted that the cluster encloses all measurements, with the circles showing the support vectors (boundary points). (b) Using a small Gaussian kernel width ($\sigma=0.3$), it is noted the presence of two regions (clusters) in the data in the LoC direction.

accuracy of 80% with 100% true positive prediction and 80% true negative prediction. In a more recent application, a support vector data description (SVDD) approach that doesn't require any labelling of the data was evaluated for machine (Linac) quality assurance using multi-institutional data of EPID images of a phantom with fiducials that provided deviation estimates between the radiation field and phantom centre at four cardinal gantry angles [36]. The algorithm was able to estimate errors that coincided with TG-142 limits and at instances exceeded that. Sample results for Leaf offset Constancy (LoC) are shown in Figure 1.6.

1.3.2 AI for Radiotherapy Predictive Analytics

1.3.2.1 Outcome Modelling

Treatment responses in radiotherapy are mainly characterized as tumour control probability (TCP) and normal tissues complication probability (NTCP), which should be maximized/minimized, respectively, to achieve desired outcomes. These models could be used during the consultation period as a guide for ranking treatment options or designing clinical decision support systems for future clinical trials. There are many methods in radiotherapy for modelling outcomes including data-driven approaches based on machine learning [77].

As an example, for machine learning outcome modelling, we will consider the application of generative (e.g., Bayesian networks) and discriminant (e.g., neural networks) models with a dataset of about 120 non-small cell lung cancer (NSCLC) patients who received radiotherapy.

Bayesian networks (BNs) are probabilistic graphical models that represent a set of biophysical variables and their conditional dependencies via a directed acyclic graph [78]. BNs are also called belief networks, where, in a graphical representation, each node represents a random variable and the edges between the nodes represent probabilistic dependencies among the interacting random variables, analogous to using nomograms for representing linear/logistic models in traditional statistical analyses. Due to their versatility and transparent nature, BNs have been widely used for modelling clinical endpoints in radiotherapy and in other domains [79,80]. BNs have also been shown to provide superior performance over traditional statistical regression methods when dealing with complex data as in radiotherapy outcomes [81]. For example, a dataset that included genetic markers (single nucleotide polymorphisms [SNPs] and microRNA) combined with clinical, dosimetric, and cytokine variables was used to generate BN models of tumour control (LC) and radiation pneumonitis (RP). An extended Markov blanket (MB) was used to identify the relevant predictors for the network. A metaheuristic search algorithm (Tabu) was applied to generate candidate BNs. The search was recursively applied to bootstrap samples to avoid overfitting pitfalls and identify the optimal structure. The performance of the resulting BN was evaluated internally using area under the receiver operating characteristics curve (AUC) on cross-validation and externally. This approach was applied for RP modelling, yielding a pre-treatment prediction AUC=0.82, which is improved by incorporating during treatment cytokine changes to an impressive AUC=0.87 on cross-validation. In the testing dataset, the pre- and during AUCs were 0.78 and 0.82, respectively [82]. A similar analysis was conducted for local control, where radiomics imaging features were added to the BN model. The resulting pre-treatment BN had an AUC=0.81, which is improved by incorporating during treatment cytokine/radiomics changes to an AUC=0.84. In the testing dataset, the pre- and during AUC values were 0.77 and 0.79, respectively, outperforming random forests (AUC=0.63). In contrast, using clinical/dosimetric metrics, as clinically practiced, yielded only AUCs of 0.67 and 0.61 for RP and local control, respectively. Recently, we demonstrated that a joint BN of LC/RP could be developed with AUCs of 0.80 and 0.85 for pre- and during, respectively, outperforming individual LC/RP networks while accounting for cross-talks as shown in Figure 1.7 [83]. In the testing dataset, the pre- and during AUC values were 0.77 and 0.79, respectively.

As opposed to the generative approaches, which would require knowledge of the system characteristics, discriminant methods, particularly based on deep learning, are garnering more attention. Using the same data, a DL-based outcome model *ADNN-com-joint* was adopted to jointly predict LC and RP in NSCLC patients after radiotherapy [84]. Specifically, patient-specific biological data (SNPs and cytokines), imaging data including radiomics features extracted from tumour PET images, as well as dosimetric data including dose-volume histogram (DVH) of GTV and lung were integrated

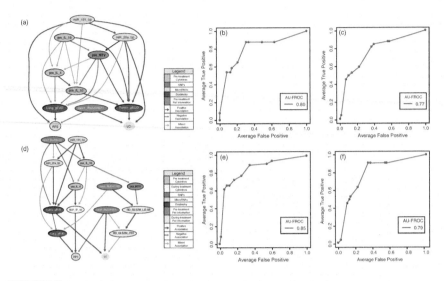

FIGURE 1.7

Top shows pre-treatment joint BN modelling of local control and RP. (a) BN structure. ROC analysis on (b) cross-validation and (c) external testing. Bottom shows during-treatment joint BN modelling. (d) BN structure. ROC analysis on (e) cross-validation and (f) external testing. This shows the novel BN ability to model competing risks.

into a composite neural network (NN) architecture to jointly predict LC/RP, as shown in Figure 1.8a. In this composite architecture, variational auto-encoders (VAEs) were adopted to reduce the dimensionality and learn the latent representation of the input biological and imaging data, and a 1D CNN was applied to the DVH input to account for the associations among adjacent pixels. The extracted representation of biological, imaging, and dosimetric data is then concatenated and fed into a Surv-net, which predicted the conditional event probability through discretized time intervals. The model and its variants were validated following the TRIPOD criteria [85] through both internal (TRIPOD level 2 – types a and b) and external validation (TRIPOD type 3), as shown in Figure 1.8b.

1.3.2.2 Knowledge-Based Adaptive Radiotherapy

In addition to predicting outcomes, a clinical decision support system would require the ability to optimize decision making [86]. Knowledge-based, response-adapted radiotherapy (KBR-ART) is an emerging area for radiation oncology personalized treatment [55]. In KBR-ART, planned dose distributions can be modified based on observed cues in patients' clinical, geometric, and physiological parameters. In a subpopulation of the previously mentioned NSCLC, FDG-avid region detected by mid-treatment positron PET was used for dose escalation and shown to improve local tumour control

(a)

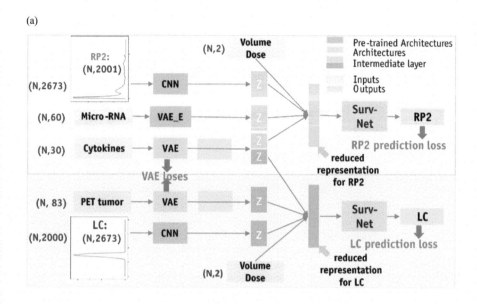

(b)

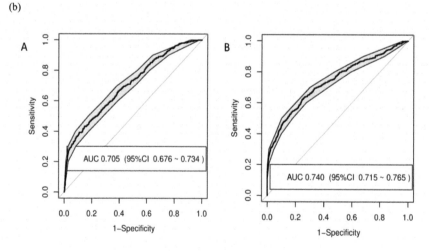

FIGURE 1.8
(a) Architecture ADNN-com-joint, which realizes the actuarial prediction of RP2 and LC. Abbreviations: CNN, convolutional neural network; DVH, dose-volume histogram; PET, positron emission tomography; VAE, variational encoder. (b) Prediction results of LC and RP [84].

at a two-year follow-up [87]. However, the dose adaptation in the study was based on the clinician's subjective assessment. Alternatively, to objectively assess the adaptive dose per fraction, a three-component deep reinforcement learning (DRL) approach with the neural network architecture was developed. The architecture was composed of (1) a generative adversarial network

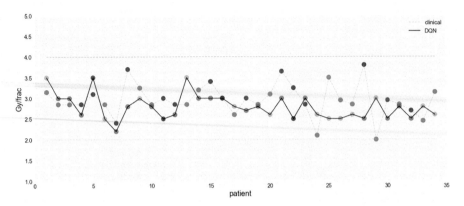

FIGURE 1.9
A deep RL for automated radiation adaptation in lung cancer. Deep Q-network (DQN) (black solid line) vs. clinical decision (blue dashed line) with RMSE error=0.5 Gy. Evaluation against eventual outcomes of good (green dots), bad (red dots), and potentially good decisions (orange dots) are shown suggesting not only comparable but also at instances better overall performance by the DQN [54].

(GAN) to learn patient population characteristics necessary for DRL training from a relatively limited sample size; (2) a radiotherapy artificial environment (RAE) reconstructed by a deep neural network (DNN) utilizing both original and synthetic data (by GAN) to estimate the transition probabilities for adaptation of personalized radiotherapy patients' treatment courses; and (3) a deep Q-network (DQN) applied to the RAE for choosing the optimal dose in a response-adapted treatment setting. The DRL was trained on large-scale patient characteristics including clinical, genetic, and imaging radiomics features in addition to tumour and lung dosimetric variables. In comparison with the clinical protocol [87], the DRL achieved a root-mean-squared error (RMSE)=0.5 Gy for dose escalation recommendation. Interestingly, the DRL seemed to suggest better decisions than the clinical ones in terms of mitigating toxicity risks and improving local control as seen in Figure 1.9 [54].

1.4 Challenges for AI in Radiotherapy and Recommendations

1.4.1 Dataset Requirements

AI training requires the availability of large and diverse data resources, which could be restricted in the medical clinical domain due to various patient privacy-related concerns, institutional restrictions, and unavailability of standardized data, all of this has limited clinical translation [88]. Recently, there has been an extensive effort to learn localized data from multiple sources using a federated learning (FL) setting that encourages decentralized learning [89]. This FL approach ensures data safety by only sharing mathematical parameters (or metadata) and not the actual data. In other words, FL algorithms iteratively analyse separate databases and return the same solution as if the data were centralized, essentially sharing research inquiries and answers between databases instead of data [89]. The advantages of FL have been demonstrated in many biomedical studies [90], including brain tumour segmentations [91,92], breast density classification [93], and in predicting radiotherapy outcomes [94,95].

1.4.2 Validation of AI Models

Retrospective validation evaluates the outcome model on the past treatments in patients who were not pre-selected for the treatment regimen in question, e.g., those recommended by the outcome models [85]. It can provide evidence to base a change in clinical practice and provide insight into designing a new clinical protocol or prospective study. More recently, a checklist for AI/ML applications in Medical Physics (CLAMP) [96] has been published to ensure rigorous and reproducible research of AI/ML in the field of medical physics and, by extension, in radiation oncology. However, recent evidence suggests that retrospective validation alone may not be adequate, especially in scenarios that require complex decision making. Moreover, physician interaction with AI algorithms seems to vary from simulated study to clinical practice. Hence, there may be a need for prospective validation strategies to evaluate a pre-existing outcome model on the newly collected data from a prospective clinical trial [97]. The validation can be conducted directly, i.e., the predictive performance of the outcome model is evaluated on patients enrolled in the new study.

1.4.3 Interpretability and Explainability

The interpretability and explainability of AI algorithms are also crucial for the transition of AI-based outcome models into clinics, as clinical implementation may require considering human–machine interactions in a practical setting [98]. Interpretability is a weaker concept than explainability, which requires a comprehensive explanation of the underlying mechanism of the model. Interpretability only requires that clinicians can discern the prediction in a scientifically sound manner without going into the details of the mechanism of the model. There are two types of interpretable methods, model-specific methods that target a specific group of models and agnostic models that can be applied to any AI model. Specific efforts have been made to improve the interpretability of DL methods. There are two types of popular methods: gradient-based backpropagation methods, e.g., class activation map (CAM) [99] and grad-CAM [100] as well as perturbation-based forward propagation methods. For instance, Wei et al. applied a combination of VAEs and CNNs to identify a new radiomics signature using imaging phenotypes and clinical variables for risk prediction of overall survival in hepatocellular carcinoma patients, as shown in Figure 1.10a. The model showed significantly better performance than traditional models. For model interpretation, grad-CAM was used to identify regions in the normal liver of high-risk patients, as shown in Figure 1.10b.

However, this could be more challenging to visualize in the case of multi-omics data (Figure 1.8), and prior knowledge along with grad-CAM were applied to generate a visual representation of the outcome models in Figure 1.11. For instance, dose regions near 20 Gy in DVHs were highlighted in grad-CAM for the prediction of RP2 (Figure 1.11a). Cytokines were found to contribute more to RP2 prediction compared to LC prediction. And PET image features were found to contribute to discriminating LC (Figure 1.11b), as would be expected.

1.4.4 Quality Assurance

A formal risk analysis assessment may be valuable to design a quality assurance program appropriate to the AI algorithms. These risks vary depending on whether or not the AI algorithm is embedded within another system such as the treatment planning system or if the algorithm is running independently with information exported from other systems. A review of QA programs for AI and different use cases was conducted in [101]. The emphasis is on using the QA effort to ensure treatments are delivered accurately, safely, and efficiently according to established tests and evaluations. It can be invaluable to use a subset of commissioning tests for performing periodic QA of AI techniques. Such QA can be used to monitor the performance of the algorithm at regular intervals as part of a continuous program that can also assess issues related to data shifts or changes in practice that may affect the algorithm too.

1.5 Conclusions

AI provides a powerful arsenal of data analytics for bringing new potentials to the radiation oncology clinic. This can be manifested in better automation of routine tasks, improved efficiency, as well as enhanced decision-making support to its complex processes from treatment planning, quality assurance, to delivery or more advanced prediction of outcomes and adaptation of daily treatment. Although the potential of AI for safer and improved radiotherapy practice seems limitless, the implementation of AI tools is still evolving from research investigations toward routine clinical practice across the spectrum of processes in radiation oncology. This process could be further accelerated

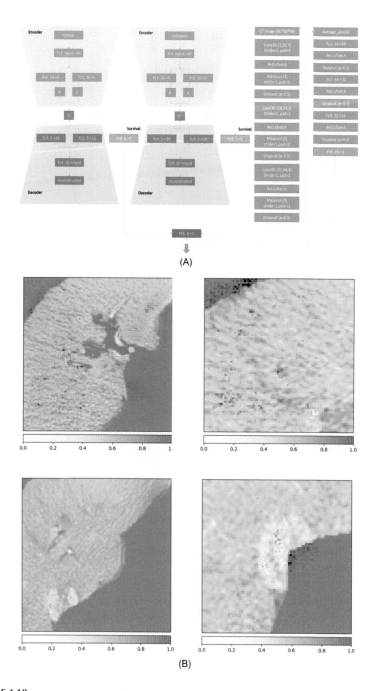

FIGURE 1.10
Deep learning prediction of survival in liver cancer. (a) VAE-SurvNet and (b) CNN-SurvNet structures. Grad-CAM interpretability of prediction. The blue dots show the critical pixels for the prediction of the neural network.

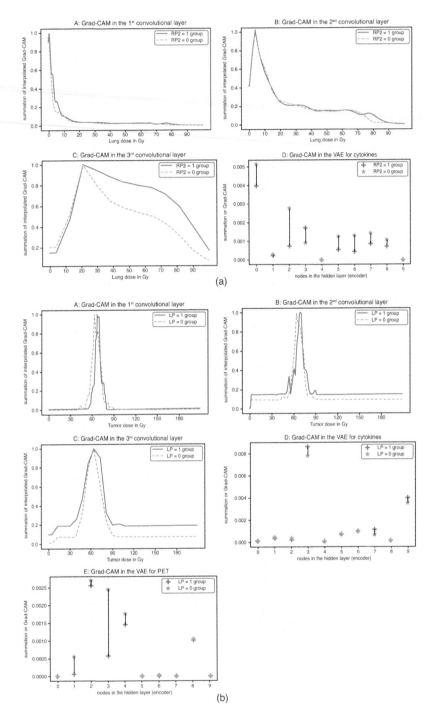

FIGURE 1.11
Grad-CAM interpretability of prediction. (a) RP2 and (b) LC of NSCLC.

by increasing available sample sizes for training via federated learning, conducting rigorous validations not only retrospectively but also prospectively, as needed, providing tools for de-puzzling AI predictions using grad-CAM and other tools, and developing comprehensive quality assurance programs for AI in the clinic. The collaboration between stakeholders (data scientists, biologists, clinical practitioners, vendors, and regulatory agencies) will allow for the safe and beneficial application of AI in radiation oncology realizing its potential for better cancer care and quality of life for its patients.

Acknowledgements

This work was partly supported by grants from the National Institute of Health (NIH), R01-CA233487. The author would like to thank Dr. Randall Ten Haken and Dr. Jean Moran for insightful discussions. The author would also like to recognize the valuable contributions of previous trainees Dr. Huan-Hsin Tseng, Dr. Yi Luo, Dr. Lise Wei, and Dr. Sunan Cui.

References

1. El Naqa I., Li R., Murphy M.J., editors. *Machine Learning in Radiation Oncology: Theory and Application*. Switzerland: Springer International Publishing; 2015.
2. El Naqa I., Haider M.A., Giger M.L., et al. Artificial Intelligence: Reshaping the practice of radiological sciences in the 21st century. *The British Journal of Radiology*. 2020 Feb;93(1106):20190855.
3. Cardenas C.E., Yang J., Anderson B.M., et al. Advances in auto-segmentation. *Seminars in Radiation Oncology*. 2019 Jul;29(3):185–197.
4. Balagopal A., Kazemifar S., Nguyen D., et al. Fully automated organ segmentation in male pelvic CT images. *Physics in Medicine and Biology*. 2018 Dec 14;63(24):245015.
5. Chan J.W., Kearney V., Haaf S., et al. A convolutional neural network algorithm for automatic segmentation of head and neck organs at risk using deep lifelong learning. *Medical Physics*. 2019 May;46(5):2204–2213.
6. Dong X., Lei Y., Tian S., et al. Synthetic MRI-aided multi-organ segmentation on male pelvic CT using cycle consistent deep attention network. *Radiotherapy and Oncology* 2019 Oct 17;141:192–199.
7. Dong X., Lei Y., Wang T., et al. Automatic multiorgan segmentation in thorax CT images using U-net-GAN. *Medical Physics*. 2019 May;46(5):2157–2168.
8. Fechter T., Adebahr S., Baltas D., et al. Esophagus segmentation in CT via 3D fully convolutional neural network and random walk. *Medical Physics*. 2017 Dec;44(12):6341–6352.

9. Feng X., Qing K., Tustison N.J., et al. Deep convolutional neural network for segmentation of thoracic organs-at-risk using cropped 3D images. *Medical Physics*. 2019 May;46(5):2169–2180.

10. Fu Y., Mazur T.R., Wu X., et al. A novel MRI segmentation method using CNN-based correction network for MRI-guided adaptive radiotherapy. *Medical Physics*. 2018 Nov;45(11):5129–5137.

11. Guo Z., Guo N., Gong K., et al. Gross tumor volume segmentation for head and neck cancer radiotherapy using deep dense multi-modality network. *Physics in Medicine and Biology*. 2019 Oct 16;64(20):205015.

12. He K., Cao X., Shi Y., et al. Pelvic organ segmentation using distinctive curve guided fully convolutional networks. *IEEE Trans Med Imaging*. 2018 Aug 13. doi: 10.1109/TMI.2018.2864958.

13. Ibragimov B., Toesca D., Chang D., et al. Combining deep learning with anatomical analysis for segmentation of the portal vein for liver SBRT planning. *Physics in Medicine and Biology*. 2017 Nov 10;62(23):8943–8958.

14. Kearney V., Chan J.W., Wang T., et al. Attention-enabled 3D boosted convolutional neural networks for semantic CT segmentation using deep supervision. *Physics in Medicine and Biology*. 2019 Jul 2;64(13):135001.

15. Liang S., Tang F., Huang X., et al. Deep-learning-based detection and segmentation of organs at risk in nasopharyngeal carcinoma computed tomographic images for radiotherapy planning. *European Radiology*. 2019 Apr;29(4):1961–1967.

16. Ma Z., Zhou S., Wu X., et al. Nasopharyngeal carcinoma segmentation based on enhanced convolutional neural networks using multi-modal metric learning. *Physics in Medicine and Biology*. 2019 Jan 8;64(2):025005.

17. Men K., Dai J., Li Y. Automatic segmentation of the clinical target volume and organs at risk in the planning CT for rectal cancer using deep dilated convolutional neural networks. *Medical Physics*. 2017 Dec;44(12):6377–6389.

18. Mylonas A., Keall P.J., Booth J.T., et al. A deep learning framework for automatic detection of arbitrarily shaped fiducial markers in intrafraction fluoroscopic images. *Medical Physics*. 2019 May;46(5):2286–2297.

19. van der Heyden B., Wohlfahrt P., Eekers D.B.P., et al. Dual-energy CT for automatic organs-at-risk segmentation in brain-tumor patients using a multi-atlas and deep-learning approach. *Scientific Reports*. 2019 Mar 11;9(1):4126.

20. van Dijk L.V., Van den Bosch L., Aljabar P., et al. Improving automatic delineation for head and neck organs at risk by Deep Learning Contouring. *Radiotherapy and Oncology: Journal of the European Society for Therapeutic Radiology and Oncology*. 2019 Oct 22;142:115–123.

21. Yang J., Veeraraghavan H., Armato S.G., 3rd, et al. Autosegmentation for thoracic radiation treatment planning: A grand challenge at AAPM 2017. *Medical Physics*. 2018 Oct;45(10):4568–4581.

22. Zaffino P., Pernelle G., Mastmeyer A., et al. Fully automatic catheter segmentation in MRI with 3D convolutional neural networks: Application to MRI-guided gynecologic brachytherapy. *Physics in Medicine and Biology*. 2019 Aug 14;64(16):165008.

23. Cardenas C.E., Anderson B.M., Aristophanous M., et al. Auto-delineation of oropharyngeal clinical target volumes using 3D convolutional neural networks. *Physics in Medicine and Biology*. 2018 Nov 7;63(21):215026.

24. Cardenas C.E., McCarroll R.E., Court L.E., et al. Deep learning algorithm for auto-delineation of high-risk oropharyngeal clinical target volumes with built-in dice similarity coefficient parameter optimization function. *International Journal of Radiation Oncology - Biology - Physics.* 2018 Jun 1;101(2):468–478.

25. Nguyen D., Long T., Jia X., et al. A feasibility study for predicting optimal radiation therapy dose distributions of prostate cancer patients from patient anatomy using deep learning. *Scientific Reports.* 2019 Jan 31;9(1):1076.

26. Willems S., Crijns W., Sterpin E., et al., editors. *Feasibility of CT-Only 3D Dose Prediction for VMAT Prostate Plans Using Deep Learning2019*; Cham: Springer International Publishing; (Artificial Intelligence in Radiation Therapy).

27. Liu Z., Fan J., Li M., et al. A deep learning method for prediction of three-dimensional dose distribution of helical tomotherapy. *Medical Physics.* 2019 May;46(5):1972–1983.

28. Moore K.L., Brame R.S., Low D.A., et al. Experience-based quality control of clinical intensity-modulated radiotherapy planning. *International Journal of Radiation Oncology – Biology – Physics.* 2011 Oct 1;81(2):545–551.

29. Wu B., Ricchetti F., Sanguineti G., et al. Data-driven approach to generating achievable dose-volume histogram objectives in intensity-modulated radio-therapy planning. *International Journal of Radiation Oncology – Biology – Physics.* 2011 Mar 15;79(4):1241–1247.

30. Wu B., Ricchetti F., Sanguineti G., et al. Patient geometry-driven information retrieval for IMRT treatment plan quality control. *Medical Physics.* 2009 Dec;36(12):5497–505.

31. Shen C., Gonzalez Y., Klages P., et al. Intelligent inverse treatment planning via deep reinforcement learning, a proof-of-principle study in high dose-rate brachytherapy for cervical cancer. *Physics in Medicine & Biology.* 2019;64(11):115013.

32. Rhee D.J., Cardenas C.E., Elhalawani H., et al. Automatic detection of contouring errors using convolutional neural networks. *Medical Physics.* 2019 Nov;46(11):5086–5097.

33. Kisling K., Zhang L., Simonds H., et al. Fully automatic treatment planning for external-beam radiation therapy of locally advanced cervical cancer: A tool for low-resource clinics. *Journal of Global Oncology.* 2019 Jan;5:1–9.

34. Shiraishi S., Moore K.L. Knowledge-based prediction of three-dimensional dose distributions for external beam radiotherapy. *Medical Physics.* 2016 Jan;43(1):378.

35. Carlson J.N., Park J.M., Park S.-Y., et al. A machine learning approach to the accurate prediction of multi-leaf collimator positional errors. *Physics in Medicine and Biology.* 2016;61(6):2514.

36. El Naqa I., Irrer J., Ritter T.A., et al. Machine learning for automated quality assurance in radiotherapy: A proof of principle using EPID data description. *Medical Physics.* 2019;46(4):1914–1921.

37. Kalet A.M., Gennari J.H., Ford E.C., et al. Bayesian network models for error detection in radiotherapy plans. *Physics in Medicine and Biology.* 2015 Apr 7;60(7):2735–2749.

38. Li Q., Chan M.F. Predictive time-series modeling using artificial neural networks for Linac beam symmetry: An empirical study. *Annals of the New York Academy of Sciences.* 2017;1387(1):84–94.

39. Valdes G., Morin O., Valenciaga Y., et al. Use of TrueBeam developer mode for imaging QA. *Journal of Applied Clinical Medical Physics.* 2015;16(4):322–333.

40. Valdes G., Scheuermann R., Hung C., et al. A mathematical framework for virtual IMRT QA using machine learning. *Medical Physics.* 2016;43(7):4323–4334.
41. Ruan D., Keall P. Online prediction of respiratory motion: Multidimensional processing with low-dimensional feature learning. *Physics in Medicine and Biology.* 2010 Jun 7;55(11):3011–3025.
42. Isaksson M., Jalden J., Murphy M.J. On using an adaptive neural network to predict lung tumor motion during respiration for radiotherapy applications. *Medical Physics.* 2005 Dec;32(12):3801–3089.
43. Guidi G., Maffei N., Meduri B., et al. A machine learning tool for re-planning and adaptive RT: A multicenter cohort investigation. *Physica Medica.* 2016;32(12):1659–1666.
44. Guidi G., Maffei N., Vecchi C., et al. A support vector machine tool for adaptive tomotherapy treatments: Prediction of head and neck patients criticalities. *Physica Medica.* 2015;31(5):442–451.
45. El Naqa I., Bradley J., Blanco A.I., et al. Multivariable modeling of radiotherapy outcomes, including dose–volume and clinical factors. *International Journal of Radiation Oncology – Biology – Physics.* 2006;64(4):1275–1286.
46. Oberije C., Nalbantov G., Dekker A., et al. A prospective study comparing the predictions of doctors versus models for treatment outcome of lung cancer patients: A step toward individualized care and shared decision making. *Radiotherapy and Oncology.* 2014;112(1):37–43.
47. Bradley J., Deasy J.O., Bentzen S., et al. Dosimetric correlates for acute esophagitis in patients treated with radiotherapy for lung carcinoma. *International Journal of Radiation Oncology – Biology – Physics.* 2004;58(4):1106–1113.
48. Hope A.J., Lindsay P.E., El Naqa I., et al. Modeling radiation pneumonitis risk with clinical, dosimetric, and spatial parameters. *International Journal of Radiation Oncology – Biology – Physics.* 2006;65(1):112–124.
49. Zhou Z., Folkert M., Cannon N., et al. Predicting distant failure in early stage NSCLC treated with SBRT using clinical parameters. *Radiotherapy and Oncology.* 119(3):501–504.
50. Dawson L.A., Biersack M., Lockwood G., et al. Use of principal component analysis to evaluate the partial organ tolerance of normal tissues to radiation. *International Journal of Radiation Oncology – Biology – Physics.* 2005 Jul 1;62(3):829–837.
51. El Naqa I., Deasy J.O., Mu Y., et al. Datamining approaches for modeling tumor control probability. *Acta Oncologica.* 2010 Nov;49(8):1363–1373.
52. El Naqa I., Bradley J.D., Lindsay P.E., et al. Predicting radiotherapy outcomes using statistical learning techniques. *Physics in Medicine and Biology.* 2009 Sep;54(18):S9–S30.
53. Sonke J.-J., Aznar M., Rasch C. Adaptive radiotherapy for anatomical changes. *Seminars in Radiation Oncology.* 2019;29(3):245–257.
54. Tseng H.H., Luo Y., Cui S., et al. Deep reinforcement learning for automated radiation adaptation in lung cancer. *Medical Physics.* 2017 Dec;44(12):6690–6705.
55. Tseng H.H., Luo Y., Ten Haken R.K., et al. The role of machine learning in knowledge-based response-adapted radiotherapy. *Frontiers in Oncology.* 2018;8:266.
56. El Naqa I., Murphy M.J., editors. *Machine and Deep Learning in Oncology, Medical Physics and Radiology.* 2nd ed. Switzerland: Springer; 2022.
57. Willoughby T.R., Starkschall G., Janjan N.A., et al. Evaluation and scoring of radiotherapy treatment plans using an artificial neural network. *International Journal of Radiation Oncology – Biology – Physics.* 1996 Mar 1;34(4):923–930.

58. Rowbottom C.G., Webb S., Oldham M. Beam-orientation customization using an artificial neural network. *Physics in Medicine and Biology*. 1999 Sep;44(9):2251–2262.

59. Wells D.M., Niederer J. A medical expert system approach using artificial neural networks for standardized treatment planning. *International Journal of Radiation Oncology – Biology – Physics*. 1998 Apr 1;41(1):173–182.

60. Gulliford S.L., Webb S., Rowbottom C.G., et al. Use of artificial neural networks to predict biological outcomes for patients receiving radical radiotherapy of the prostate. *Radiotherapy and Oncology*. 2004;71(1):3–12.

61. Munley M.T., Lo J.Y., Sibley G.S., et al. A neural network to predict symptomatic lung injury. *Physics in Medicine and Biology*. 1999;44:2241–2249.

62. Su M., Miften M., Whiddon C., et al. An artificial neural network for predicting the incidence of radiation pneumonitis. *Medical Physics*. 2005;32(2):318–325.

63. Cui S., Tseng H.H., Pakela J., et al. Introduction to machine and deep learning for medical physicists. *Medical Physics*. 2020 Jun;47(5):e127–e147.

64. El Naqa I., Yang D., Apte A., et al. Concurrent multimodality image segmentation by active contours for radiotherapy treatment planning. *Medical Physics*. 2007 Dec;34(12):4738–4749.

65. Yang D., Zheng J., Nofal A., et al. Techniques and software tool for 3D multimodality medical image segmentation. *Journal of Radiation Oncology Informatics*. 2009;1:1–22.

66. Sharp G., Fritscher K.D., Pekar V., et al. Vision 20/20: Perspectives on automated image segmentation for radiotherapy. *Medical Physics*. 2014;41(5):050902.

67. Delpon G., Escande A., Ruef T., et al. Comparison of automated atlas-based segmentation software for postoperative prostate cancer radiotherapy [Original Research]. *Frontiers in Oncology*. 2016 Aug 03; 6:178.

68. Ibragimov B., Xing L. Segmentation of organs-at-risks in head and neck CT images using convolutional neural networks. *Medical Physics*. 2017 Feb;44(2):547–557.

69. Nikolov S., Blackwell S., Mendes R., et al. Deep learning to achieve clinically applicable segmentation of head and neck anatomy for radiotherapy. arXiv e-prints. 2018 [cited]. https://ui.adsabs.harvard.edu/abs/2018arXiv180904430N.

70. Appenzoller L.M., Michalski J.M., Thorstad W.L., et al. Predicting dose-volume histograms for organs-at-risk in IMRT planning. *Medical Physics*. 2012 Dec;39(12):7446–7461.

71. Scaggion A., Fusella M., Roggio A., et al. Reducing inter- and intra-planner variability in radiotherapy plan output with a commercial knowledge-based planning solution. *Physica Medica : PM: An International Journal Devoted to the Applications of Physics to Medicine and Biology: Official Journal of the Italian Association of Biomedical Physics (AIFB)*. 2018 Sep;53:86–93.

72. Babier A., Boutilier J.J., McNiven A.L., et al. Knowledge-based automated planning for oropharyngeal cancer. *Medical Physics*. 2018;45(7):2875–2883.

73. Shiraishi S., Moore K.L. Knowledge-based prediction of three-dimensional dose distributions for external beam radiotherapy. *Medical Physics*. 2016;43(1):378–387.

74. Nguyen D., Jia X., Sher D., et al. Three-dimensional radiotherapy dose prediction on head and neck cancer patients with a hierarchically densely connected U-net deep learning architecture. arXiv:180510397 [physicsmed-ph]. 2018.

75. Kazemifar S., Balagopal A., Nguyen D., et al. Segmentation of the prostate and organs at risk in male pelvic CT images using deep learning. arXiv:180209587 [physicsmed-ph. 2018.

76. Nguyen D., Jia X., Sher D., et al. 3D radiotherapy dose prediction on head and neck cancer patients with a hierarchically densely connected U-net deep learning architecture. *Physics in Medicine & Biology.* 2019; 64(6):065020.

77. El Naqa I. *A Guide to Outcome Modeling in Radiotherapy and Oncology: Listening to the Data.* Boca Raton, FL: CRC Press, Taylor & Francis Group; 2018. (Series in medical physics and biomedical engineering).

78. Pearl J. *Probabilistic Reasoning in Intelligent Systems: Networks of Plausible Inference.* San Francisco, CA: Morgan Kaufmann Publishers Inc.; 1988. (Kaufmann M., editor. Representation and Reasoning).

79. Oh J.H., Craft J., Al Lozi R., et al. A Bayesian network approach for modeling local failure in lung cancer. *Physics in Medicine and Biology.* 2011 Mar;56(6):1635–1651.

80. Oh J.H., Craft J.M., Townsend R., et al. A bioinformatics approach for biomarker identification in radiation-induced lung inflammation from limited proteomics data. *Journal of Proteome Research.* 2011 Mar;10(3):1406–1415.

81. Lee S., Ybarra N., Jeyaseelan K., et al. Bayesian network ensemble as a multivariate strategy to predict radiation pneumonitis risk. *Medical Physics.* 2015 May;42(5):2421–2430.

82. Luo Y., El Naqa I., McShan D.L., et al. Unraveling biophysical interactions of radiation pneumonitis in non-small-cell lung cancer via Bayesian network analysis. *Radiotherapy and Oncology.* 2017;123(1):85–92.

83. Luo Y., McShan D.L., Matuszak M.M., et al. A multi-objective bayesian networks approach for joint prediction of tumor local control and radiation pneumonitis in non-small-cell lung cancer (NSCLC) for response-adapted radiotherapy. *Medical Physics.* 2018. doi: 10.1002/mp.13029.

84. Cui S., Ten Haken R.K., El Naqa I. Integrating multiomics information in deep learning architectures for joint actuarial outcome prediction in non-small cell lung cancer patients after radiation therapy. *International Journal of Radiation Oncology - Biology – Physics.* 2021 Feb 1;110:893–904.

85. Collins G.S., Reitsma J.B., Altman D.G., et al. Transparent reporting of a multivariable prediction model for individual prognosis or diagnosis (TRIPOD): The TRIPOD Statement. *BMC Medicine.* 2015;13(1):1.

86. El Naqa I., Kosorok M.R., Jin J., et al. Prospects and challenges for clinical decision support in the era of big data. *JCO Clinical Cancer Informatics.* 2018;2:1–12.

87. Kong F., Ten Haken R.K., Schipper M., et al. Effect of midtreatment pet/ct-adapted radiation therapy with concurrent chemotherapy in patients with locally advanced non–small-cell lung cancer: A phase 2 clinical trial. *JAMA Oncology.* 2017;3(10):1358–1365.

88. Balagurunathan Y., Mitchell R., El Naqa I. Requirements and reliability of AI in the medical context. *Physica Medica.* 2021 Mar;83:72–78.

89. Rieke N., Hancox J., Li W., et al. The future of digital health with federated learning. *NPJ Digital Medicine.* 2020;3(1):119.

90. Zerka F., Barakat S., Walsh S., et al. Systematic review of privacy-preserving distributed machine learning from federated databases in health care. *JCO Clinical Cancer Informatics.* 2020;4:184–200.

91. Sheller M.J., Reina G.A., Edwards B., et al., editors. Multi-institutional Deep Learning Modeling Without Sharing Patient Data: A Feasibility Study on Brain Tumor Segmentation. Cham: Springer International Publishing; 2019 (Brain lesion: Glioma, Multiple Sclerosis, Stroke and Traumatic Brain Injuries).

92. Li W., Milletarì F., Xu D., et al. Privacy-preserving Federated Brain Tumour Segmentation2019 [cited arXiv:1910.00962 p.]. https://ui.adsabs.harvard.edu/abs/2019arXiv191000962L.
93. Roth H.R., Chang K., Singh P., et al., editors. *Federated Learning for Breast Density Classification: A Real-World Implementation. Domain Adaptation and Representation Transfer, and Distributed and Collaborative Learning.* Cham: Springer International Publishing; 2020.
94. Jochems A., Deist T.M., El Naqa I., et al. Developing and validating a survival prediction model for NSCLC patients through distributed learning across 3 countries. *International Journal of Radiation Oncology – Biology – Physics.* 2017;99(2):344–352.
95. Jochems A., El-Naqa I., Kessler M., et al. A prediction model for early death in non-small cell lung cancer patients following curative-intent chemoradiotherapy. *Acta Oncologica.* 2018 Feb;57(2):226–230.
96. El Naqa I., Boone J.M., Benedict S.H., et al. AI in medical physics: Guidelines for publication. *Medical Physics.* 2021 Sep;48(9):4711–4714.
97. El Naqa I. Prospective clinical deployment of machine learning in radiation oncology. *Nature Reviews Clinical Oncology.* 2021 Oct;18(10):605–606.
98. Luo Y., Tseng H.-H., Cui S., et al. Balancing accuracy and interpretability of machine learning approaches for radiation treatment outcomes modeling. *BJR|Open.* 2019;1(1):20190021.
99. Zhou B., Khosla A., Lapedriza A., et al. Learning Deep Features for Discriminative Localization2015 [cited arXiv:1512.04150 p.]. https://ui.adsabs.harvard.edu/abs/2015arXiv151204150Z.
100. Selvaraju R.R., Cogswell M., Das A., et al. Grad-CAM: Visual Explanations from Deep Networks via Gradient-based Localization2016 [cited arXiv:1610.02391 p.]. https://ui.adsabs.harvard.edu/abs/2016arXiv161002391S.
101. El Naqa I., Moran J., Ten Haken R. Machine learning in radiation oncology: What have we learned so far? In: van Dyk J., editor. *The Modern Technology of Radiation Oncology.* Madison, WI: Medical Physics Publishing; 2020.

2

Machine Learning for Image-Based Radiotherapy Outcome Prediction

Bulat Ibragimov

University of Copenhagen

CONTENTS

2.1 Introduction

Medical images play an essential role in both cancer diagnoses and cancer radiation therapy (RT) planning. For the last couple of decades, it has been a

DOI: 10.1201/9781003094333-2

routine practice to manually or semi-automatically annotate the tumor and surrounding tissues, the so-called organs-at-risk (OARs), in order to quantitatively estimate the tumor volume coverage with the radiation dose and to minimize the risks of post-RT toxicities originated from over-irradiation of OARs. The tumor control probability and toxicity risks are usually estimated from the dose–volume histograms (DVHs) that qualify the dose coverage for each tissue. The clinical community has established a set of DVH thresholds and recommendations for successful treatments, which were validated against representative RT databases with outcomes [1]. The DVHs are easy to compute and visually comprehend but can oversimplify dose distribution plans. Indeed, the DVHs collapse volumetric dose distribution plans into several vectors resulting in the loss of spatial dose distribution information. Such information loss limits the predictive powers of DVHs, and more than 30% of RTs end up with acute or late post-RT complications [2–5]. At the same time, the modern dose delivery equipment nowadays offers many opportunities for treatment design, including precise radiation beam angulation and dose delivery fractionation. As a consequence, several RT plans can be designed for a particular patient that will satisfy the clinical DVH-based constraints. The outcomes of such RT plans could be different. There is therefore an urgent unmet need for RT personalization considering that the technical opportunity for such personalization exists.

Pre-RT images contain much more data than just the spatial relationships between tumor and OARs. Some of the image features, or the so-called biomarkers, are clearly visible to the human eye and their importance has been well documented, turning the quantitate assessment of these biomarkers into routine clinical practice of cancer treatment planning. The biomarkers of such type include response evaluation criteria in solid tumors (RECIST) [6] or World Health Organization criteria [7]. The advances in imaging equipment reduced imaging dose, speeded up image acquisition, improved image resolution, and overall improved cancer visualization. At the same time, the abilities of the human eye remain the same limiting the opportunities for visual identification of complex non-trivial imaging biomarkers. The development of computational equipment overcomes the deficiency of the human eye and opens an opportunity for automated identification and quantification of imaging biomarkers.

The imaging biomarkers are usually extracted from the tumor or/and OARs using pre-RT medical images. Considering the fact that tumors and OARs are always segmented prior to RT, the biomarkers can be extracted and analyzed with no extra manual labor. The challenge remains to identify the biomarkers that are important for treatment planning and outcome prediction and can be robustly computed from the commonly-used RT image modalities.

There is no technological limit to the complexity of imaging biomarkers. The main challenge is to estimate which biomarkers are useful for the prediction of an RT outcome of interest. Several questions need to be answered before a biomarker is ready to be integrated into clinical practice. One of the first questions is how sensitive is a biomarker value when computed from different pre-RT images of the same patient. If a biomarker is not invariant to imaging equipment installed at different hospitals or varies dramatically when images are segmented by different observers, its clinical applicability will be limited. The second question goes to the predictive or prognostic power a biomarker potentially exhibits. The estimation of biomarker predictive powers needs to be performed against large and potentially multi-institutional patient cohorts. Existing research papers, however, are often restricted by the data available at their institutions and follow different evaluation protocols. The third question is about biomarker explainability, i.e., mapping the biomarker with the clinical and anatomical knowledge.

In this book chapter, I go through the current developments in machine learning-based image analysis for the prediction of RT outcomes. The chapter summarizes various aspects of this rapidly developing field including the methodology of biomarker extraction and outcome prediction, and the main RT types and RT outcomes targeted by the researchers.

2.2 Imagining Modalities

Computed tomography (CT) is currently the main imaging modality for RT planning. The existing commercial CT scanners can produce images of an exceptionally high resolution, which allows visualization of small structures for precise dose coverage calculation. Moreover, the attenuation of radiation by a specific tissue is invariant to the type of CT scanner used, so we can expect CT images generated by different scanners to have the same distribution of image intensities. This attenuation information is valuable for calculating the dose distribution during RT. The fact that CT images represent the main modality for RT planning means that the tumor and surrounding OARs will be always segmented by a human expert as a part of the standard RT planning protocol. The availability of reliable image segmentations at no cost significantly simplifies the research in the field of image-based RT outcome prediction. Most of the studies in the field are therefore performed on CT images [8–55]. In some studies, it was explicitly stated that CT images were contrast enhanced [9,12,40]. Two recent studies on non-small-cell lung cancers (NSCLCs) worked with cone-beam CTs instead of conventional CTs [16,17]. Fave et al. developed a framework for the registration-based analysis of four-dimensional CT images acquired during the breathing cycle in order to robustly capture the appearance properties of NSCLC tumors and predict overall survival, distant metastases, and recurrence after lung RT.

Magnetic resonance (MR) imaging has been rapidly gaining popularity as a diagnostic modality due to no radiation involvement during imaging and high contrast of soft tissues. The resolution of commonly used MR scanners, however, remains way lower than the resolution of the CT scanner. Despite this obstacle, the applicability of MR imaging for RT planning has been established and its adoption in clinical practice will be accelerated with the release of MR-based Linacs. As MR is radiation-free, it can safely be used to track tumor motion during abdominal or lung RTs, which opens a pathway for the online adaptive RT [56]. The improved contrast of soft tissues in MR in comparison to CT images can result in more accurate tumor delineation and consequently more precise dose delivery especially when the tumor is surrounded by soft tissues [57,58]. Naturally, the studies on MR-based prediction of radiotherapy outcomes [22,25,28,40,59–73] are mainly focused on head-and-neck cancer [25,28,62,68,74,75], brain cancer [63,66,69,76], and prostate cancer [60,64,71,73], where tumors are usually surrounded by soft tissues and therefore poorly-visible on CTs.

Positron emission tomography (PET) measures metabolic activity in the cells and improves visualization of malignant tumors that take up more fluorodeoxyglucose – a typical radioisotope tracer utilized in PET – than other tissues. Combined PET/CT scanners can simultaneously acquire both CT and PET images in one session, which guarantees the images to be perfectly aligned and allows reliable image biomarker extraction without the need for CT-PET registration. The nature of PET images facilitated the development of PET-specific image biomarkers such as standardized uptake value (SUV), which strongly correlates with the tumor aggressiveness and treatment outcomes. The resolution of PET images is, however, fundamentally restricted by the positron range and acollinearity factor and remains way lower than the resolution of CT images [77]. The predictions of RT outcomes can rely on biomarkers extracted from PET images alone [78–86] and both CT and PET images [10,15,19,28,35,48]. A few studies analyzed three RT modalities, i.e., CT, PET, and MR, for the prediction of disease recurrence after chemoradiotherapy (CRT) for cervical cancer [65] and nasopharyngeal carcinoma [24].

The CT, MR, and PET modalities define the three most commonly used RT planning modalities (Figure 2.1a). Other imaging modalities, such as ultrasound, can be used for the diagnosis of cancer before designing the treatment regimen [87]. In the field of machine learning-based prediction of RT outcomes, Saednia et al. [88] discovered that pre-RT thermal images of breast contain quantitative biomarkers with predictive powers for post-RT skin toxicity.

2.3 Quantitative Image Biomarkers

2.3.1 Image Standardization

Machine learning in medicine has advanced significantly in recent decades, and novel mathematical models were found to be effective in cancer diagnosis and RT planning. The growing predictive powers of machine learning

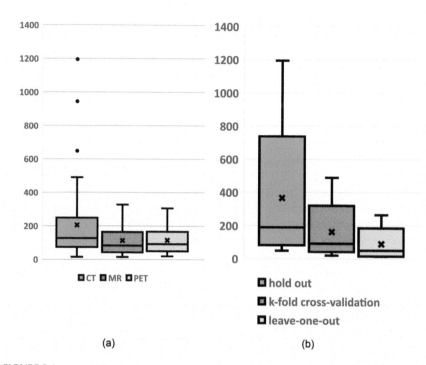

(a)   (b)

FIGURE 2.1

Statistics of the existing work on machine learning-based image analysis for radiotherapy outcome prediction. (a) The box whiskers diagram with the number of images used in studies of biomarkers extracted from CT, MR, and PET images. Note that studies that use multiple image modalities are included into statistics for each individual modality. (b) The box whiskers diagram with the number of images used in studies that utilized hold-out, k-fold cross-validation, and leave-one-out validation strategies. The crosses indicate mean values.

models, however, come with the price of a potentially reduced generalizability. It was shown that the performance of machine learning models can dramatically drop from 0.9 of the area under the receiving operator curve (AUC), when trained and tested on the databases from the same hospital, to 0.59 AUC, when tested on a database from a different hospital [89]. This overfitting-to-training issue is one of the main obstacles toward the clinical integration of machine learning models. A number of steps and tests must be performed to reduce the risks of overfitting including data standardization, model regularization, and statistical analysis.

Data standardization in medical image analysis is largely associated with image preprocessing. Different hospitals are usually equipped with different image scanners resulting in pre-RT images with different properties. The National Institutes of Health and Radiological Society of North America funded initiatives to improve the standardization of the image acquisition protocol and quantitative image biomarker calculation [90]. Despite certain progress, the lack of state-of-the-art imaging equipment at different hospitals does not allow the adoption of a unified standardization protocol. Even when a standardization protocol is adopted, it will not affect the historical RT records with non-standardized data, which are needed to train machine learning models for RT outcome prediction.

The first image preprocessing step is isotropic image rescaling that compensates for varying in-plane image resolution and slice thickness [91]. The reduction of tube voltage or projection numbers in low-dose CT results in image noise and reconstruction artifacts. Image denoising and sparse-view CT reconstruction can be performed to compensate for such image imperfections by utilizing one of the most recent deep learning-based algorithms [92,93]. Kim et al. [94] analyzed how image biomarkers change when different image reconstruction algorithms are used and concluded that 60% of common image biomarkers are statistically significantly affected by the reconstruction algorithms. Along a similar line, the presence of metallic implants, catheters, or vasculature stents near the tumor area may result in CT image artifacts, which will significantly compromise image biomarker extraction. This issue is likely to be addressed via projection-based metal artifact reduction technologies integrated into modern CT scanners [95]. While intensity values for each tissue type are the same for all CT images, they significantly vary in MR due to the manufacturer settings, sequence type, and acquisition parameters. Bias field correction can be adopted to compensate for low-frequency signals that corrupt MR images [91]. This issue is usually pronounced when old MR scanners are used. Intensity inhomogeneity cannot be completely fixed with the bias field correction, and anatomy-specific solutions are preferred. The basic idea of such solutions is to roughly recognize the location of organs of interest and standardize their appearance using a reference appearance atlas. For brain imaging, this procedure involves the algorithmic detection and removal of the skull and recognition of the brain tissue region [96]. Similarly to MR, PET image intensities are not standardized and depend on the utilized radioisotope tracers and acquisition and reconstruction protocols. PET standardization is often performed against images of phantoms with known physical properties. Not all variability in imaging data can be compensated with image preprocessing. For example, various patient immobilization equipment, contrast injection regimens, and image acquisition protocols can significantly affect a pre-RT image appearance and biomarker values but cannot be compensated with universal image preprocessing techniques.

2.3.2 Image Delineation

The majority of studies on image-based RT outcome prediction extract quantitative biomarkers from tumors depicted on pre-RT images [8–13,15–18,20,22–24,28–30,32–35,37,38,40,41,43–49,51–55,59,61,62,65–70,72,74–76,78–86,97,98]. The accuracy of tumor delineation is paramount for robust and reliable outcome prediction models. Without ensuring accurate tumor delineation, it is impossible to conclude whether a biomarker does not have predictive powers or it has predictive powers but their calculation was unreliable. Manual delineation of the gross tumor volume in CT images is a standard-of-care step in RT planning. The results, however, are subjected to inter- and intra-rater variability, especially when the tumor appearance is compromised by poor image contrast or artifacts. Eminowicz and McCormack estimated the inter-observer variability in cervical cancer delineation in CT and observed that the overlap value ranged from 0.51 to 0.81 with a maximum of 4 cm absolute difference [99]. Low accuracy of tumor annotation in CT could be potentially mitigated by MR images where the soft tissue contrast is higher. The inclusion of MR images shown to reduce the inter-observer variability in prostate and head-and-neck tumors delineation, i.e., in the anatomical regions where tumors are surrounded by soft tissues [58,100]. The implications of inter-observer variability and consensus-based delineation on RT outcome were investigated for nasopharyngeal carcinoma [62,75], pancreatic adenocarcinoma [12], esophageal squamous cell carcinoma [78], head-and-neck squamous cell carcinoma (HNSCC) [37], NSCLC [37], and rectal cancer [67].

An alternative to manual delineation is the automated or semi-automated delineation of tumors. The introduction of deep learning boosted this research field, and most of the top-performing algorithms use convolutional neural networks (CNNs) for tumor delineation [101,102]. Semi-automated tumor delineation has been successfully used for the prediction of survival after lung RT [24] and disease progression after brain RT. Despite all the potential advantages of automated tumor delineation, its current accuracy is usually insufficient for clinical use. The delineation errors are often manifested when tumors are small and have a poor signal-to-background intensity ratio. The most significant advances are observed for breast cancer, where several automated delineation solutions have been approved for clinical use [103]. The outcome of RT depends both on the irradiation of the tumor and the surrounding OARs. A significant number of studies investigated the usability of image biomarkers extracted from automatically segmented OARs. The outcomes of interest in such studies include post-RT toxicities of the OARs [21,25,27,31,39,42,43,50,88], survival [18], and cancer recurrence [60,71,73].

2.3.3 Biomarker Extraction

The results of manual, semi-automated, or automated segmentations are used to calculate quantitative image biomarkers. Many quantitative biomarkers originate from qualitative biomarkers, i.e., characteristics used by physicians to describe tumors, such as tumor heterogeneity or the presence of necrotic regions. Qualitative biomarkers are subjective and often insufficient to predict RT outcomes. Quantitative biomarkers can be subdivided into several categories: intensity-based, histogram-based, and shape-based. The biomarkers are not restricted to any particular image modality and all of them can be computed for CT, MR, and PET images. The predictive powers of biomarkers, however, vary for different modalities. Recently, Dissaux et al. [10] investigated the predictive powers of biomarkers computed from PET and CT images for the NSCLC RT outcome prediction. The authors discovered that out of 191 biomarkers only two PET and two CT biomarkers were significantly predictive for post-RT local cancer control. It then turned out that only two biomarkers from four significant biomarkers were needed to maximize the prediction accuracy, i.e., the remaining two biomarkers were redundant. The authors did not find any image biomarkers associated with overall survival or distant metastases. Similarly, Simpson et al. [61] analyzed the predictive powers of MR image biomarkers. Out of 42 biomarkers tested, the gray-level co-occurrence matrix energy was found to be necessary and sufficient for the response prediction after pancreatic RT.

Several hundreds of quantitative image biomarker types exist. To avoid errors in the biomarker calculation, the Image Biomarker Standardization Initiative (ISBI) has been established [104]. Teams from 19 research institutions united to test the performance of their biomarker extraction tools on a common database of images. They found that out of 174 common image biomarkers, 169 biomarkers were almost invariant against various implementations. The Initiative also released a 3D phantom image and a segmented lung cancer CT for new researchers in the fields. The authors recommend to test in-house implementations of biomarker calculation on the reference data and ensure that the generated biomarker values agree with the reference biomarker values. Among the four most widely used public toolboxes for image biomarker calculation, three were compliant with the ISBI verification protocol, namely, PyRadiomics [105], LIFEx [106], and CERR [107], while IBEX [108] toolbox was not compliant. The compliant toolboxes exhibited statistically significant agreement on 70% of the common biomarkers and partially agreed on 6% of the biomarkers. The only non-compliant IBEX toolbox exhibited statistically significant agreement with other toolboxes on 47% of the biomarkers. It can be concluded that the use of an ISBI-compliance protocol is beneficial for the reliability and robustness of the biomarker calculation [109].

Often, biomarkers are simple to compute and usually require the execution of small code snippets [108]. Several biomarkers of a more complex nature, however, exist. Hao et al. [97] proposed an algorithm for the extraction of biomarkers from the tumor surface instead of tumor volume and demonstrated that such biomarkers can be beneficial for the prediction of distant failure after NSCLC stereotactic body RT (SBRT) and cervical RT. Torheim et al. [70] evaluated how the MR image intensity increased during the time after the contrast agent injection using the Tofts and Brix models. The aim was to find longitudinal image patterns associated with locoregional cervical cancer relapse after CRT. The longitudinal changes in tumor appearance in PET were investigated by Tan et al. [86] to predict the pathological response after esophageal CRT. Simple shape properties of the tumor, e.g., ellipticity, volume, and length, are included in biomarker calculation packages and demonstrated a potential to predict outcomes of breast [13,72], head-and-neck [11,46], and NSCLC [16,17] RTs. More complex models are, however, needed to analyze the shapes of irradiated OARs for the prediction of radiation-induced toxicities of these OARs. Lakshminarayanan et al. [27] developed a coherent point drift-based framework for characterizing the shape of parotid glands and doses delivered to individual parotid gland regions. Van Luijk et al. [110] found that sparring consistently located regions in parotid glands can significantly reduce the risks of post-RT xerostomia. Ibragimov et al. [111] applied rigid registration on portal veins to find parts of the liver vasculature that must be spared from high doses to reduce the risks of hepatobiliary toxicity after liver SBRT.

The above-mentioned biomarkers share the common property that their signature is predefined by human experts. Modern machine learning solutions offer mechanisms for automated biomarker generation [4,5,23,24,29,63]. The core idea is to train CNNs to map pre-RT images and RT outcomes and then investigate the consistent patterns in network neurons. It is possible to check the network behavior on different pre-RT images and extract the image patterns, i.e., biomarkers, that are predicted to be associated with RT outcomes. On a large cohort of patients with lung cancer, Lou et al. [23] have demonstrated that predictive powers of biomarkers automatically extracted by CNNs are higher than the predictive powers of standard imaging biomarkers. Hosny et al. [29] applied to CNNs to identify imaging biomarkers associated with 2-year survival after NSCLC RT using seven patient cohorts from different institutions. The authors found out that CNNs not only accurately predicted lung RT outcomes but also highlighted the image regions of interest that were associated with poor survival prognosis.

2.3.4 Biomarker Repeatability

It has been long understood that apart from having high predictable powers, a biomarker must be invariant to input image variability as long as the image follows an appropriate acquisition protocol [104]. As it was shown in the previous section, the biomarker calculation implementation by itself can compromise the biomarker value. However, a more significant and difficult-to-mitigate source of errors comes from inconsistencies in image acquisition and target object delineation. Aerts et al. performed a test–retest biomarker analysis using CT images acquired in the 15-minute time interval [112]. The authors observed that the predictive powers of a biomarker are correlated with its repeatability. The existence of such correlation leaves a question of whether biomarkers with low predictive powers truly have low predictive powers or were not robustly calculated. A similar analysis was performed with CT images acquired with different scanners and at different times [113]. Only 2% of biomarkers had a concordance correlation coefficient of >0.85 in that test–retest study. Traverso et al. performed a literature review to understand which biomarkers are found to be reproducible in the field [114]. The authors observed that the first-order statistic-based biomarkers are more reproducible than morphology-based biomarkers. The image entropy was concluded to be one of the most reproducible biomarkers.

Humans and algorithms can be imprecise when delineating poorly-visible or small tumors. The biomarkers extracted from such delineations could therefore be unreliable. Pavic et al. [37] recruited three radiologists to annotate HNSCC, malignant pleural mesotheliomas (MPM), and NSCLC and studied the differences in biomarkers computed from such annotations. The authors found out that the agreement between annotations ranges from 0.86 for NSCL to 0.26 for MPM, which in turn propagated to the agreement between biomarkers ranging from 90% for NSCLC to 36% for MPM. Kim et al. [94] observed that inter-observer variability on average has a more significant impact on biomarker values than intra-observer variability or image reconstruction technique. The unreliability of single-observer-based biomarkers has been acknowledged in the research field and some studies recruit multiple observers to annotate target objects before biomarker extraction [12,37,62,67,75,78].

2.4 RT Outcome Prediction Methodology

2.4.1 Biomarker Selection

There are hundreds and sometimes thousands of imaging biomarkers that are computed in each study. Most of the biomarkers are redundant, do not exhibit any predictive powers, or/and have very low clinical meaning. The extraction of relevant biomarkers is often the first step of the predictive model development, which can be achieved by biomarker selection or pruning [12,13,15,18,20,21,25,28,35,39,52,60–62,67,68,73,80,81]. The least absolute shrinkage and selection operator (LASSO) is most commonly used for biomarker selection [20,25,28,39,61,62,67]. The LASSO imposes the L1 regularization to the biomarkers selected by the machine learning predictor. As a result, the fewer biomarkers the predictor utilizes – the lower will be the regularization penalty during predictor training. The elastic net-based feature selection augments LASSO with L2 regularization to make biomarker selection less restrictive and allow the inclusion of mutually-dependent and therefore partially redundant biomarkers. Adding some redundancy to the selected biomarkers increases the predictor robustness against potential noise in the data. Mostafaei et al. [21] used the elastic nets for biomarker selection for the prediction of radiation-induced cystitis after prostate RTs. Principal component analysis (PCA) is an alternative strategy to reduce biomarker collection dimensionality. The PCA algorithm searches for the orthogonal linear combinations of biomarkers that capture the most variability in the data. The most contributive linear combinations are then used as new features. The PCA was shown to be effective for the outcome prediction after the prostate [60], head-and-neck [15,28], and lung [35,52] RTs. Lian et al. [83] adopted the Dempster–Shafer theory for evidence-based biomarker selection and demonstrated its practical applicability on post-CRT survival prediction using PET image biomarkers.

2.4.2 Machine Learning Methodology for Image-Based RT Outcome Prediction

To predict an outcome of a newly planned RT, the biomarkers from previous RTs with known outcomes need to be analyzed. The machine learning field offers various algorithms and methodological concepts for finding consistent patterns in historical data and mapping such patterns with outcomes of interest. The selection of an appropriate algorithm depends on several factors including the size of the RT database, the type of the outcome of interest, and the database imbalance. The four most-commonly used machine learning algorithms for RT outcome prediction include support vector machines (SVMs) [13,21,28,32,36,40,48,54,55,59,63,66,67,69,74,76,85,97,98], naïve Bayesian classifier (NBC) [13,39,50,53–55,64], random forests (RFs) [8,11,21,30,34,36,38, 41,51,54,55,61,64,71,79,82,88], and artificial neural networks (ANNs) [21,23, 24,26,28,29,32,40,54,63,74,75]. The SVMs search for an N-dimensional hyperplane that best separates RT data samples according to the RT outcomes. The SVMs are best suited for the problems with binary RT outcomes of interest, e.g., toxicity/no toxicity, but a k-1 nested SVM can be used for k-class outcome prediction. The NBC evaluates the probability of observing specific biomarker values for different RT outcomes and multiplies such probabilities to predict the outcome of a new RT sample. The RFs iteratively study the predictive powers of individual biomarkers and automatically create a hierarchy of binary biomarker tests for making the final prediction. At each iteration of the RF classifier training, a random subset of biomarkers is analyzed to reduce the risks of classifier overfitting. The RF can work with k-class outcome prediction as well as with RT outcomes of continuous type, e.g., survival. The ANNs can automatically learn complex patterns in biomarkers and, in the case of CNN, automatically generate image biomarkers. The ANNs exhibit high predictive powers, work well with multi-type input, but may easily overfit on training data. Less commonly used machine learning methodology for RT outcome prediction includes gradient boosting [12], bagging [54], AdaBoost [64], k-nearest neighbors [64,75,83], k-means clustering [43,70], artificial immune systems [48], and multiple adaptive regression splines [54]. Parmar et al. [54] compared the performance of 12 machine learning predictors against the prediction of overall survival after NSCLC CRT using a large database of 647 patients. The authors observed that most of the predictors exhibit similar performance with RFs being slightly superior to other predictors.

2.4.3 Predictor Explainability

Machine learning predictors are able to find complex patterns in RT image biomarkers, whereas the abilities of human observers are way more limited, so humans mainly focus on evident biomarkers. The more complex patterns an algorithm can capture, the more likely the algorithm to find some of them to be predictive and potentially overfit on the training RT data. It is therefore important to perform an explainability test for a predictor and check the explainability of all biomarkers that were selected as significant. NBC has high explainability as it statistically studies the predictive powers of individual biomarkers. The explainability of RF is also high, as each decision tree stores the information gain associated with the selected biomarkers. Biomarkers with high predictive powers have high mean information gain over all trees and are often selected during training as the best data separator. The explainability of SVMs and ANNs is lower, and non-trivial computational techniques need to be applied to analyze biomarker importance. There is, however, a universal permutation method that can measure a predicted biomarker association with an RT outcome. The idea of the permutation method is to artificially change the values of a biomarker and measure how the prediction results change. If the prediction results change significantly, the biomarker is estimated to be strongly associated with the RT outcome of interest. In contrast, small changes suggest that the biomarker exhibits low predictive powers.

2.4.4 Predictor Training Design

Machine learning studies are all about data. The studies on machine learning-based analysis of image biomarkers for RT outcome prediction often work with limited-size databases (Figures 2.2 and 2.3a). The median database size is 127, 84, and 94 images for CT-, MR-, and PET-based studies, respectively. Acquiring large image databases is very challenging as each patient must follow a similar treatment protocol and be monitored for a lengthy period of time for late RT outcomes to manifest. The problem with small databases is especially pronounced when researchers work with thousands of biomarkers. For example, let's say we have a database of 100 RTs with a binary outcome of interest. How many, on average, randomly generated fake pseudo-biomarkers are needed to find at least one pseudo-biomarker that will be able to "predict" the RT outcomes with more than 66% of success? It turns out that 500 random pseudo-biomarkers are enough to have a 50% chance to find a "predictive" pseudo-biomarker. To reduce the risks of such false predictions, the training and testing protocols should be correctly designed.

Prior to predictor training, the RT data needs to be split into training, validation, and testing subparts. The training process has full access to the training subpart and can use it to infer any biomarker patterns in the pre-RT images associated with RT outcomes. The validation part is not used to learn any biomarker patterns but to estimate the quality of the trained predictor.

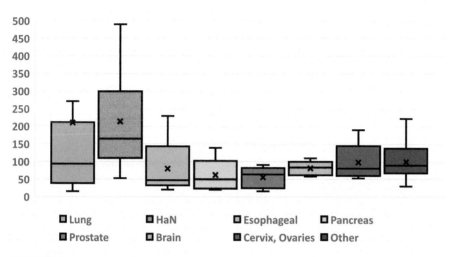

FIGURE 2.2
Statistics of the existing work on machine learning-based image analysis for radiotherapy (RT) outcome prediction. The box whiskers diagram with the number of images used in studies against different cancer types. The crosses indicate mean values. Three studies on machine learning-based lung RT outcome prediction analyzing 647, 944 and 1,194 CT image are not included into the box whiskers diagram to preserve fine details for other cancer types.

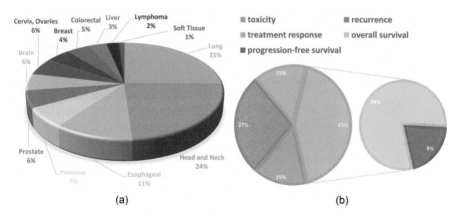

FIGURE 2.3
Statistics of the existing work on machine learning-based image analysis for radiotherapy outcome prediction. (a) The pie chart with the distribution of cancer types analyzed by the research community. (b) The pie chart with the treatment outcomes analyzed by the research community.

The validation subpart is essential to recognize predictor overfitting, i.e., when the performance on the training subpart is substantially higher than the performance on the validation subpart. Overfitting on validation data indicates that the predictor is likely to fail on unseen test data and the overall predictor design must be changed. The performance on that validation sub-part can be calculated multiple times during the predictor design. The testing subpart should only be used once to quantitatively access the final predictor performance. There are two main strategies for splitting the data into training, validation, and testing subparts. The first strategy is to randomly or semi-randomly perform the split, which is called a hold-out validation. The second strategy is to split the data into N equal subparts and iteratively use them as training, validation, and testing. The second strategy is called N-fold cross-validation, or when N equals the number of samples, leave-one-out validation. The data splitting protocol is less critical for predictors that are resistant against overfitting, for example, SVMs, but extremely critical for predictors that tend to overfit, for example, ANNs and RFs.

Both validation approaches were used in machine learning-based studies on RT outcome prediction. In the studies that selected the hold-out validation approach, the median database size was 190 RTs [8,10,11,14,15,20,23, 24,26,29,30,34,40,41,46,53,62,65,67,68,74,78,81,88]. In the studies that selected the N-fold cross-validation approach, the median database size was 91 RTs [12,13,21,25,28,31–33,35,36,38,39,43,44,48,50–52,60,63,64,66,69,75,76,80,85,97], whereas the studies that selected the leave-one-out cross-validation approach had the median database size of 51 RTs [22,25,49,55,61,73,83,98] (Figure 2.1b). One can observe that there is a tendency to select cross-validation over hold-out for studies with fewer subjects. Such a tendency is statistically justified, as there are high risks of selecting easy-to-analyze test cases when using hold-out validation with small databases. Validation bias can be minimized and the study conclusions strengthened when training and testing are performed on data from different hospitals. Kitamura and Deible have recently demonstrated that the accuracy of computer-aided diagnosis with machine learning drops from 0.9 to 0.59, if a machine learning model is tested on data from a different hospital. The data from different hospitals was used for validation of machine learning-based image biomarkers for survival prediction after lung [10,23,29,54], head-and-neck [11,15,53], cervical [65], and esophageal [34] RTs. The studies with validation on external data are usually larger and more comprehensive than other studies.

2.5 RT Outcomes of Interest Targeted by Machine Learning Predictors

2.5.1 Toxicities

Toxicities of healthy OARs represent the main limiting factor towards dose escalation during RT [2,115] (Figure 2.3b). The manifestation of toxicities is very poorly predictable as it depends on various factors including the patient's disease history, dose delivery regimen, motion compensation technique, and demographics [3,116]. Radiation-induced xerostomia is one of the most common toxicities after head-and-neck RTs due to the fact that salivary glands are often located in close proximity to the tumors. Radiation-induced xerostomia can range from mild and very treatable acute disease or tissue fibrosis associated with permanent xerostomia. Several attempts have been made to predict xerostomia from pre-RT CT and MR images using machine learning [25,36,42,50]. Van Dijk et al. [42] correlated post-RT xerostomia with the short-run emphasis CT image biomarker that, when computed over parotid glands, captures fat saturation of the glands. Gabrys et al. [36] have observed that the parotid gland volume and eccentricity are predictive anatomical biomarkers for late post-RT xerostomia. Sheikh et al. [25] found that the appearance of CT and MR biomarkers extracted from submandibular glands and the elongation of the parotid gland can significantly predict xerostomia, which is in agreement with the previously mentioned studies.

Moran et al. [47] searched for image biomarkers correlated with radiation-induced lung disease. The only biomarker with a statistically significant correlation was the GLCM-correlation biomarker computed over lung tumor volume. Abdollahi et al. [39] applied NBC to study 490 biomarkers and discovered 10 biomarkers extracted from cochlea segmentation that correlate with sensorineural hearing loss after head-and-neck CRT. Krafft et al. [31] have demonstrated that the combination of image biomarkers with dosimetric factors can predict radiation-induced pneumonitis with 0.68 AUC. Mostafaei et al. [21] used RFs and ANNs to demonstrate that image biomarkers exhibit higher predictive powers than clinical biomarkers for radiation-induced cystitis. RFs were able to find an early thermal signal in longitudinal thermal infrared images of breast acquired before individual RT fractions that predicted the development of radiation-induced dermatitis [88]. Recently, RFs were adapted for the prediction of radiation-induced temporal lobe injury using more than 10,000 biomarkers extracted from brain T1 and T2 MR images [8].

2.5.2 Complete Pathological Response

The lack of cancer cells in tissue samples extracted after RT, i.e., pathological response, is the earliest treatment outcome that can be measured (Figure 2.3b). Machine learning-based image biomarker analysis was performed for the prediction of treatment response after esophageal [40,74,78,79,84–86], nasopharyngeal [75], lung [24,51], rectal [32,67], pancreatic [18,26,61] CRTs, prostate intensity modulated RT [64], and brain stereotactic radiosurgery [33]. Despite seven studies on predicting esophageal CRT response, no biomarker was found to exhibit consistent predictive power, e.g., the tumor shape was found predictive [79] and not-predictive by different groups [74,78]. In contrast, the tumor volume is found to be predictive of pathological response after lung CRT by both studies that investigated this topic [24,51].

2.5.3 Cancer Recurrence

Although a pathological complete response after RT strongly correlates with favorable outcomes, certain patients will still have cancer recurrence (Figure 2.3b). Machine learning algorithm has been applied to associate image biomarkers with local, regional, or distant cancer recurrence. The researchers tried to identify biomarkers for the recurrence prediction after prostate [60,71,73], cervical [65,82,97], brain [63,66,69], lung [10,17,23,35,48,49,97], head-and-neck [11,14,15,20,28,38,44,46], and liver [45] RTs.

All three studies on cervical cancer concluded that tumor volume/size and tumor intensity entropy are among the most predictive PET image biomarkers for cancer recurrence RT outcome [65,82,97]. It is important to note that similar findings were observed on cervical cancer data from the Centre Eugene Marquis in France [82], Southwestern Medical Center in the USA [97], University Hospital of Brest in France [65], University Hospitals of Nantes in France [65], and McGill in Canada [65]. The conclusions on recurrence prediction after lung RTs varied in different studies. If Fave et al. [49] found no predictive CT image biomarkers [49], Hao et al. detected predictive powers in intensity, geometry, and texture CT biomarker types [97]. There was, however, a consistent conclusion about the predictive powers of tumor elongation biomarker [10,23,35]. The existing studies on head-and-neck cancer recurrence prediction mainly work with CT image biomarkers [11,14,20,38,46], with one study analyzing MR image biomarkers [28] and one study analyzing PET-CT image biomarkers [15]. In total, 1,073 oropharyngeal, 488 nasopharyngeal, 194 hypopharyngeal, 197 laryngeal, and 32 oral cavity cancers were analyzed by the studies on the topic. The conclusions are in general agreement with each other. The tumor intensity entropy [28,46], large area gray-level emphasis [15,20,46], tumor size [14,46], and local intensity maximum [20,38] were selected as predictive by more than one research study. In contrast to the enthusiasm shown by most of the studies on the topic, Keek et al. [11] observed that the predictive powers of CT head-and-neck image biomarkers could disappear when machine learning algorithms are tested on external RT databases.

2.5.4 Survival

The survival after cancer treatment is one of the most important outcomes for RT success evaluation (Figure 2.3b). The research community has been applying machine learning to search for consistent patterns in image biomarkers for survival prediction after lung [10,16,19,22,24,29,35,49,52,54,55,83,98], esophageal [34,79,83,98], head and neck [11,20,30,41,44,53,62,68], breast [72], pancreas [12,18,80,81], and liver [45]. The studies are focused on predicting disease-free survival or overall survival.

The researchers have tested the applicability of RF [54,55], naïve Bayesian [54,55], SVMs [54,55,98], and ANN [24,29,54] trained on CT, MR, and PET biomarkers for predicting survival after lung RTs. The highest intensity value in the tumor volume is considered to be a highly predictive PET [35,83,98] and CT [16,22,35] biomarker. The size, elongation, and overall tumor shape are generally considered to be predictive biomarkers for post-lung-RT survival [19,35,49,52]. In contrast, Shi et al. [16] did not observe any predictive power in tumor volume biomarkers. The homogeneity of tumors in both PET [83,98] and CT [35] images is a biomarker associated with a positive survival prognosis. Hawkins et al. [55] statistically confirmed the significance of tumor location and observed the predictive powers of the tumor touching the lung borders or pleural wall. Independently, CNNs confirmed these observations and automatically highlighted the tumors that touched the lung outer walls as the tumors with poor survival prognosis [29]. The most predictive biomarkers for esophageal cancer were the SUV [83,98] and tumor homogeneity [79,98] on PET images. The observations for head-and-neck cancers are very similar to the observations for other cancer types. In particular, the large area gray-level emphasis and the tumor size were predictive for survival after head-and-neck RTs [20,62].

2.6 Discussion

The technical developments in machine learning significantly advanced the field of image-based prediction of RT outcomes. In recent years, we have observed an explosive growth of papers on the topic. Naturally, it took some time before standardized protocols in the field have been developed. Despite the standardized protocols and interest from the community, none of the above-mentioned studies transitioned to clinical practice due to various obstacles. First, it was demonstrated that the image biomarkers significantly depend on image quality [94], image annotation quality [22], implementation protocol [108], etc. Second, around 50% of all research on the topic works with relatively small databases containing less than 100 patients treated at a single institution. Validation on small databases precludes the adoption of the developed predictors in clinical practice. It is very much expected to face challenges when collecting databases for RT outcome prediction. In contrast to the computer-aided diagnosis field where images are easy to label and databases, therefore, contain hundreds and thousands of images [117,118], the database of RTs with outcomes is very difficult to collect because outcome analysis requires the patients to have the same treatment protocol and have lengthy follow-ups. There is also no guarantee that a patient will be treated and followed up at the same hospital. These restrictions shrink the pool of patients accessible to individual research groups. Third, the treatment endpoint definitions vary among studies. It is therefore a common scenario when different studies arrive at contradictory conclusions.

Another conclusion that can be made from the literature review is that the biomarkers found to be predictive of different RT outcomes are also considered predictive by non-machine learning clinical studies. The machine learning methods often select maximum tumor intensity, which in PET image case is replaced with SUV [119], or tumor volume, i.e., biomarkers with established clinical predictive powers. On one hand, this observation supports the correctness of machine learning predictors design. On the other hand, this observation may suggest that complex image biomarkers do not exhibit any predictive powers and therefore not needed. Many complex image biomarkers serve to capture some statistical properties of tumor appearance. Such statistical properties do not always correspond to an anatomical or clinical tumor property. Moreover, the existing biomarkers are designed to capture the appearance of a single object of interest, e.g., tumors, and ignore inter-object relationships. The development of deep learning allowed to move away from pre-defined image biomarkers to machine-generated image biomarkers. Several research groups trained CNNs to find consistent patterns in pre-RT images and highlight image regions associated with negative treatment outcomes [23,29]. Hosny et al. [29] trained CNNs to predict survival after HSCLC RT or surgery using 754 cases. The authors then tested CNNs on 408 cases from different institutions and generated CNN activation maps for cases with predicted poor survival. It was observed that CNNs focus their attention on the interface between the tumor and parenchyma or pleura. Lou et al. [23] studied 944 lung RT patients using CNNs and found out that 38% of image voxels that summon CNNs attention are located at peritumoral regions and tumor margins. Although the authors did not find the exact pattern in such outside voxels, they concluded that the imaging biomarker should extend beyond tumor borders.

The prediction of RT outcomes using only image biomarkers is insufficient. The treatment outcome is mostly based on the treatment design while the image biomarkers should play an axillary role in outcome prediction. The prescribed treatment dose, dose delivery fractionation, the use of immobilization equipment, and the quality of dose distribution plans are the key factors affecting RT outcomes. The understanding of the importance of treatment features is also reflected in a number of studies mentioned in this book chapter [12–15,21,23,25,31,32,36,38,39,43–45,48,50,51,80,88]. The most common strategy for the inclusion of treatment features into the analysis is to convert treatment features into numerical values and concatenate them to image biomarkers and then provide all features to a machine learning predictor. The main treatment feature of interest is whether RT was combined with chemotherapy or/and surgery. Parr et al. [12] observed that a successful pancreatic tumor resection is a stronger predictor for survival after pancreatic SBRT than any image biomarker. Machine learning predictors observed that the information about concurrent-to-RT chemotherapy can augment image biomarkers for the prediction of head-and-neck cancer [38,39], esophageal cancer [43], and lung cancer [51] treatment outcomes. The different authors observed no statistically significant predictive powers of the inclusion of chemotherapy into the treatment regimen for head-and-neck cancer [14,44] and pancreatic cancer [80,81] treatment outcomes. The potentially contradictory conclusions for head-and-neck cancer can be explained by different study design and study population. Moreover, the inclusion of chemotherapy into the treatment may not be predictive by itself but be of importance in combination with other treatment features and image biomarkers. Machine learning predictors can discover such complex patterns and indicate the benefits of concurrent chemotherapy for RT outcome prediction for specific patients.

The dose distribution plans are of extreme significance for the prediction of RT outcomes. All studies that analyzed the dose plans in combination with image biomarkers found such synergy to improve the outcome prediction accuracy [4,5,13,15,21,23,25,31,32,36,43,45,48,50,51,88,111]. The dose plans are defined as 3D volumes of the same size as the treatment images. The dose plans can therefore be analyzed with the same methodology that is used for image biomarker extraction. The synergistic analysis of image biomarkers and doses delivered to the skin improves the prediction of skin toxicity after breast radiotherapy [88], doses delivered to bladders – the prediction of radiation-induced cystitis [21], doses delivered to the rectum – the prediction of proctitis [21], doses delivered to parotids (D_{40}) and submandibular (D_{60}) glands – the prediction of xerostomia [25], and doses delivered to heart and lung improve the prediction of pneumonitis [31]. Avanzo et al. [13] observed that run-length non-uniformity dose and 10th percentile PTV 3D biologically effective dose (BED) biomarkers, which roughly capture the uniformity of dose distribution and the presence of dose hot spots, respectively, computed over breast tissue can predict radiation-induced fibrosis. Similarly, Gabrys et al. [36] demonstrated that spatial dose distribution metrics, which can be computed using image biomarker extraction toolboxes, exhibit stronger predictive powers that dose–volume metrics conventionally used for RT planning.

2.7 Conclusion

Machine learning has been expanding to all areas of research for the last decade. The expansion is especially pronounced in the fields, where there is a need to analyze large amounts of multitype data, e.g. image-based prediction of RT outcomes. In the last years, this field witnessed an explosive growth of publications. This growth stimulated the development of research standards including standardized methodology for image biomarker extraction, image preprocessing, data curation, and statistical result evaluation. This book chapter presented a summary of the methodological and clinical achievements in this rapidly growing field of research.

Acknowledgements

Bulat Ibragimov is supported by the Novo Nordisk Foundation under grant NFF20OC0062056.

References

1. J. O. Deasy et al., "Improving normal tissue complication probability models: The need to adopt a 'data-pooling' culture," *Int. J. Radiat. Oncol. Biol. Phys.*, vol. 76, no. 3 Suppl, pp. S151–154, Mar. 2010, doi: 10.1016/j.ijrobp.2009.06.094.
2. C. Terrones-Campos, B. Ledergerber, I. R. Vogelius, L. Specht, M. Helleberg, and J. Lundgren, "Lymphocyte count kinetics, factors associated with the end-of-radiation-therapy lymphocyte count, and risk of infection in patients with solid malignant tumors treated with curative-intent radiation therapy," *Int. J. Radiat. Oncol.*, vol. 105, no. 4, pp. 812–823, Nov. 2019, doi: 10.1016/j.ijrobp.2019.07.013.
3. D. A. S. Toesca et al., "Central liver toxicity after SBRT: An expanded analysis and predictive nomogram," *Radiother. Oncol.*, vol. 122, no. 1, pp. 130–136, Jan. 2017, doi: 10.1016/j.radonc.2016.10.024.
4. B. Ibragimov et al., "Deep learning for identification of critical regions associated with toxicities after liver stereotactic body radiation therapy," *Med. Phys.*, vol. 47, no. 8, pp. 3721–3731, 2020, doi: 10.1002/mp.14235.
5. B. Ibragimov, D. A. S. Toesca, Y. Yuan, A. C. Koong, D. T. Chang, and L. Xing, "Neural networks for deep radiotherapy dose analysis and prediction of liver SBRT outcomes," *IEEE J. Biomed. Health Inform.*, vol. 23, no. 5, pp. 1821–1833, Sep. 2019, doi: 10.1109/JBHI.2019.2904078.
6. E. A. Eisenhauer et al., "New response evaluation criteria in solid tumours: revised RECIST guideline (version 1.1)," *Eur. J. Cancer Oxf. Engl. 1990*, vol. 45, no. 2, pp. 228–247, Jan. 2009, doi: 10.1016/j.ejca.2008.10.026.
7. P. Therasse et al., "New guidelines to evaluate the response to treatment in solid tumors," *JNCI J. Natl. Cancer Inst.*, vol. 92, no. 3, pp. 205–216, Feb. 2000, doi: 10.1093/jnci/92.3.205.
8. B. Zhang et al., "Machine-learning based MRI radiomics models for early detection of radiation-induced brain injury in nasopharyngeal carcinoma," *BMC Cancer*, vol. 20, no. 1, p. 502, Jun. 2020, doi: 10.1186/s12885-020-06957-4.
9. M. C. Korpics et al., "A validated T cell radiomics score is associated with clinical outcomes following multisite SBRT and pembrolizumab," *Int. J. Radiat. Oncol. Biol. Phys.*, vol. 108, no. 1, pp. 189–195, Sep. 2020, doi: 10.1016/j.ijrobp.2020.06.026.
10. G. Dissaux et al., "Pretreatment 18F-FDG PET/CT radiomics predict local recurrence in patients treated with stereotactic body radiotherapy for early-stage non-small cell lung cancer: A multicentric study," *J. Nucl. Med. Off. Publ. Soc. Nucl. Med.*, vol. 61, no. 6, pp. 814–820, Jun. 2020, doi: 10.2967/jnumed.119.228106.
11. S. Keek et al., "Computed tomography-derived radiomic signature of head and neck squamous cell carcinoma (peri)tumoral tissue for the prediction of locoregional recurrence and distant metastasis after concurrent chemo-radiotherapy," *PLOS ONE*, vol. 15, no. 5, p. e0232639, May 2020, doi: 10.1371/journal.pone.0232639.

12. E. Parr et al., "Radiomics-based outcome prediction for pancreatic cancer following stereotactic body radiotherapy," *Cancers*, vol. 12, no. 4, Apr. 2020, doi: 10.3390/cancers12041051.
13. M. Avanzo et al., "Electron density and biologically effective dose (BED) radiomics-based machine learning models to predict late radiation-induced subcutaneous fibrosis," *Front. Oncol.*, vol. 10, 2020, doi: 10.3389/fonc.2020.00490.
14. T.-T. Zhai et al., "Pre-treatment radiomic features predict individual lymph node failure for head and neck cancer patients," *Radiother. Oncol.*, vol. 146, pp. 58–65, May 2020, doi: 10.1016/j.radonc.2020.02.005.
15. A. Wu et al., "Dosiomics improves prediction of locoregional recurrence for intensity modulated radiotherapy treated head and neck cancer cases," *Oral Oncol.*, vol. 104, p. 104625, May 2020, doi: 10.1016/j.oraloncology.2020.104625.
16. L. Shi et al., "Cone-beam computed tomography-based delta-radiomics for early response assessment in radiotherapy for locally advanced lung cancer," *Phys. Med. Biol.*, vol. 65, no. 1, p. 015009, 2020, doi: 10.1088/1361-6560/ab3247.
17. Q. Qin et al., "Cone-beam CT radiomics features might improve the prediction of lung toxicity after SBRT in stage I NSCLC patients," *Thorac. Cancer*, vol. 11, no. 4, pp. 964–972, 2020, doi: 10.1111/1759-7714.13349.
18. H. Nasief et al., "Improving treatment response prediction for chemoradiation therapy of pancreatic cancer using a combination of delta-radiomics and the clinical biomarker CA19-9," *Front. Oncol.*, vol. 9, Jan. 2020, doi: 10.3389/fonc.2019.01464.
19. M. M. K. Krarup et al., "Heterogeneity in tumours: Validating the use of radiomic features on 18F-FDG PET/CT scans of lung cancer patients as a prognostic tool," *Radiother. Oncol. J. Eur. Soc. Ther. Radiol. Oncol.*, vol. 144, pp. 72–78, Mar. 2020, doi: 10.1016/j.radonc.2019.10.012.
20. X. Mo et al., "Prognostic value of the radiomics-based model in progression-free survival of hypopharyngeal cancer treated with chemoradiation," *Eur. Radiol.*, vol. 30, no. 2, pp. 833–843, Feb. 2020, doi: 10.1007/s00330-019-06452-w.
21. S. Mostafaei et al., "CT imaging markers to improve radiation toxicity prediction in prostate cancer radiotherapy by stacking regression algorithm," *Radiol. Med. (Torino)*, vol. 125, no. 1, pp. 87–97, Jan. 2020, doi: 10.1007/s11547-019-01082-0.
22. R. N. Mahon, G. D. Hugo, and E. Weiss, "Repeatability of texture features derived from magnetic resonance and computed tomography imaging and use in predictive models for non-small cell lung cancer outcome," *Phys. Med. Biol.*, Apr. 2019, doi: 10.1088/1361-6560/ab18d3.
23. B. Lou et al., "An image-based deep learning framework for individualising radiotherapy dose: A retrospective analysis of outcome prediction," *Lancet Digit. Health*, vol. 1, no. 3, pp. e136–e147, Jul. 2019, doi: 10.1016/S2589-7500(19)30058-5.
24. Y. Xu et al., "Deep learning predicts lung cancer treatment response from serial medical imaging," *Clin. Cancer Res. Off. J. Am. Assoc. Cancer Res.*, vol. 25, no. 11, pp. 3266–3275, 2019, doi: 10.1158/1078-0432.CCR-18-2495.
25. K. Sheikh et al., "Predicting acute radiation induced xerostomia in head and neck Cancer using MR and CT Radiomics of parotid and submandibular glands," *Radiat. Oncol.*, vol. 14, no. 1, p. 131, Jul. 2019, doi: 10.1186/s13014-019-1339-4.
26. H. Nasief et al., "A machine learning based delta-radiomics process for early prediction of treatment response of pancreatic cancer," *NPJ Precis. Oncol.*, vol. 3, no. 1, Art. no. 1, Oct. 2019, doi: 10.1038/s41698-019-0096-z.

27. P. Lakshminarayanan et al., "Radio-morphology: Parametric shape-based features in radiotherapy," *Med. Phys.*, vol. 46, no. 2, pp. 704–713, Feb. 2019, doi: 10.1002/mp.13323.

28. S. Li et al., "Use of radiomics combined with machine learning method in the recurrence patterns after intensity-modulated radiotherapy for nasopharyngeal carcinoma: A preliminary study," *Front. Oncol.*, vol. 8, p. 648, 2018, doi: 10.3389/fonc.2018.00648.

29. A. Hosny et al., "Deep learning for lung cancer prognostication: A retrospective multi-cohort radiomics study," *PLoS Med.*, vol. 15, no. 11, p. e1002711, Nov. 2018, doi: 10.1371/journal.pmed.1002711.

30. S. Leger et al., "CT imaging during treatment improves radiomic models for patients with locally advanced head and neck cancer," *Radiother. Oncol. J. Eur. Soc. Ther. Radiol. Oncol.*, vol. 130, pp. 10–17, 2019, doi: 10.1016/j.radonc.2018.07.020.

31. S. P. Krafft et al., "The utility of quantitative CT radiomics features for improved prediction of radiation pneumonitis," *Med. Phys.*, vol. 45, no. 11, pp. 5317–5324, Nov. 2018, doi: 10.1002/mp.13150.

32. J.-E. Bibault et al., "Deep Learning and Radiomics predict complete response after neo-adjuvant chemoradiation for locally advanced rectal cancer," *Sci. Rep.*, vol. 8, no. 1, Art. no. 1, Aug. 2018, doi: 10.1038/s41598-018-30657-6.

33. Y. J. Cha et al., "Prediction of response to stereotactic radiosurgery for brain metastases using convolutional neural networks," *Anticancer Res.*, vol. 38, no. 9, pp. 5437–5445, Sep. 2018, doi: 10.21873/anticanres.12875.

34. R. T. H. M. Larue et al., "Pre-treatment CT radiomics to predict 3-year overall survival following chemoradiotherapy of esophageal cancer," *Acta Oncol. Stockh. Swed.*, vol. 57, no. 11, pp. 1475–1481, Nov. 2018, doi: 10.1080/0284186X.2018.1486039.

35. A. Oikonomou et al., "Radiomics analysis at PET/CT contributes to prognosis of recurrence and survival in lung cancer treated with stereotactic body radiotherapy," *Sci. Rep.*, vol. 8, no. 1, p. 4003, 2018, doi: 10.1038/s41598-018-22357-y.

36. H. S. Gabryś, F. Buettner, F. Sterzing, H. Hauswald, and M. Bangert, "Design and selection of machine learning methods using radiomics and dosiomics for normal tissue complication probability modeling of xerostomia," *Front. Oncol.*, vol. 8, p. 35, 2018, doi: 10.3389/fonc.2018.00035.

37. M. Pavic et al., "Influence of inter-observer delineation variability on radiomics stability in different tumor sites," *Acta Oncol. Stockh. Swed.*, vol. 57, no. 8, pp. 1070–1074, Aug. 2018, doi: 10.1080/0284186X.2018.1445283.

38. H. Elhalawani et al., "Investigation of radiomic signatures for local recurrence using primary tumor texture analysis in oropharyngeal head and neck cancer patients," *Sci. Rep.*, vol. 8, no. 1, Art. no. 1, Jan. 2018, doi: 10.1038/s41598-017-14687-0.

39. H. Abdollahi, S. Mostafaei, S. Cheraghi, I. Shiri, S. Rabi Mahdavi, and A. Kazemnejad, "Cochlea CT radiomics predicts chemoradiotherapy induced sensorineural hearing loss in head and neck cancer patients: A machine learning and multi-variable modelling study," *Phys. Medica PM Int. J. Devoted Appl. Phys. Med. Biol. Off. J. Ital. Assoc. Biomed. Phys. AIFB*, vol. 45, pp. 192–197, Jan. 2018, doi: 10.1016/j.ejmp.2017.10.008.

40. Z. Hou et al., "Radiomic analysis in contrast-enhanced CT: predict treatment response to chemoradiotherapy in esophageal carcinoma," *Oncotarget*, vol. 8, no. 61, pp. 104444–104454, Nov. 2017, doi: 10.18632/oncotarget.22304.

41. S. Leger et al., "A comparative study of machine learning methods for time-to-event survival data for radiomics risk modelling," *Sci. Rep.*, vol. 7, no. 1, Art. no. 1, Oct. 2017, doi: 10.1038/s41598-017-13448-3.
42. L. V. van Dijk et al., "Geometric image biomarker changes of the parotid gland are associated with late xerostomia," *Int. J. Radiat. Oncol. Biol. Phys.*, vol. 99, no. 5, pp. 1101–1110, Dec. 2017, doi: 10.1016/j.ijrobp.2017.08.003.
43. J. S. Niedzielski et al., "A novel methodology using CT imaging biomarkers to quantify radiation sensitivity in the esophagus with application to clinical trials," *Sci. Rep.*, vol. 7, Jul. 2017, doi: 10.1038/s41598-017-05003-x.
44. D. Ou et al., "Predictive and prognostic value of CT based radiomics signature in locally advanced head and neck cancers patients treated with concurrent chemoradiotherapy or bioradiotherapy and its added value to Human Papillomavirus status," *Oral Oncol.*, vol. 71, pp. 150–155, 2017, doi: 10.1016/j.oraloncology.2017.06.015.
45. L. Cozzi et al., "Radiomics based analysis to predict local control and survival in hepatocellular carcinoma patients treated with volumetric modulated arc therapy," *BMC Cancer*, vol. 17, no. 1, p. 829, Dec. 2017, doi: 10.1186/s12885-017-3847-7.
46. M. Bogowicz et al., "Computed tomography radiomics predicts HPV status and local tumor control after definitive radiochemotherapy in head and neck squamous cell carcinoma," *Int. J. Radiat. Oncol. Biol. Phys.*, vol. 99, no. 4, pp. 921–928, 2017, doi: 10.1016/j.ijrobp.2017.06.002.
47. A. Moran, M. E. Daly, S. S. F. Yip, and T. Yamamoto, "Radiomics-based assessment of radiation-induced lung injury after stereotactic body radiotherapy," *Clin. Lung Cancer*, vol. 18, no. 6, pp. e425–e431, 2017, doi: 10.1016/j.cllc.2017.05.014.
48. Z. Zhou et al., "Multi-objective radiomics model for predicting distant failure in lung SBRT," *Phys. Med. Biol.*, vol. 62, no. 11, pp. 4460–4478, 2017, doi: 10.1088/1361-6560/aa6ae5.
49. X. Fave et al., "Delta-radiomics features for the prediction of patient outcomes in non-small cell lung cancer," *Sci. Rep.*, vol. 7, no. 1, p. 588, 2017, doi: 10.1038/s41598-017-00665-z.
50. M. Pota et al., "Early prediction of radiotherapy-induced parotid shrinkage and toxicity based on CT radiomics and fuzzy classification," *Artif. Intell. Med.*, vol. 81, pp. 41–53, Sep. 2017, doi: 10.1016/j.artmed.2017.03.004.
51. T. P. Coroller et al., "Radiomic-based pathological response prediction from primary tumors and lymph nodes in NSCLC," *J. Thorac. Oncol. Off. Publ. Int. Assoc. Study Lung Cancer*, vol. 12, no. 3, pp. 467–476, 2017, doi: 10.1016/j.jtho.2016.11.2226.
52. E. Huynh *et al.*, "CT-based radiomic analysis of stereotactic body radiation therapy patients with lung cancer," *Radiother. Oncol. J. Eur. Soc. Ther. Radiol. Oncol.*, vol. 120, no. 2, pp. 258–266, 2016, doi: 10.1016/j.radonc.2016.05.024.
53. C. Parmar, P. Grossmann, D. Rietveld, M. M. Rietbergen, P. Lambin, and H. J. W. L. Aerts, "Radiomic machine-learning classifiers for prognostic biomarkers of head and neck cancer," *Front. Oncol.*, vol. 5, 2015, doi: 10.3389/fonc.2015.00272.
54. C. Parmar, P. Grossmann, J. Bussink, P. Lambin, and H. J. W. L. Aerts, "Machine learning methods for quantitative radiomic biomarkers," *Sci. Rep.*, vol. 5, no. 1, Art. no. 1, Aug. 2015, doi: 10.1038/srep13087.
55. S. H. Hawkins et al., "Predicting outcomes of nonsmall cell lung cancer using CT image features," *IEEE Access*, vol. 2, pp. 1418–1426, 2014, doi: 10.1109/ACCESS.2014.2373335.

56. B. Slotman and C. Gani, "Online MR-guided radiotherapy – A new era in radiotherapy," *Clin. Transl. Radiat. Oncol.*, vol. 18, pp. 102–103, Apr. 2019, doi: 10.1016/j.ctro.2019.04.011.

57. J. Jonsson, T. Nyholm, and K. Söderkvist, "The rationale for MR-only treatment planning for external radiotherapy," *Clin. Transl. Radiat. Oncol.*, vol. 18, pp. 60–65, Apr. 2019, doi: 10.1016/j.ctro.2019.03.005.

58. N.-N. Chung, L.-L. Ting, W.-C. Hsu, L. T. Lui, and P.-M. Wang, "Impact of magnetic resonance imaging versus CT on nasopharyngeal carcinoma: Primary tumor target delineation for radiotherapy," *Head Neck*, vol. 26, no. 3, pp. 241–246, 2004, doi: 10.1002/hed.10378.

59. Y. Gao et al., "Treatment effect prediction for sarcoma patients treated with preoperative radiotherapy using radiomics features from longitudinal diffusion-weighted MRIs," *Phys. Med. Biol.*, vol. 65, no. 17, p. 175006, Aug. 2020, doi: 10.1088/1361-6560/ab9e58.

60. Q.-Z. Zhong et al., "Radiomics of multiparametric MRI to predict biochemical recurrence of localized prostate cancer after radiation therapy," *Front. Oncol.*, vol. 10, 2020, doi: 10.3389/fonc.2020.00731.

61. G. Simpson et al., "Predictive value of 0.35 T magnetic resonance imaging radiomic features in stereotactic ablative body radiotherapy of pancreatic cancer: A pilot study," *Med. Phys.*, vol. 47, no. 8, pp. 3682–3690, 2020, doi: 10.1002/mp.14200.

62. H. Shen et al., "Predicting progression-free survival using MRI-based radiomics for patients with nonmetastatic nasopharyngeal carcinoma," *Front. Oncol.*, vol. 10, May 2020, doi: 10.3389/fonc.2020.00618.

63. M. Li, H. Tang, M. D. Chan, X. Zhou, and X. Qian, "DC-AL GAN: Pseudoprogression and true tumor progression of glioblastoma multiform image classification based on DCGAN and AlexNet," *Med. Phys.*, vol. 47, no. 3, pp. 1139–1150, Mar. 2020, doi: 10.1002/mp.14003.

64. H. Abdollahi et al., "Machine learning-based radiomic models to predict intensity-modulated radiation therapy response, Gleason score and stage in prostate cancer," *Radiol. Med. (Torino)*, vol. 124, no. 6, pp. 555–567, Jun. 2019, doi: 10.1007/s11547-018-0966-4.

65. F. Lucia et al., "External validation of a combined PET and MRI radiomics model for prediction of recurrence in cervical cancer patients treated with chemoradiotherapy," *Eur. J. Nucl. Med. Mol. Imaging*, vol. 46, no. 4, pp. 864–877, Apr. 2019, doi: 10.1007/s00259-018-4231-9.

66. S. Rathore et al., "Radiomic signature of infiltration in peritumoral edema predicts subsequent recurrence in glioblastoma: Implications for personalized radiotherapy planning," *J. Med. Imaging Bellingham Wash*, vol. 5, no. 2, p. 021219, Apr. 2018, doi: 10.1117/1.JMI.5.2.021219.

67. Z. Liu et al., "Radiomics analysis for evaluation of pathological complete response to neoadjuvant chemoradiotherapy in locally advanced rectal cancer," *Clin. Cancer Res. Off. J. Am. Assoc. Cancer Res.*, vol. 23, no. 23, pp. 7253–7262, Dec. 2017, doi: 10.1158/1078-0432.CCR-17-1038.

68. B. Zhang et al., "Radiomics features of multiparametric MRI as novel prognostic factors in advanced nasopharyngeal carcinoma," *Clin. Cancer Res. Off. J. Am. Assoc. Cancer Res.*, vol. 23, no. 15, pp. 4259–4269, Aug. 2017, doi: 10.1158/1078-0432.CCR-16-2910.

69. P. Tiwari et al., "Computer-extracted texture features to distinguish cerebral radionecrosis from recurrent brain tumors on multiparametric MRI: A feasibility study," *Am. J. Neuroradiol.*, Sep. 2016, doi: 10.3174/ajnr.A4931.
70. T. Torheim et al., "Cluster analysis of dynamic contrast enhanced MRI reveals tumor subregions related to locoregional relapse for cervical cancer patients," *Acta Oncol. Stockh. Swed.*, vol. 55, no. 11, pp. 1294–1298, Nov. 2016, doi: 10.1080/0284186X.2016.1189091.
71. K. Gnep et al., "Haralick textural features on T2-weighted MRI are associated with biochemical recurrence following radiotherapy for peripheral zone prostate cancer," *J. Magn. Reson. Imaging JMRI*, vol. 45, no. 1, pp. 103–117, 2017, doi: 10.1002/jmri.25335.
72. M. D. Pickles, M. Lowry, and P. Gibbs, "Pretreatment prognostic value of dynamic contrast-enhanced magnetic resonance imaging vascular, texture, shape, and size parameters compared with traditional survival indicators obtained from locally advanced breast cancer patients," *Invest. Radiol.*, vol. 51, no. 3, pp. 177–185, Mar. 2016, doi: 10.1097/RLI.0000000000000222.
73. S. B. Ginsburg, M. Rusu, J. Kurhanewicz, and A. Madabhushi, "Computer extracted texture features on T2w MRI to predict biochemical recurrence following radiation therapy for prostate cancer," in *Medical Imaging 2014: Computer-Aided Diagnosis*, Mar. 2014, vol. 9035, p. 903509, doi: 10.1117/12.2043937.
74. Z. Hou, S. Li, W. Ren, J. Liu, J. Yan, and S. Wan, "Radiomic analysis in T2W and SPAIR T2W MRI: Predict treatment response to chemoradiotherapy in esophageal squamous cell carcinoma," *J. Thorac. Dis.*, vol. 10, no. 4, pp. 2256–2267, Apr. 2018, doi: 10.21037/jtd.2018.03.123.
75. J. Liu et al., "Use of texture analysis based on contrast-enhanced MRI to predict treatment response to chemoradiotherapy in nasopharyngeal carcinoma," *J. Magn. Reson. Imaging JMRI*, vol. 44, no. 2, pp. 445–455, 2016, doi: 10.1002/jmri.25156.
76. L. Peng et al., "Distinguishing true progression from radionecrosis after stereotactic radiation therapy for brain metastases with machine learning and radiomics," *Int. J. Radiat. Oncol. Biol. Phys.*, vol. 102, no. 4, pp. 1236–1243, 2018, doi: 10.1016/j.ijrobp.2018.05.041.
77. W. W. Moses, "Fundamental limits of spatial resolution in PET," *Nucl. Instrum. Methods Phys. Res. Sect. Accel. Spectrometers Detect. Assoc. Equip.*, vol. 648, no. Supplement 1, pp. S236–S240, Aug. 2011, doi: 10.1016/j.nima.2010.11.092.
78. Q. Cao, Y. Li, Z. Li, D. An, B. Li, and Q. Lin, "Development and validation of a radiomics signature on differentially expressed features of 18F-FDG PET to predict treatment response of concurrent chemoradiotherapy in thoracic esophagus squamous cell carcinoma," *Radiother. Oncol. J. Eur. Soc. Ther. Radiol. Oncol.*, vol. 146, pp. 9–15, May 2020, doi: 10.1016/j.radonc.2020.01.027.
79. P. Desbordes et al., "Predictive value of initial FDG-PET features for treatment response and survival in esophageal cancer patients treated with chemoradiation therapy using a random forest classifier," *PLoS One*, vol. 12, no. 3, p. e0173208, 2017, doi: 10.1371/journal.pone.0173208.
80. Y. Yue et al., "Identifying prognostic intratumor heterogeneity using pre- and post-radiotherapy 18F-FDG PET images for pancreatic cancer patients," *J. Gastrointest. Oncol.*, vol. 8, no. 1, Art. no. 1, Feb. 2017.

81. Y. Cui et al., "Quantitative analysis of (18)F-fluorodeoxyglucose positron emission tomography identifies novel prognostic imaging biomarkers in locally advanced pancreatic cancer patients treated with stereotactic body radiation therapy," *Int. J. Radiat. Oncol. Biol. Phys.*, vol. 96, no. 1, pp. 102–109, 2016, doi: 10.1016/j.ijrobp.2016.04.034.

82. G. Roman-Jimenez et al., "Random forests to predict tumor recurrence following cervical cancer therapy using pre- and per-treatment 18F-FDG PET parameters," in *2016 38th Annual International Conference of the IEEE Engineering in Medicine and Biology Society (EMBC)*, Aug. 2016, pp. 2444–2447, doi: 10.1109/EMBC.2016.7591224.

83. C. Lian, S. Ruan, T. Denœux, F. Jardin, and P. Vera, "Selecting radiomic features from FDG-PET images for cancer treatment outcome prediction," *Med. Image Anal.*, vol. 32, pp. 257–268, 2016, doi: 10.1016/j.media.2016.05.007.

84. S. S. F. Yip et al., "Use of registration-based contour propagation in texture analysis for esophageal cancer pathologic response prediction," *Phys. Med. Biol.*, vol. 61, no. 2, pp. 906–922, Jan. 2016, doi: 10.1088/0031-9155/61/2/906.

85. H. Zhang et al., "Modeling pathologic response of esophageal cancer to chemoradiotherapy using spatial-temporal 18F-FDG PET features, clinical parameters, and demographics," *Int. J. Radiat. Oncol. Biol. Phys.*, vol. 88, no. 1, Jan. 2014, doi: 10.1016/j.ijrobp.2013.09.037.

86. S. Tan et al., "Spatial-temporal [18F]FDG-PET features for predicting pathologic response of esophageal cancer to neoadjuvant chemoradiation therapy," *Int. J. Radiat. Oncol. Biol. Phys.*, vol. 85, no. 5, pp. 1375–1382, Apr. 2013, doi: 10.1016/j.ijrobp.2012.10.017.

87. R. T. H. M. Larue, G. Defraene, D. De Ruysscher, P. Lambin, and W. van Elmpt, "Quantitative radiomics studies for tissue characterization: A review of technology and methodological procedures," *Br. J. Radiol.*, vol. 90, no. 1070, p. 20160665, Feb. 2017, doi: 10.1259/bjr.20160665.

88. K. Saednia et al., "Quantitative thermal imaging biomarkers to detect acute skin toxicity from breast radiation therapy using supervised machine learning," *Int. J. Radiat. Oncol. Biol. Phys.*, vol. 106, no. 5, pp. 1071–1083, Apr. 2020, doi: 10.1016/j.ijrobp.2019.12.032.

89. G. Kitamura and C. Deible, "Retraining an open-source pneumothorax detecting machine learning algorithm for improved performance to medical images," *Clin. Imaging*, vol. 61, pp. 15–19, May 2020, doi: 10.1016/j.clinimag.2020.01.008.

90. L. P. Clarke et al., "The quantitative imaging network: NCI's historical perspective and planned goals," *Transl. Oncol.*, vol. 7, no. 1, pp. 1–4, Feb. 2014, doi: 10.1593/tlo.13832.

91. M. Schwier et al., "Repeatability of multiparametric prostate MRI radiomics features," *Sci. Rep.*, vol. 9, no. 1, Art. no. 1, Jul. 2019, doi: 10.1038/s41598-019-45766-z.

92. S. Xie et al., "Artifact removal using improved GoogLeNet for sparse-view CT reconstruction," *Sci. Rep.*, vol. 8, no. 1, p. 6700, Dec. 2018, doi: 10.1038/s41598-018-25153-w.

93. P. Després and X. Jia, "A review of GPU-based medical image reconstruction," *Phys. Med.*, vol. 42, pp. 76–92, Oct. 2017, doi: 10.1016/j.ejmp.2017.07.024.

94. H. Kim et al., "Impact of reconstruction algorithms on CT radiomic features of pulmonary tumors: Analysis of intra- and inter-reader variability and inter-reconstruction algorithm variability," *PLoS One*, vol. 11, no. 10, p. e0164924, 2016, doi: 10.1371/journal.pone.0164924.

95. M. Katsura, J. Sato, M. Akahane, A. Kunimatsu, and O. Abe, "Current and novel techniques for metal artifact reduction at CT: Practical guide for radiologists," *RadioGraphics*, vol. 38, no. 2, pp. 450–461, Mar. 2018, doi: 10.1148/rg.2018170102.

96. P. O. Zinn et al., "A coclinical radiogenomic validation study: Conserved magnetic resonance radiomic appearance of periostin-expressing glioblastoma in patients and xenograft models," *Clin. Cancer Res.*, vol. 24, no. 24, pp. 6288–6299, Dec. 2018, doi: 10.1158/1078-0432.CCR-17-3420.

97. H. Hao et al., "Shell feature: A new radiomics descriptor for predicting distant failure after radiotherapy in non-small cell lung cancer and cervix cancer," *Phys. Med. Biol.*, vol. 63, no. 9, p. 095007, 2018, doi: 10.1088/1361-6560/aabb5e.

98. H. Mi, C. Petitjean, B. Dubray, P. Vera, and S. Ruan, "Robust feature selection to predict tumor treatment outcome," *Artif. Intell. Med.*, vol. 64, no. 3, pp. 195–204, Jul. 2015, doi: 10.1016/j.artmed.2015.07.002.

99. G. Eminowicz and M. McCormack, "Variability of clinical target volume delineation for definitive radiotherapy in cervix cancer," *Radiother. Oncol.*, vol. 117, no. 3, pp. 542–547, Dec. 2015, doi: 10.1016/j.radonc.2015.10.007.

100. C. Ménard et al., "Role of prostate MR imaging in radiation oncology," *Radiol. Clin.*, vol. 56, no. 2, pp. 319–325, Mar. 2018, doi: 10.1016/j.rcl.2017.10.012.

101. S. Bakas et al., "Identifying the Best Machine Learning Algorithms for Brain Tumor Segmentation, Progression Assessment, and Overall Survival Prediction in the BRATS Challenge," *ArXiv181102629 Cs Stat*, Apr. 2019, Accessed: Sep. 04, 2020. [Online]. Available: http://arxiv.org/abs/1811.02629.

102. O. Ronneberger, P. Fischer, and T. Brox, "U-Net: Convolutional networks for biomedical image segmentation," in *Medical Image Computing and Computer-Assisted Intervention – MICCAI 2015*, Cham, 2015, pp. 234–241, doi: 10.1007/978-3-319-24574-4_28.

103. H. J. W. L. Aerts, "The potential of radiomic-based phenotyping in precision medicine: A review," *JAMA Oncol.*, vol. 2, no. 12, pp. 1636–1642, Dec. 2016, doi: 10.1001/jamaoncol.2016.2631.

104. A. Zwanenburg, S. Leger, M. Vallières, and S. Löck, "Image biomarker standardisation initiative," *Radiology*, vol. 295, no. 2, pp. 328–338, May 2020, doi: 10.1148/radiol.2020191145.

105. J. J. M. van Griethuysen et al., "Computational radiomics system to decode the radiographic phenotype," *Cancer Res.*, vol. 77, no. 21, pp. e104–e107, Nov. 2017, doi: 10.1158/0008-5472.CAN-17-0339.

106. C. Nioche et al., "LIFEx: A freeware for radiomic feature calculation in multimodality imaging to accelerate advances in the characterization of tumor heterogeneity," *Cancer Res.*, vol. 78, no. 16, pp. 4786–4789, 2018, doi: 10.1158/0008-5472.CAN-18-0125.

107. A. P. Apte et al., "Technical note: Extension of CERR for computational radiomics: A comprehensive MATLAB platform for reproducible radiomics research," *Med. Phys.*, Jun. 2018, doi: 10.1002/mp.13046.

108. L. Zhang, D. V. Fried, X. J. Fave, L. A. Hunter, J. Yang, and L. E. Court, "IBEX: An open infrastructure software platform to facilitate collaborative work in radiomics," *Med. Phys.*, vol. 42, no. 3, pp. 1341–1353, Mar. 2015, doi: 10.1118/1.4908210.

109. I. Fornacon-Wood et al., "Reliability and prognostic value of radiomic features are highly dependent on choice of feature extraction platform," *Eur. Radiol.*, Jun. 2020, doi: 10.1007/s00330-020-06957-9.

110. P. van Luijk et al., "Sparing the region of the salivary gland containing stem cells preserves saliva production after radiotherapy for head and neck cancer," *Sci. Transl. Med.*, vol. 7, no. 305, Art. no. 305, Sep. 2015, doi: 10.1126/scitranslmed. aac4441.

111. B. Ibragimov, D. Toesca, D. Chang, Y. Yuan, A. Koong, and L. Xing, "Development of deep neural network for individualized hepatobiliary toxicity prediction after liver SBRT," *Med. Phys.*, vol. 45, no. 10, Art. no. 10, 2018, doi: 10.1002/mp.13122.

112. H. J. W. L. Aerts et al., "Decoding tumour phenotype by noninvasive imaging using a quantitative radiomics approach," *Nat. Commun.*, vol. 5, no. 1, Art. no. 1, Jun. 2014, doi: 10.1038/ncomms5006.

113. J. E. van Timmeren et al., "Test–retest data for radiomics feature stability analysis: generalizable or study-specific?," *Tomography*, vol. 2, no. 4, pp. 361–365, Dec. 2016, doi: 10.18383/j.tom.2016.00208.

114. A. Traverso, L. Wee, A. Dekker, and R. Gillies, "Repeatability and reproducibility of radiomic features: A systematic review," *Int. J. Radiat. Oncol. Biol. Phys.*, vol. 102, no. 4, pp. 1143–1158, 2018, doi: 10.1016/j.ijrobp.2018.05.053.

115. M. Hoyer et al., "Phase-II study on stereotactic radiotherapy of locally advanced pancreatic carcinoma," *Radiother. Oncol. J. Eur. Soc. Ther. Radiol. Oncol.*, vol. 76, no. 1, pp. 48–53, Jul. 2005, doi: 10.1016/j.radonc.2004.12.022.

116. L. J. Isaksson et al., "Machine learning-based models for prediction of toxicity outcomes in radiotherapy," *Front. Oncol.*, vol. 10, Jun. 2020, doi: 10.3389/fonc.2020.00790.

117. V. Gulshan et al., "Development and validation of a deep learning algorithm for detection of diabetic retinopathy in retinal fundus photographs," *JAMA*, vol. 316, no. 22, Art. no. 22, Dec. 2016, doi: 10.1001/jama.2016.17216.

118. A. Esteva et al., "Dermatologist-level classification of skin cancer with deep neural networks," *Nature*, vol. 542, no. 7639, Art. no. 7639, Feb. 2017, doi: 10.1038/nature21056.

119. P. E. Kinahan and J. W. Fletcher, "PET/CT Standardized Uptake Values (SUVs) in clinical practice and assessing response to therapy," *Semin. Ultrasound. CT MR*, vol. 31, no. 6, pp. 496–505, Dec. 2010, doi: 10.1053/j.sult.2010.10.001.

3

Metric Predictions for Machine and Patient-Specific Quality Assurance

Alon Witztum and Gilmer Valdes

University of California

Maria F. Chan

Memorial Sloan Kettering Cancer Center

CONTENTS

3.1 Introduction

Machine learning (ML), which focuses on designing algorithms that can learn from and make predictions on data, has the potential to modernize the field of radiation oncology and its ability to improve the quality and efficiency of radiotherapy workflows has made it a major area of research.[1] Quality assurance (QA) is integrated into every step in the radiotherapy workflow in order to prevent errors and ensure accurate and safe treatment delivery. With the increasing complexity of modern radiotherapy, the number of QA tasks has also increased, which has led to efforts to prioritize those tasks most associated with delivering the safest treatment by the American Association of Physicists in Medicine (AAPM) in Task Group 100.[2] The current clinical practice utilizes QA data as a one-time test with the results evaluated against a tolerated

DOI: 10.1201/9781003094333-3

threshold but recent research into the application of machine learning to QA has produced a variety of proof-of-concept, often with encouraging results.[3]

This chapter will demonstrate the power of machine learning with examples of direct applications to machine and patient-specific QA.

3.2 Machine Learning Applications to Quality Assurance

The use of ML for QA of multiple elements of the radiotherapy workflow will be covered in this section. First, the use of ML in the chart review process will be discussed, followed by its application to treatment delivery machines, then to proton plan QA, and finally to photon plan QA. Table 3.1 can be found at the end of this section summarizing all the studies presented on machine, proton plan, and photon plan QA.

3.2.1 Automated Chart Review

Verification of the integrity of plans before they are delivered to the patient is just one of the QA tasks that falls under the responsibility of the medical physicist. These chart reviews occur both prior to and during the course of treatment. The AAPM Task Group 275 has reported on this process and includes some of the different aspects of the plan to be reviewed: technical parameters (data integrity), calculation accuracy, image guidance, plan quality, and consideration of technical clinical factors.[4] The importance of this check should not be underestimated as it has been suggested that over half of incident reports[5] and 33% of near-miss incidents[6] originate in the treatment preparation process. However, due to the amount of information that requires attention for each chart, the repetitive nature of the work, and the time-crunch often faced, it has been reported in some studies that only 25%–38% of detectable errors were actually identified at this stage.[7,8] While even simply rule-based logic can be applied to improve this process, statistical process control and machine learning tools have a role here too. Some examples of these include the use of clustering methods to find outliers based on plan comparisons[9,10] and Bayesian network architecture to detect links in the workflow that are more likely to introduce errors.[11]

3.2.2 Treatment Delivery Systems

A linear accelerator (Linac) is used to deliver radiation to the patient and QA is performed on this machine to ensure consistent delivery. Machine learning has been used to predict Linac performance as well as discrepancies in multi-leaf collimator (MLC) positioning and this section will review both elements.

The Linac performance over time, specifically the beam symmetry, was predicted by Li and Chan using Artificial Neural Network (ANN) time-series

TABLE 3.1

Summary of Studies on Machine QA, Proton Plan QA, and Photon Plan QA Using Machine Learning Techniques

	Group	QA Source	Dataset	ML Model
Machine Quality Assurance	Carlson et al.[15]	DICOM_RT, Dynalog files	74 VMAT plans	Regression, Random Forest, Cubist
	Li & Chan[12]	Daily QA Device	Five-year Daily QA Data	ANN time-series, ARMA models
	Naqa et al.[13]	EPID	119 Images from 8 Linacs	Support Vector Data Description, Clustering
	Chuang et al.[16]	Trajectory log files	116 IMRT plans, 125 VMAT plans	Boosted tree outperformed LR
	Zhao et al.[14]	Water Tank Measurement	43 TrueBeam PDD, Profiles	Multivariate Regression (Ridge)
Proton QA	Sun et al.[17]	Ion Chamber	1754 Proton Fields	Random Forrest, XGBoost, Cubist
	Grewal et al.[18]	Ion Chamber	4231 Proton Fields	Gaussian Processes, Shallow NN
Photon Plan QA	Valdes et al.[19]	MapCHECK2	498 IMRT Plans	Poisson Regression
	Valdes et al.[20]	Portal Dosimetry	203 IMRT Beams	Poisson Regression
	Interian et al.[21]	MapCHECK2	498 IMRT Plans	Convolutional Neural Network
	Tomori et al.[22]	EBT3 film	60 IMRT Plans	Convolutional Neural Network
	Nyflot et al.[23]	EPID	186 IMRT Beams	Convolutional Neural Network
	Granville et al.[24]	Delta4	1620 VMAT Beams	Support Vector Classifier
	Li et al.[26]	MatriXX	255 VMAT Beams	Poisson Lasso & Random Forest
	Wang et al.[27]	MatriXX	400 VMAT Beams	Hybrid model ACLR
	Wall et al.[28]	MapCHECK2	500 VMAT Plans	Linear model, SVM, tree-based, NNs
	Hirashima et al.[29]	ArcCHECK	1255 VMAT Plans	XGBoost

Source: Adapted from Chan et al.[30]

prediction modeling to longitudinal daily Linac QA data over a five-year period.[12] The network architecture, which was selected using a trial-and-error process, consisted of a set of one hidden layer, six hidden neurons, and two input delays. The developed ANN model was compared to an autoregressive integrated moving average (ARIMA) model as a benchmark and found to be more accurate. Naqa et al. used 119 electronic portal imaging device (EPID) images from 8 Linacs to predict QA results that were outside of the AAPM suggested tolerances of Task Group 142 by using a Support Vector Data Description approach.[13] Schuler et al. built a machine learning model using commissioning and annual QA water tank beam data to predict the percent depth dose (PDD) and beam profiles for other field sizes with an accuracy of 1% using $10 \times 10 \, cm^2$ field size.[14] This work has the potential of reducing beam data acquisition time as well as allowing for fast periodic Linac QA.

MLC position discrepancies were first predicted using machine learning techniques by Carlson et al. who used predictive parameters such as leaf position and speed to predict the difference in position between the DICOM-RT and DynaLog files.[15] This group used three ML algorithms – linear regression, random forest, and a cubist model – and found that the cubist model performed best in terms of accuracy. Chuang et al. also predicted these MLC discrepancies from log files using multiple machine learning models including linear regression, decision tree, and ensemble methods.[16] The ability of all these models to predict MLC discrepancy could allow for future integration with the treatment planning system to use during optimization or for more realistic dose distribution displays which can be shown to clinicians.

3.2.3 Proton QA

Proton patient-specific QA results are inherently linked to the machine output. Three machine learning ensemble approaches (Random Forest, XGBoost, and Cubist) were developed by Sun et al. to predict output and derive monitor units for a double-scatter proton delivery system.[17] The Cubist-based solution performed best with a mean absolute discrepancy of 0.62% and a maximum discrepancy of 3.17% between measured and predicted output factors. Similarly, Grewal et al. also built models to predict output factors and monitor units for a uniform scanning proton delivery system using two algorithms – Gaussian process regression (GPR) and a shallow neural network (SNN).[18] Both GPR and SNN algorithms outperformed the empirical model currently used in the clinic and the GPR model outperformed the SNN with a smaller number of training datasets. The work described in this section is a promising development of predictive secondary checks for proton patient plans that could also eventually be used to reduce the need for proton patient-specific output factor measurements.

3.2.4 Patient-Specific QA

While the previous section discussed machine learning approaches specific to proton patient-specific QA, this section will focus on photon treatment plans, specifically IMRT (intensity-modulated radiation therapy) and

VMAT (volumetric-modulated arc therapy) QA. In the clinic, these plans can undergo QA in a variety of ways including single ion chamber measurement, diode or ion chamber array, EPID, and log files. Machine learning can play a crucial role in this area if it is able to predict these QA results using plan parameters. The studies described in this section involve extracting features from patient plans and calculating multiple complexity metrics that are associated with QA results. The models built using these features and metrics can be used to predict QA results for new treatment plans.

Virtual IMRT QA was first developed by Valdes et al. using a Poisson regression ML model to predict QA results from a MapCHECK (Sun Nuclear Corporation, Melbourne, FL) diode array using an initial dataset of 498 clinical IMRT plans.[19] There was a strong correlation between MapCHECK QA results and the predicted results with a maximum error of 3%. An additional dataset of 203 plans was obtained with QA results from EPID.[20] Plans from both datasets were obtained from Eclipse (Varian Medical System, Palo Alto, CA). By querying the Eclipse database using SQL, plan parameters were extracted for all plans and scripts were developed to extract MLC and collimator information. MATLAB (The MathWorks Inc, Natick, MA) was used to calculate features for each beam and the machine learning model was built to predict QA results. Learning curves showed that approximately 200 plans are needed for training the MapCHECK model and 100 fields are needed for training the EPID model. From the 78 extracted features for the MapCHECK model, the most important features included the fraction of area delivered outside a circle with a 20 cm radius (accounting for symmetry disagreements), duty cycle, and the fraction of opposed MLCs with an aperture smaller than 5 mm (accounting for the rounded leaf shape of the MLC). Out of the 88 extracted features for the EPID model (the original 78 and 10 more to account for portal dosimetry characteristics), the most important features included the Complete Irradiated Area Outline (CIAO) area, the fraction of MLC leaves with gaps smaller than 20 or 5 mm, and the fraction of area receiving less than 50% of the total calibrated MUs.

The virtual IMRT studies described involve finding and calculating plan features that will correlate with QA results. Interian et al. compared a Deep Neural Network against the previously described Poisson regression model using the same data.[21] Fluence maps from patient plans were used as input into a convolution neural network (CNN), a specialized neural network designed to analyze images, and models trained to predict MapCHECK QA results using TensorFlow and Keras. This study demonstrated that the CNN and the Poisson regression model had comparable results even though the latter used features designed by physicists, meaning that QA prediction models can be built without subject expert supervision.

Tomori et al. also used deep learning to predict IMRT QA results by applying a 15-layer CNN to learn the planar dose distributions from a QA phantom using 60 patient plans. Inputs included the volume of the PTV, rectum, and the overlapping region, as well as the monitor units for each field.[22] Radiochromic EBT3 film was used to measure the QA gamma passing rate result. The CNN model, built with five-fold cross-validation, predicted gamma passing rates at various thresholds: 2%/2 mm, 3%/2 mm, 2%/3 mm, and 3%/3 mm. A linear correlation was found for all thresholds, further suggesting that deep learning can be used to predict IMRT QA results. Deep learning was also used to classify treatment delivery errors and predict QA results using image and texture featured from 186 EPID images by Nyflot et al.[23] In this study, three sets of planar doses were exported for each QA plan corresponding to an error-free case, a random MLC error case, and a systematic MLC error case. All plans were then delivered to an EPID panel and the gamma analysis was performed by the device's software package. Two radiomic approaches were used to identify input metrics for the machine learning classifiers: (1) image features selected using a CNN and (2) texture features selected by human experts. The performance of the CNN features was superior to the texture features, and both of these image-based approaches were superior at predicting clinically relevant errors compared to the traditional gamma passing rate method.

Granville et al. built a machine learning VMAT QA prediction model on 1620 VMAT Elekta plans using both treatment plan characteristics and Linac performance metrics.[24] A linear Support Vector Classifier (SVC) was used to classify QA results with the output classes representing the median dose difference (±1%) between measured and expected dose distributions rather than passing rates. A recursive feature elimination (RFE) cross-validation technique was used during model development to eliminate unimportant features. Of the ten most predictive features of VMAT QA results, half represented treatment plan characteristics and half represented Linac performance metrics. This study demonstrated the feasibility of adding machine performance characteristics to the usual plan characteristics to predict QA results.

The impact of plan characteristics on the dosimetric accuracy of VMAT plans was investigated by Li et al. using 344 QA plans.[25] It was found that the leaf speed is the most important factor affecting the dose accuracy of gynecologic, rectal, and head and neck plans, while the field complexity, small aperture score, and MU are most important for prostate plans. The same group also used two machine learning models, a Poisson regression model and a Random Forest classification model, to predict VMAT QA results.[26] A ten-fold cross-validated model was built using 255 Varian VMAT plans and 48 VMAT plans were used as an independent validation set without cross-validation. Model performance was assessed under different gamma analysis thresholds and the authors showed that the prediction accuracy was affected by both the absolute measured gamma passing rates and gamma thresholds. The regression model was able to accurately predict VMAT QA results but the classification model had better sensitivity to detecting failed QA plans. In a later study, the same group used an autoencoder-based classification-regression (ACLR) model to improve their QA prediction of three different gamma thresholds using 54 complexity metrics for input.[27] Clinical validation was performed with an additional 150 VMAT plans and the group reported that this hybrid model significantly improved prediction accuracy over the classic Poisson regression model. Wall et al. trained four machine learning algorithms on 500 VMAT plans with MapCHECK results and found that the SVM model, trained with the 100 most important features found with linear regression, gave the best cross-validated mean-absolute-error of 3.75% compared to linear models, tree-based models, and neural networks.[28] Gradient Boosting, considered the most accurate algorithm to date for tabular data analysis, was recently applied by Hirashima et al. to predict ArcCHECK (Sun Nuclear Corporation, Melbourne, FL) diode array QA results using plan complexity and dosiomic features from 1255 VMAT plans.[29]

As demonstrated in this section, there have been numerous studies showing the validity and accuracy of using machine learning models to predict a multitude of IMRT and VMAT QA results. In most cases, the workflow is standard, consisting of collection of QA data, extraction of plan parameters, features, and complexity metrics, and then building a model to predict results.

3.3 Future Directions

Reports on machine learning methods being applied to predict QA metrics started as recently as 2016 and in this time the field has grown significantly with multiple new studies reported each year and with increasingly complex and accurate models being used. These developments have come at a time when there has been a sharp rise in the number of QA tasks in the field and the need for prioritization of these tasks has been recognized by the American Association of Physicists in Medicine through Task Group 100.[2] It would seem that machine learning techniques, with their powerful ability to process a large amount of data, have the potential to become an invaluable tool for QA. While this chapter has presented the extensive work to date in this area, it is important to understand the limitations of predicted QA. There have been discussions about some of the major issues faced by machine learning tools including data quality, model adaptability, and model limitations by Kalet et al.[3] as well as the misuse of deep learning in the field by Kearney et al.[31]

Data quality is the primary requirement for accurate machine learning models and in the ever-changing field of radiotherapy QA, it is likely that prediction accuracy will decrease over time. It is therefore of paramount importance to see these models as additional tools to assist in the QA tasks and not allow them to automate decisions. Processes through which QA can be performed on these algorithms to ensure consistent and accurate results are still being formulated and these must be firmly in place before the transition to using predicted QA results to assist in making clinical decisions.

The development of machine learning models to predict QA results will doubtlessly continue and it is important to combine these studies with a deep understanding of contributing factors of QA failures in order to successfully implement risk-based QA programs. Future development could also allow for QA result predictions to be integrated into the treatment planning system to ensure plans will pass QA. This can allow physicists to focus their efforts only on the most complex plans and will also shift QA failures upstream in the treatment planning process, allowing time for rescheduling and replanning if necessary. It is clear that a sufficiently validated clinical implementation of QA result prediction will have a profound impact on the current radiotherapy treatment workflow and can lead to improved patient care.

Conflict of Interest

The authors declare they have read this chapter and there are no competing interests.

References

1. Feng, M., Valdes, G., Dixit, N., Solberg, T.D. (2018). Machine learning in radiation oncology: Opportunities, requirements, and needs. *Front Oncol.* doi: 10.3389/fonc.2018.00110.
2. Huq, M.S., Fraass, B.A., Dunscombe, P.B., Gibbons Jr., J.P., Ibbott, G.S., Mundt, A.J., et al. (2016). The report of task group 100 of the AAPM: Application of risk analysis methods to radiation therapy quality management. *Med Phys* 43:4209–62. doi:10.1118/1.4947547.
3. Kalet, A.M., Luk, S.M.H., Phillips, M.H. (2020). Radiation therapy quality assurance tasks and tools: The many roles of machine learning. *Med Phys* 47(5):e168–77. doi:10.1002/mp.13445.
4. Ford, E., Conroy, L., Dong, L., et al. (2020) Strategies for effective physics plan and chart review in radiation therapy: Report of AAPM Task Group 275. *Med Phys* 47(6):e236–72.
5. Clark, B.G., Brown, R.J., Ploquin, J.L., Kind, A.L., Grimard, L. (2010) The management of radiation treatment error through incident learning. *Radiother Oncol* 95(3):344–49.
6. Novak, A., Nyflot, M.J., Ermoian, R.P., Jordan, L.E., et al. (2016) Targeting safety improvements through identification of incident origination and detection in a near-miss incident learning system. *Med Phys* 43(5):2053–62.

7. Ezzell, G., Chera, B., Dicker, A., et al. (2018) Common error pathways seen in the RO-ILS data that demonstrate opportunities for improving treatment safety. *Pract Rdiat Oncol* 8:123–32.

8. Gopan, O., Zeng, J., Novak, A., et al. (2016) The effectiveness of pretreatment physics plan review for detecting errors in radiation therapy. *Med Phys* 43:5181.

9. Azmandian, F., Kaeli, D., Dy J.G., et al. (2007) Towards the development of an error checker for radiotherapy treatment plans: A preliminary study. *Phy Med Biol* 52:6511–24.

10. Furhang, E.E., Dolan, J., Sillanpaa, J.K., et al. (2009) Automating the initial physics chart-checking process. *J Appl Clin Med Phys* 10:129–35.

11. Bojechko, C., Philips, M., Kalet, A., et al. (2015) A quantification of the effectiveness of EPID dosimetry and software-based plan verification systems in detecting incidents in radiotherapy. *Med Phys* 42:5363.

12. Li, Q., Chan, M.F. (2017) Predictive time series modeling using artificial neural networks for Linac beam symmetry – An empirical study. *Ann NY Acad Sci* 1387:84–94. doi: 10.1111/nyas.13215.

13. Naqa, I.E., Irrer, J., Ritter, T.A., et al. (2019). Machine learning for automated quality assurance in radiotherapy: A proof of principle using EPID data description. *Med Phys* 46(4):1914–21. doi: 10.1002/mp.13433.

14. Zhao, W., Patil, I., Han, B., Yang, Y., Xing, L., Schüler, E. (2020). Beam data modeling of linear accelerators (linacs) through machine learning and its potential applications in fast and robust linac commissioning and quality assurance. *Radiother Oncol* 153:122–129.

15. Carlson, J.N., Park, J.M., Park, S.Y., et al. (2016). A machine learning approach to the accurate prediction of multi-leaf collimator positional errors. *Phys Med Biol* 61:2514. doi:10.1088/0031-9155/61/6/2514.

16. Chuang, K.C., Adamson, J., Giles, W. (2021, In Press). A tool for patient specific prediction of delivery discrepancies in machine parameters using trajectory log files. *Med Phys* 48(3):978–990.

17. Sun, B., Lam, D., Yang, D., et al. (2018). A machine learning approach to the accurate prediction of monitor units for a compact proton machine. *Med Phys* 45(5):2243–51.

18. Grewal, H.S., Chacko, M.S., Ahmad, S., et al. (2020). Prediction of the output factor using machine and deep learning approach uniform scanning proton therapy. *J Appl Clin Med Phys.* doi:10.1002/acm2.12899.

19. Valdes, G., Scheuermann, R., Hung, C.Y., et al. (2016). A mathematical framework for virtual IMRT QA using machine learning. *Med Phys* 43(7):4323–34. doi:10.1118/1.4953835.

20. Valdes, G., Chan, M.F., Lim, S., Scheuermann, R., Deasy, J.O., Solberg, T.D. (2017). IMRT QA using machine learning: A multi-institutional validation. *J Appl Clin Med Phys* 18(5):278–84. doi: 10.1002/acm2.12161.

21. Interian, Y., Rideout, V., Kearney, V.P., et al. (2018). Deep nets vs expert designed features in medical physics: An IMRT QA case study. *Med Phys* 45(6):2672–80. doi: 10.1002/mp.12890.

22. Tomori, S., Kadoya, N., Takayama, Y., et al. (2018). A deep learning-based prediction model for gamma evaluation in patient-specific quality assurance. *Med Phys* 45(9): 4055–65. doi: 10.1002/mp.13112.

23. Nyflot, M.J., Thammasorn, P., Wooton, L.S., et al. (2019). Deep learning for patient-specific quality assurance: Identifying errors in radiotherapy delivery by radiomic analysis of gamma images with convolutional neural networks. *Med Phys* 46(2):456–64. doi:10.1002/mp.13338.
24. Granville, D.A., Sutherland, J.G., Belec, J.G., et al. (2019). Predicting VMAT patient-specific QA results using a support vector classifier trained on treatment plan characteristics and linac QC metrics. *Phys Med Biol* 64:095017. doi:10.1088/1361-6560/ab142e.
25. Li, J., Zhang, X., Li, J., et al. (2019). Impact of delivery characteristics on dose accuracy of volumetric modulated arc therapy for different treatment sites. *J Radiat Res.* doi:10.1093/jrr/rrz033.
26. Li, J., Wang, L., Zhang, X., et al. (2019). Machine learning for patient-specific quality assurance of VMAT: Prediction and classification accuracy. *Int J Rad Onc Biol Phys* 105(4):893–902. doi:10.1016/j.ijrobp.2019.07.049.
27. Wang, L., Li, J., Zhang, S., et al. (2020). Multi-task autoencoder based classification-regression (ACLR) model for patient-specific VMAT QA. Phys Med Biol 65(23):235023. doi:10.1088/1361-6560/abb31c.
28. Wall, P.D.H., Fontenot, J.D. (2020). Application and comparison of machine learning models for predicting quality assurance outcomes in radiation therapy treatment planning. *Inform Med Unlocked* 18:100292. doi:10.1016/j.imu.2020.100292.
29. Hirashima, H., Iramina, H., Mukumoto, N., et al. (2020). Improvement of prediction and classification performance for gamma passing rate by using plan complexity and dosiomics features. *Radiat Oncol.* doi:10.1016/j.radonc.2020.07.031.
30. Chan, M.F., Witztum, A., Valdes, G. (2020). Integration of AI and machine learning in radiotherapy QA. *Front Artif Intell.* doi: 10.3389/frai.2020.577620.
31. Kearney, V., Valdes, G., Solberg, T.D. (2018). Deep learning misuse in radiation oncology. *Int J Radiat Oncol Biol Phys* 102:S62.

4

Data-Driven Treatment Planning, Plan QA, and Fast Dose Calculation

Yong Yang, Lei Xing, Nataliya Kovalchuk, Charles Huang, and Yusuke Nomura
Stanford University

Weigang Hu and Jiawei Fan
Fudan University Shanghai Cancer Center
Shanghai Medical College Fudan University
Shanghai Key Laboratory of Radiation Oncology

CONTENTS

4.1 Radiation Therapy and Treatment Planning

Radiation therapy (RT) aims to eradicate cancerous cells while maximally sparing the organs at risks (OARs). Treatment planning is an important step in achieving the clinical goal of RT. In general, treatment planning is a complex process and depends on multiple factors, such as the machine and dose delivery technique, tumor and anatomy characteristics, physician- and patient-specific factors, software tools used for planning, and the training

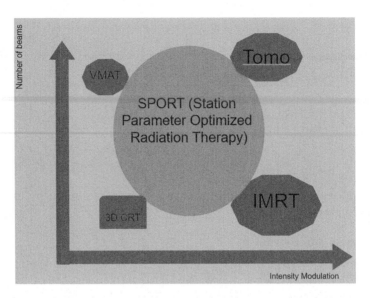

FIGURE 4.1
A schematic drawing of different types of therapy modalities in relation to SPORT.

and experience of the planner.[1,2] Several important clinical and technical advances in the last decade call for innovations in new dose optimization and delivery strategies. Clinically, SBRT/SRS of various diseases, such as oligometastatic diseases and ventricular tachycardia (VT), is becoming increasingly important in radiation oncology and greatly elevates the need for improved dose conformality, adaptive therapy, and more efficient workflow.[3-5] Technically, a new generation of digital linac, which has a number of important features such as auto-field sequencing, programmable gantry, collimator and couch motions, and high-dose rate (HDR) flattening-filter free (FFF) beam, has become widely adopted.[6] The new types of digital linacs not only support traditional IMRT and VMAT but also allow us to develop a framework, referred to as station parameter optimized radiation therapy (SPORT),[7,8] to overcome many of the limitations of the existing RT techniques and greatly augment the efficacy of modern RT. Figure 4.1 shows a schematic plot of SPORT in relationship with some of the currently employed RT approaches. We note that, while the concept of SPORT is quite general, it can be implemented in a variety of formats. For example, SPORT implementation can be confined in a coplanar or a pre-selected trajectory to enhance the current VMAT or RapidArc™ treatment by enabling (1) non-uniform sampling of station points (i.e., nodes);[8] (2) modulation of collimator angle during the process of gantry rotation;[9] and (3) optimal placement of a single or multiple iso-center.[10] This will provide a ready-to-implement technology to greatly enhance the existing VMAT or RapidArc™ solution for both C-arm linacs (e.g., TrueBeam™) and ring-gantry linac (Halcyon™).

It will also help us to gain comprehensive knowledge and practical experience on SPORT and better prepare us for the next logical step of developing a fully-fledged SPORT with non-conventional beam trajectory[11] in the future.

Considering the fact that IMRT and VMAT are currently the most commonly used modalities to produce conformal dose distribution for patient care,[12-31] this chapter will be focused on the applications of DL for IMRT/VMAT planning. Broadly speaking, IMRT and VMAT are considered special cases of SPORT. Thus, the methodology presented in the following can be extended to SPORT in the future. In current IMRT/VMAT treatments, inverse treatment planning is typically required to design treatment plans and is one of the key features that distinguishes IMRT/VMAT from other more traditional radiotherapy techniques, such as 3D conformal radiotherapy. In inverse planning, after treatment beams are set, the desired plan outcome is first specified in terms of the tumor dose and normal structure dose limits, and the inverse treatment planning system (TPS) then adjusts each beam intensity to find a configuration that best matches the desired plan.

Although IMRT/VMAT has been widely used in the clinic and considerably improved the quality of RT, its planning process involves non-intuitively iterative steps based on planners' subjective decisions. Planners might spend days to achieve an acceptable treatment plan, yet the resulting plan quality highly depends on planners' experience due to the variations in the chosen optimization constraints and their relative priorities. This may lead to the variable quality of the radiotherapy treatment and compromise the quality of patient care.

In recent years, a great deal of effort has been devoted to knowledge-based techniques in assisting treatment planning. It is arguable that the knowledge-based planning originated from the concept of class solution in IMRT treatment planning.[32] Data-driven and machine learning-based are developed by a few groups.[33-36] It should be noted that a double-blind clinical assessment of the machine learning approach has been reported recently by the University of Toronto group.[37] Mardani et al.[2] from Stanford University pioneered the use of deep learning (DL) for dose/dose volume histogram (DVH) prediction and applied the algorithm to prostate IMRT dose prediction, which had generated tremendous interest in DL-driven or artificial intelligence (AI)-based treatment planning. The key steps of these methods include predicting achievable DVHs[38-61] or dose distributions for an individual patient based on prior knowledge extracted from a high-quality treatment plans database[62-65] and establishing an algorithm to identify the correlation between the IMRT plan complexity metrics and gamma passing rates for virtual IMRT QA.[66,67] In addition to dose optimization, DL has also been applied to many other problems in RT, including, to name a few, image segmentation and analysis,[1,68-70] image reconstruction,[71-73] quality assurance,[74-77] outcome prediction,[78,79] proton therapy,[80,81] and so forth.

4.2 Anatomy-Based Dose Distribution Prediction

The machine-learning methods, such as support vector regression with principal component analysis and artificial neural network, which are based on several hand-crafted features, have been studied intensively in the literature to predict the DVH or dose distribution.[62–65] The model is established to illustrate the correlation between the features of the DVH and anatomic information.[62] Artificial neural networks have been developed to predict dose distributions for pancreatic cancer,[63] prostate cancer,[64] and stereotactic radiosurgery. However, these studies extracted features manually and some low-level information may not be captured, resulting in non-enough prediction accuracy.[65] More accurate and effective dose prediction technique needs to be investigated.

Data-driven DL methods[82] which benefit from recent technologic improvements in computing hardware have brought significant breakthroughs in medicine.[83,84] Chen et al. developed a data-driven method to predict optimal dose distributions by applying DL inferring model to correlate the given planning CT images and segmented anatomy with previously optimized and approved dose distribution.[85] They used transfer learning to fine-tune a ResNet101 model[86] that was pretrained on a large dataset (ImageNet). The proposed model was implemented on the early-stage nasopharyngeal cancer patients and the overall mean MAE_{body} was comparable (5.5%±6.8% vs 5.3%±6.4%, $P = 0.181$) between TPS calculation and prediction. Ma et al. implemented a deep CNN-based framework for dose prediction using a concept of isodose feature-preserving voxelization (IFPV).[87] IFPV is a sparse voxelization scheme that partitions the voxels into subgroups according to their geometric, anatomical, and dosimetric features.[88] The contours of six structures in CT images were imported into the CNN model to predict the achievable dose distribution for prostate cases. And the proposed approach achieved mean SARs of 0.029±0.020 and 0.077±0.030 for bladder and rectum, respectively, compared with mean SARs of 0.039±0.029 and 0.069±0.028 in the conventional voxel-based method as shown in Figure 4.2.

Fan et al.[89] developed an automated treatment planning strategy for IMRT, including a DL-based dose prediction and a dose distribution-based plan generation algorithm. It is the first to implement a data-driven method to perform an accurate prediction of the 3D dose distribution in head-and-neck cancer patients with the "ResNet-antiResNet" DL model trained from scratch as shown in Figure 4.3. A novel auto-planning strategy was also proposed in this study, it uses the predicted 3D dose distribution as the objective function, and the results come close to match the clinically acceptable plans without any post-optimization as shown in Figure 4.4.

In addition to the prediction of IMRT dose, Liu et al.[90] implemented a DL model to predict a 3D dose distribution by using previously treated Helical Tomotherapy plans as training data. For 20 tested patients, the prediction bias ranged from −2.0% to 2.3% and the prediction error varied from 1.5%

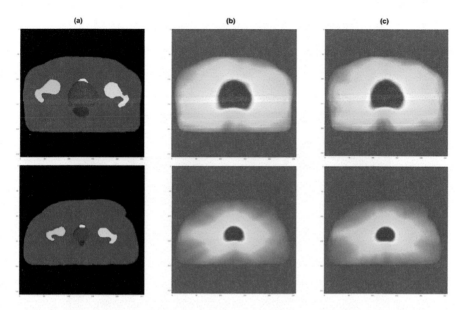

FIGURE 4.2
Comparison of predicted dose distributions between the voxel-based method and the iso-dose feature-preserving voxelization (IFPV)-based method on two test cases. (a) Contours. (b) Predicted dose distributions by the voxel-based method. (c) Predicted dose distributions by the IFPV-based method.

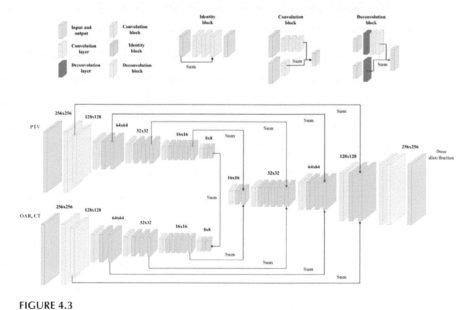

FIGURE 4.3
The illustration of the network architecture used in this analysis. Different colors represent different layers or blocks; different sizes of the cubes with numbers on them represent different dimensions of the layer.

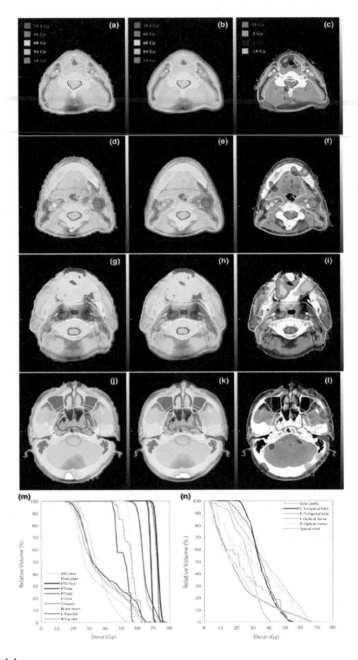

FIGURE 4.4

The dose distribution and DVH comparison between the predicted plan and the automatic generated plan for a patient. Top left is the predicted plan, top middle is the automatic generated plan, and top right is voxel-by-voxel difference maps. The color bars representing different dose levels are shown in the top of the figure. In the bottom two plots, the solid line represents the predicted plan, while the dashed line is the automatic generated plan.

to 4.5% (relative to prescription) for 3D dose differences. These mentioned studies use only patient anatomy as input and assume consistent beam configuration for all patients in the training database. Nguyen et al.[91] developed a more general model that considers variable beam configurations in addition to patient anatomy to achieve more comprehensive automatic planning with a potentially easier clinical implementation, without the need to train specific models for different beam settings. The beam setup information is represented by a 3D matrix of the non-modulated beam's eye view ray-tracing dose distribution. The proposed *anatomy and beam* (AB) model based on a hierarchically densely connected U-Net outperformed the *anatomy only* (AO) model of about 1%–2% in terms of dose–volume metrics.

4.3 Dose Distribution Prediction Based on Prior Geometric, Anatomic, and Dosimetric Properties of the Patients

Since the seminal work by Mardani et al.[2] on using imaging information and contours to predict dose distribution, the field has become one of the most active areas of research in AI applications in RT. However, in all these methods, including the original work by Mardani et al., only geometric/anatomic features were learned for building the dose prediction model and few features that characterize the dosimetric properties of the patients were utilized. The purely data-driven approach influences the accuracy and reliability of the dose prediction model. As has been shown in many related research studies, especially research in image reconstruction, inclusion of prior knowledge can significantly improve the robustness and trustworthiness of DL-based applications.

We have proposed a CNN-based method to include the dosimetric features in the construction of a more reliable dose prediction model.[92] In our work, in addition to the anatomic features, the dosimetric features learned from the dose distribution of PTV-only treatment plan (i.e., the plan with the best PTV coverage by sacrificing the OARs sparing) are also incorporated in modelling. Our rationale was that the dosimetric features inherently measure the capability of satisfying the dosimetric goals for a given case.[93] The greater the difference between the dose distribution of the PTV-only plan and the clinical plan, the more difficult for the plan to meet the dosimetric constraints. Thus, the PTV-only plan provides useful information for leveraging the dosimetric features to train a more reliable prediction model. By integrating the dosimetric features, our method can predict the achievable dose distribution with much better accuracy.[92] In contrast to the existing methods, the proposed framework has the potential of more accurately predict the dose distribution by harnessing learned features. Thus, it may enable guiding the clinical plan optimization process to achieve high-quality plans with high efficiency. We note that, in addition to the dosimetric features, many other types of prior knowledge can and should be included in DL-based planning to enhance its performance.

4.4 Prediction of Machine Delivery Parameters or Fluence Maps for Treatment Planning

While the prediction of DVHs or dose distribution is useful and can be used as input to "warm stat" an existing inverse planning calculation, it is important to emphasize that these predicted quantities may or may not be achievable by the delivery machine. To truly benefit from the state-of-the-art DL techniques and improve the clinical workflow, it is highly desirable to obtain the machine parameters directly so that the DL predictions can be utilized directly for patient treatment after adequate quality assurance. Along this line, we have recently developed a generative adversarial network (GAN)-based DL approach to estimate the VMAT multileaf collimator (MLC) aperture and corresponding monitor units (MUs) from a given 3D dose distribution.[75] The proposed design of the adversarial network, which integrates a residual block into pix2pix framework, jointly trains a "U-Net"-like architecture as the generator and a convolutional "PatchGAN" classifier as the discriminator. Along the same line, MA et al.[94] and Hoyeon et al.[95] have investigated the use of DL for fluence map prediction in inverse treatment planning. In principle, the predicted fluence map can be converted directly to MLC segment for downstream plan delivery.

4.5 Adjusting Treatment Planning Parameters Directly

In the presence of prediction errors, DL-based predictions of the dose distribution, DVH, etc. can result in plans that are either unachievable or inefficient. As an alternative to predicting dose distributions, DVHs, machine delivery parameters, etc., adjustments to the inverse planning objectives and constraints can be made directly. One popular method for automatically adjusting these inverse planning parameters is multicriteria optimization (MCO),[96–99] which navigates the various tradeoffs in treatment planning to produce efficient and clinically acceptable plans. Adjusting inverse planning parameters can also be performed using reinforcement learning (RL),[100] where the treatment planning problem is formulated as a Markov decision process. Through training, an RL agent learns an optimal policy (i.e., how to best adjust the various objective weights and constraints) to maximize reward (i.e., produce high-quality treatment plans). While the feasibility of using these RL agents in the clinic may currently be limited, due to the high computational cost of training, future improvements to the computational efficiency of RL algorithms could make these agents viable for clinical deployment.

4.6 Data-Driven Treatment Plan QA

For IMRT/VMAT treatment, measurement-based patient-specific QA is an important clinical process to ensure safe treatments due to its planning and delivery complexity. It is typically performed by comparing the measured and calculated dose distributions using a detector array. The most commonly used metric to assess the agreement between the two distributions is the gamma index, which combines both percentage dose-difference and distance-to-agreement (DTA). While practically useful, the measurement is performed in a surrogate phantom instead of the actual patients, which may not fully reflect the actual clinical treatment and patient-specific dose errors may not be detected.[101–103]

Recently, a machine learning-based prediction model that uses a set of treatment plan parameters, such as the MLC apertures, gantry/collimator angles, and couch positions, as input, to predict the dosimetric gamma passing rate, has been proposed.[104–107] Valdes et al.[105] extracted 78 different complexity metrics from five main sources of errors, including MLC leaf transmission, leaf end leakage (Dosimetric Leaf Gap, DLG), transmission through the jaws, tongue and groove effect, and charged particle equilibrium failure. A generalized linear model using the Poisson regression with Lasso regularization was trained to learn the relationship between these metrics and the passing rates, and the passing rates 3%/3 mm local dose/DTA can be predicted with an error smaller than 3%. This virtual IMRT QA technique can also predict passing rates using different measurement techniques and across multiple institutions. Lam et al.[104] demonstrated that gamma passing rates for portal dosimetry IMRT QA can be accurately predicted using three widely used tree-based algorithms: Random Forest, Adaboost, and XGBoost. Instead of using the linear regression model, Tomori et al.[107] present a gamma evaluation tool by using a 15-layer convolutional neural networks inferring model. The model was trained to learn the correlation between the sagittal planar dose distributions, volume of the PTV, monitor unit values for each field, and the gamma pass rate. And the results demonstrated a strong or moderate correlation between the predicted and measured values.

However, a potential drawback of these approaches is that the QA decision based purely on the gamma passing rate may not be interpretable and robust enough for practical applications. The reason is that the passing rate for given Gamma index criteria is heavily dependent on the selected region of interest.[108] Fan et al.[109] developed a generative adversarial network (GAN)-based DL approach to estimate the MU/MLC shapes from a given 3D dose distribution. Since the MU/MLC shapes are fundamental machine delivery parameters, this approach is significantly different from previous studies and allows us to verify the plan from the machine parameter level in a more intuitive and accurate way. The average deviation of predicted MUs from the planned MUs normalized to each beam or arc was within 2% for all the testing patients and the MLC position prediction error is around one pixel as shown in Figures 4.5 and 4.6. The results show that the proposed strategy is highly promising and may find valuable applications in verifying the treatment plan on the machine parameter level.

Extending a similar idea to brachytherapy, Fan et al.[110] developed a data-driven strategy for HDR brachytherapy treatment plan check and verification. The proposed model was trained to verify the dwell positions and times for a given input brachytherapy isodose distribution. An important contribution of this study is the introduction of the concept of Gaussian heatmap to characterize the dwell position. Compared with the regression of discretized numbers, the heatmap retains the spatial information of the dwell position and avoids the adoption of a more complex neural network, which makes the model training much easier. The proposed model achieved the excellent predictive performance, the deviation of the predicted dwell position coordinates was around one pixel from the planned positions (on average, a pixel is $\sim 0.5\,mm$), and the relative deviations of the predicted dwell times were within 2% as shown in Figures 4.7 and 4.8. The proposed method is promising and can be easily extended to other types of brachytherapy, such as Utrecht/Venezia type applicators with various ovoid–intrauterine tube combinations, interstitial brachytherapy, or LDR brachytherapy.

4.7 Data-Driven Dose Calculation

A DL architecture has been successfully applied to predict dose distributions from patients' anatomy. Some studies aim to predict a dose distribution by establishing a DL model based on the beam fluence map or a different dose calculation algorithm. Dong and Xing[111] pioneered to introduce a novel DL strategy to obtain a highly accurate dose by transforming from a dose distribution calculated using a low-cost algorithm. They constructed a deep DoseNet to model the relation between Eclipse calculated AAA and AXB dose. The average mean-square-error decreased from 4.7×10^{-4} between

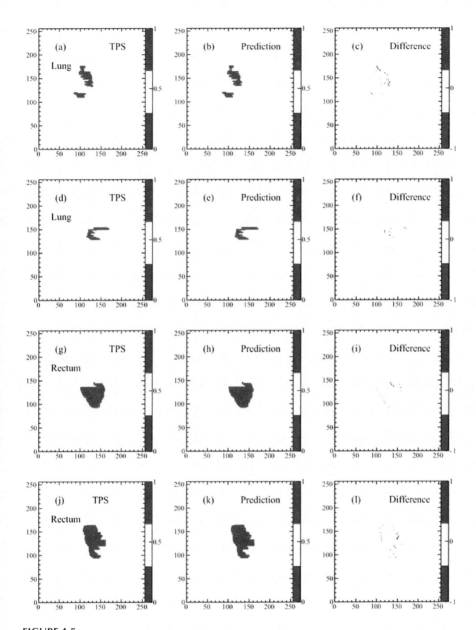

FIGURE 4.5
Comparison between the planned and predicted MLC apertures for four segments from a lung IMRT and a rectum IMRT case.

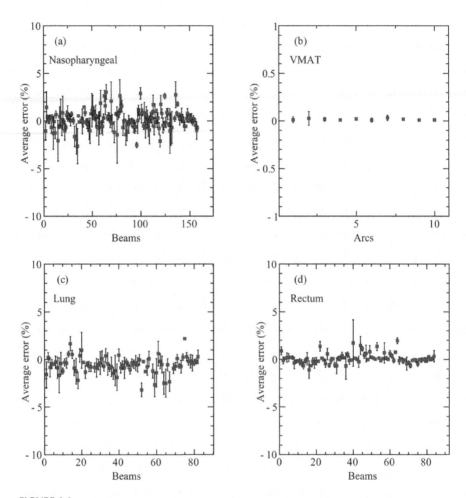

FIGURE 4.6

Average relative error and standard deviations in predicted MUs (normalized to each beam or arc) for each beam (or arc in VMAT) in the nasopharyngeal, VMAT, lung, and rectum patients.

AAA and AXB to 7.0×10^{-5} between DL calculated and AXB, with an average improvement of ~12 times. Figure 4.9 shows a typical dose distribution in the validation study obtained using the DL model.

Xing et al.[112] developed a new radiotherapy dose calculation engine based on a modified Hierarchically Densely Connected U-net model and tested its feasibility with prostate IMRT cases. The ray-tracing dose calculation is used to obtain a pre-calculated inaccurate dose distribution from the fluence maps; a DL model was established to correlate this pre-calculated dose distribution with the TPS-approved results. The average Gamma passing rates

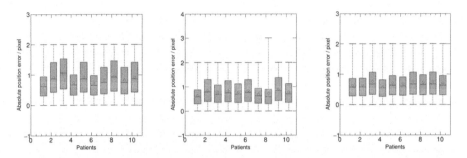

FIGURE 4.7
The absolute errors in X (a), Y (b), and Z (c) coordinates of the prediction relative to the TPS calculation for all testing patients.

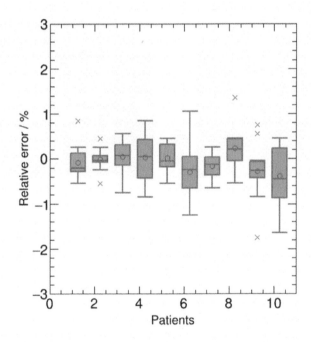

FIGURE 4.8
The whiskers plot illustrating the relative errors of the predicted times of all the dwell points in the ten testing patients.

between predicted and TPS dose distributions for the testing patients are 98.5% (±1.6%) at 1 mm/1% and 99.9% (±0.1%) at 2 mm/2%. Kontaxis et al.[113] extended the method to calculate the Monte Carlo dose distribution. The trained DL model can provide a Monte Carlo dose from five 3D volumes modelling the physical quantity/feature calculated from the fluence map.

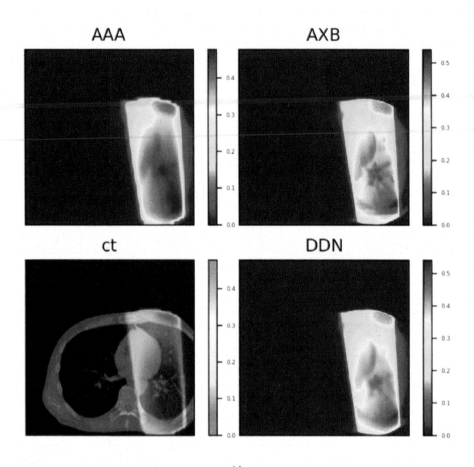

FIGURE 4.9
A typical dose distribution in the validation study obtained using the DDN. For visualization/comparison, the AAA dose overlaid on CT, AAA, and AXB doses is also displayed.

It yields on average 99.9%±0.3% for the forward calculated patient plans at 3%/3 mm gamma tests.

Fan et al.[114] proposed a general technique to convert the fluence map to 3D volume and proved that a common DL model, shown in Figure 4.10, was good enough to calculate the dose distribution using the converted 3D volume. The feasibility and reliability of the proposed model was demonstrated by four different cancer sites, including nasopharyngeal, lung, rectum, and breast cancer cases. The performance of the proposed model is effective and the average per-voxel bias of the DL calculated value and standard deviation (normalized to the prescription), relative to the TPS calculation, is 0.17%±2.28%. An example of dose calculation result is shown in Figure 4.11 for a nasopharyngeal patient.

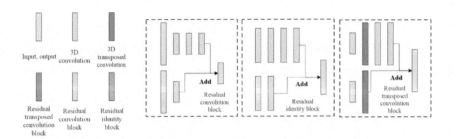

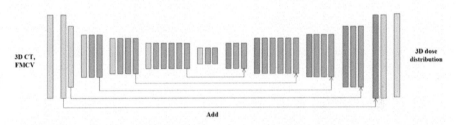

FIGURE 4.10
The architecture of the proposed DL model.

4.8 Summary

Treatment planning is a process to search for the optimal machine parameters to create a desired dose distribution in the context of the 3D anatomy of the patient. The state-of-the-art DL technology has significant advantages in learning voxelized data and dramatically promoted the development of automatic planning, plan QA, and data-driven dose calculation investigation. DL technology can independently mine data characteristics and capture deep-level data information that cannot be obtained by traditional machine learning methods. It can also greatly reduce the influence of human factors and improve data mining efficiency. Recent advances in deep neural networks to incorporate physical and clinical data into treatment planning and plan QA are discussed in detail. Studies on data-driven methods for contour/fluence-based dose calculation are emerging and incorporation of the Monte Carlo dose may provide new ideas for rapid application of Monte Carlo method in radiotherapy. Meanwhile, integrating the dose prediction method with the MU/MLC shape prediction method is expected to realize a new data-driven treatment planning process, innovate the concept of traditional manual treatment planning, reduce the interference of human factors, and promote the development of the homogeneous radiotherapy industry. Finally, we emphasize that the incorporation of newly available radiomics and other clinical data is an important area of research in data-driven treatment planning for the years to come.

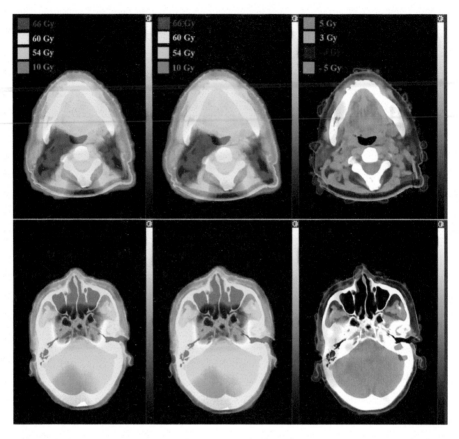

FIGURE 4.11
Dose distributions comparison in two axial planes for a nasopharyngeal patient: TPS calculated (a), DL calculated (b), and pixel-wise differences (c).

Acknowledgements

Part of this research was supported by NIH grants (1R01 CA176553 and 1R01 256890), a Google faculty research award, and Varian Medical Systems.

References

1. Ibragimov B., Pernus F., Strojan P., Xing L. Machine-learning based segmentation of organs at risks for head and neck radiotherapy planning. *Med Phys* 2016; 43(6 Part32):3883.

2. Mardani Korani M., Dong P., Xing L. Deep-learning based prediction of achievable dose for personalizing inverse treatment planning. *Med Phys* 2016; 43(6 Part32):3724.

3. Xing L., Giger M.L., Min J.K., eds. *Artificial Intelligence in Medicine: Technical Basis and Clinical Applications*. London, UK: Academic Press; 2020.

4. Timmerman R., Xing L. *Image Guided and Adaptive Radiation Therapy*. Baltimore, MD: Lippincott Williams & Wilkins; 2009.

5. Xing L., Giger M.L., Min J.K. *Artificial Intelligence in Medicine: Technical Basis and Clinical Applications*. London, UK: Academic Press; 2020.

6. Fahimian B., Yu V., Horst K., Xing L., Hristov D. Trajectory modulated prone breast irradiation: A LINAC-based technique combining intensity modulated delivery and motion of the couch. *Radiother Oncol*. 2013; 109(3):475–81.

7. Li R., Xing L. Bridging the gap between IMRT and VMAT: Dense angularly sampled and sparse intensity modulated radiation therapy. *Med Phys* 2011; 38(9):4912–9.

8. Li R., Xing L. "An adaptive planning strategy for station parameter optimized radiation therapy (SPORT): Segmentally boosted VMAT". *Med Phys Lett* 2013 May; 40(5): 050701.

9. Zhang P., Happersett L., Yang Y., Yamada Y., Mageras G., Hunt M. Optimization of collimator trajectory in volumetric modulated arc therapy: Development and evaluation for paraspinal SBRT. *Int J Radiat Oncol Biol Phys* 2010; 77(2):591–9.

10. Li R., Xing L., Horst K.C., Bush K. Nonisocentric treatment strategy for breast radiation therapy: A proof of concept study. *Int J Radiat Oncol Biol Phys* 2014; 88(4):920–6.

11. Dong P., Liu H., Xing L. Monte Carlo tree search -based non-coplanar trajectory design for station parameter optimized radiation therapy (SPORT). *Phys Med Biol* 2018; 63(13):135014.

12. AAPM IMRT Sub-committee. Guidance document on delivery, treatment planning, and clinical implementation of IMRT: Report of the IMRT subcommittee of the AAPM radiation therapy committee. *Med Phys* 2003; 30:2089–115.

13. Bortfeld T. Optimized planning using physical objectives and constraints. *Semin Radiat Oncol* 1999; 9:20–34.

14. Xing L., Chen G.T.Y. Iterative algorithms for Inverse treatment planning. *Phys Med Biol* 1996; 41:2107–23.

15. Yu C.X. Intensity-modulated arc therapy with dynamic multileaf collimation: an alternative to tomotherapy. *Phys Med Biol* 1995; 40:1435–49.

16. Otto K. Volumetric modulated arc therapy: IMRT in a single gantry arc. *Med Phys* 2008; 35:310–7.

17. Crooks S.M., Wu X., Takita C., Matzich M., Xing L. Aperture modulated arc therapy. *Phys Med Biol* 2003; 48:1333–44.

18. Xing L., Li J.G., Donaldson S., Le Q.T., Boyer A.L. Optimization of importance factors in inverse planning. *Phys Med Biol* 1999; 44:2525–36.

19. Xing L., Li J.G., Pugachev A., Le Q.T., Boyer A.L. Estimation theory and model parameter selection for therapeutic treatment plan optimization. *Med Phys* 1999; 26:2348–58.

20. Yu Y., Zhang J.B., Cheng G., Schell M.C., Okunieff P. Multi-objective optimization in radiotherapy: Applications to stereotactic radiosurgery and prostate brachytherapy. *Artif Intell Med* 2000; 19:39–51.

21. Zarepisheh M., Long T., Li N., Tian Z., Romeijn H.E., Jia X., Jiang S.B. A DVH-guided IMRT optimization algorithm for automatic treatment planning and adaptive radiotherapy replanning. *Med Phys* 2014; 41:061711.
22. Reinstein L.E., Hanley J., Meek A.G. A feasibility study of automated inverse treatment planning for cancer of the prostate. *Phys Med Biol* 1996; 41:1045–58.
23. Schreibmann E., Xing L. Feasibility study of beam orientation class-solutions for prostate IMRT. *Med Phys* 2004; 31:2863–70.
24. Pugachev A., Li J.G., Boyer A.L., Hancock S.L., Le Q.T., Donaldson S.S., Xing L. Role of beam orientation optimization in intensity-modulated radiation therapy. *Int J Radiat Oncol Biol Phys* 2001; 50:551–60.
25. Pugachev A., Xing L., Boyer A.L. Beam orientation optimization in IMRT: to optimize or not to optimize? *XII International Conference on the Use of Computers in Radiation Therapy.* Heidelberg, Germany, 2000.
26. Pugachev A., Xing L. Incorporating prior knowledge into beam orientation optimization. *Int J Radiat Oncol Biol Phys* 2002; 54:1565–74.
27. Cotrutz C., Xing L. Using voxel-dependent importance factors for interactive DVH-based dose optimization. *Phys Med Biol* 2002; 47:1659–69.
28. Yang Y., Xing L. Inverse treatment planning with adaptively evolving voxel-dependent penalty scheme. *Med Phys* 2004; 31:2839–44.
29. Bortfeld T. IMRT: A review and preview. *Phys Med Biol* 2006; 51:R363–79.
30. Kim H., Li R., Lee R., Xing L. Beam's-eye-view dosimetrics (BEVD) guided rotational station parameter optimized radiation therapy (SPORT) planning based on reweighted total-variation minimization. *Phys Med Biol* 2015; 60:N71–82.
31. Dong P., Ungun B., Boyd S., Xing L. Optimization of rotational arc station parameter optimized radiation therapy. *Med Phys* 2016; 43:4973.
32. Schreibmann E., Xing L. Feasibility study of beam orientation class-solutions for prostate IMRT. *Med Phys* 2004; 31(10):2863–70.
33. Wu B., Ricchetti F., Sanguineti G., et al. Data-driven approach to generating achievable dose-volume histogram objectives in intensity-modulated radiotherapy planning. *Int J Radiat Oncol Biol Phys* 2011; 79(4):1241–7.
34. Zhu X., Ge Y., Li T., Thongphiew D., Yin F.F., Wu Q.J. A planning quality evaluation tool for prostate adaptive IMRT based on machine learning. *Med Phys* 2011; 38(2):719–26.
35. Babier A., Zhang B., Mahmood R., et al. OpenKBP: The open-access knowledge-based planning grand challenge and dataset. *Med Phys* 2021; 48:5549–61.
36. McIntosh C., Welch M., McNiven A., Jaffray D.A., Purdie T.G. Fully automated treatment planning for head and neck radiotherapy using a voxel-based dose prediction and dose mimicking method. *Phys Med Biol* 2017; 62(15):5926–44.
37. McIntosh C., Conroy L., Tjong M.C., et al. Clinical integration of machine learning for curative-intent radiation treatment of patients with prostate cancer. *Nat Med* 2021; 27(6):999–1005.
38. Fan J., Wang J., Zhang Z., Hu W. Iterative dataset optimization in automated planning: Implementation for breast and rectal cancer radiotherapy. *Med Phys* 2017 Jun; 44(6):2515–31.
39. McIntosh C., Welch M., McNiven A., Jaffray D.A., Purdie T.G. Fully automated treatment planning for head and neck radiotherapy using a voxel-based dose prediction and dose mimicking method. *Phys Med Biol* 2017; 62:5926–44.

40. Zarepisheh M., Shakourifar M., Trigila G., Ghomi P.S., Couzens S., Abebe A., Norena L., Shang W., Jiang S.B., Zinchenko Y. A moment-based approach for DVH-guided radiotherapy treatment plan optimization. *Phys Med Biol* 2013; 58:1869–87.

41. Liu H., Dong P., Xing L. Using measurable dosimetric quantities to characterize the inter-structural tradeoff in inverse planning. *Phys Med Biol* 2017; 62:6804–21.

42. Kang J., Schwartz R., Flickinger J., Beriwal S. Machine learning approaches for predicting radiation therapy outcomes: A clinician's perspective. *Int J Radiat Oncol Biol Phys* 2015; 93:1127–35.

43. Lee T., Hammad M., Chan T.C., Craig T., Sharpe M.B. Predicting objective function weights from patient anatomy in prostate IMRT treatment planning. *Med Phys* 2013; 40:121706.

44. Li T., Wu Q., Yang Y., Rodrigues A., Yin F.F., Wu Q.J. Quality assurance for online adapted treatment plans: Benchmarking and delivery monitoring simulation. *Med Phys* 2015; 42:381–90.

45. Fogliata A., Nicolini G., Bourgier C., Clivio A., De Rose F., Fenoglietto P., Lobefalo F., Mancosu P., Tomatis S., Vanetti E., Scorsetti M., Cozzi L. Performance of a knowledge-based model for optimization of volumetric modulated arc therapy plans for single and bilateral breat irradiation. *PloS One* 2015; 10:e0145137.

46. Purdie T.G., Dinniwell R.E., Letourneau D., Hill C., Sharpe M.B. Automated planning of tangential breast intensity-modulated radiotherapy using heuristic optimization. *Int J Radiat Oncol Biol Phys* 2011; 81:575–83.

47. Purdie T.G., Dinniwell R.E., Fyles A., Sharpe M.B. Automation and intensity modulated radiation therapy for individualized high-quality tangent breast treatment plans. *Int J Radiat Oncol Biol Phys* 2014; 90:688–95.

48. Lian J., Yuan L., Ge Y., Chera B.S., Yoo D.P., Chang S., Yin F., Wu Q.J. Modeling the dosimetry of organ-at-risk in head and neck IMRT planning: An intertechnique and interinstitutional study. *Med Phys* 2013; 40:121704.

49. Liu H., Wu Q. Evaluations of an adaptive planning technique incorporating dose feedback in image-guided radiotherapy of prostate cancer. *Med Phys* 2011; 38:6362–70.

50. Shiraishi S., Tan J., Olsen L.A., Moore K.L. Knowledge-based prediction of plan quality metrics in intracranial stereotactic radiosurgery. *Med Phys* 2015; 42:908.

51. Amit G., Purdie T.G., Levinshtein A., Hope A.J., Lindsay P., Marshall A., Jaffray D.A., Pekar V. Automatic learning-based beam angle selection for thoracic IMRT. *Med Phys* 2015; 42:1992–2005.

52. Schreibmann E., Fox T. Prior-knowledge treatment planning for volumetric arc therapy using feature-based database mining. *J Appl Clin Med Phys* 2014; 15:4596.

53. Cotrutz C., Lahanas M., Kappas C., Baltas D. A multiobjective gradient-based dose optimization algorithm for external beam conformal radiotherapy. *Phys Med Biol* 2001; 46:2161–75.

54. Kamran S.C., Mueller B.S., Paetzold P., Dunlap J., Niemierko A., Bortfeld T., Willers H., Craft D. Multi-criteria optimization achieves superior normal tissue sparing in a planning study of intensity-modulated radiation therapy for RTOG 1308-eligible non-small cell lung cancer patients. *Radiother Oncol* 2016; 118:515–20.

55. Unkelbach J., Bortfeld T., Craft D., Alber M., Bangert M., Bokrantz R., Chen D., Li R., Xing L., Men C., Nill S., Papp D., Romeijn E., Salari E. Optimization approaches to volumetric modulated arc therapy planning. *Med Phys* 2015; 42:1367–77.
56. Mardani M., Dong P., Xing L. Personalized dose prescription for treatment planning via deep convolutional neural networks. Annual Meeting of American Society of Radiation Oncology, Boston, September 25–28, 2016, 2016.
57. Mardani M., Dong P., Xing L. Deep-learning based prediction of achievable dose for personalizing inverse treatment planning. Annual Meeting of American Association of Physicists in Medicine, Boston, July 31-August 4 2015, 2016.
58. Appenzoller L.M., Michalski J.M., Thorstad W.L., Mutic S., Moore K.L. Predicting dose-volume histograms for organs-at-risk in IMRT planning. *Med Phys* 2012; 39:7446–61.
59. Wu Q., Yuan L., Li T., Ying F., Ge Y. Knowledge-based organ-at-risk sparing models in IMRT planning. *Pract Radiat Oncol* 2013; 3:S1–2.
60. Yuan L., Ge Y., Lee W.R., Yin F.F., Kirkpatrick J.P., Wu Q.J. Quantitative analysis of the factors which affect the interpatient organ-at-risk dose sparing variation in IMRT plans. *Medical Physics* 2012; 39:6868–78.
61. Good D., Lo J., Lee W.R., Wu Q.J., Yin F.F., Das S.K. A knowledge-based approach to improving and homogenizing intensity modulated radiation therapy planning quality among treatment centers: An example application to prostate cancer planning. *Int J Radiat Oncol Biol Phys* 2013; 87:176–81.
62. Zhu X., Ge Y., Li T., Thongphiew D., Yin F.F., Wu Q.J. A planning quality evaluation tool for prostate adaptive IMRT based on machine learning. *Med Phys* 2011; 38:719–26.
63. Campbell W.G., Miften M., Olsen L., et al. Neural network dose models for knowledge-based planning in pancreatic SBRT. *Med Phys* 2017; 44:6148–58.
64. Shiraishi S., Moore K.L. Knowledge-based prediction of three-dimensional dose distributions for external beam radiotherapy. *Med Phys* 2016; 43:378.
65. Wei L., Su R., Wang B., Li X., Zou Q. Integration of deep feature representations and handcrafted features to improve the prediction of N 6-methyladenosine sites. *Neurocomputing* 2019; 324:3–9.
66. Valdes G., Chan M.F., Lim S.B., Scheuermann R., Deasy J.O., Solberg T.D. IMRT QA using machine learning: A multi-institutional validation. *J Appl Clin Med Phys* 2017 Sep; 18(5):279–84.
67. Lam D., Zhang X., Li H., Deshan Y., Schott B., Zhao T., Zhang W., Mutic S., Sun B. Predicting gamma passing rates for portal dosimetry-based IMRT QA using machine learning. *Med Phys* 2019 Oct; 46(10):4666–75.
68. Ibragimov B., Xing L. Segmentation of organs-at-risks in head and neck CT images using convolutional neural networks. *Med Phys* 2017; 44(2):547–57.
69. Liang X., Zhao W., Hristov D.H., et al. A deep learning framework for prostate localization in cone beam CT-guided radiotherapy. *Med Phys* 2020; 47(9):4233–40.
70. Liang X., Bibault J.E., Leroy T., et al. Automated contour propagation of the prostate from pCT to CBCT images via deep unsupervised learning. *Med Phys* 2021; 48:1764–70.
71. Shen L., Zhao W., Xing L. Patient-specific reconstruction of volumetric computed tomography images from a single projection view via deep learning. *Nat Biomed Eng* 2019; 3(11):880–8.

72. Mardani M., Gong E., Cheng J.Y., et al. Deep generative adversarial neural networks for compressive sensing MRI. *IEEE Trans Med Imaging* 2019; 38(1):167–79.
73. Wu Y., Ma Y., Liu J., Du J., Xing L. Self-attention convolutional neural network for improved MR image reconstruction. *Inf Sci (N Y)* 2019; 490:317–28.
74. Fan J., Xing L., Dong P., Wang J., Hu W., Yang Y. Data-driven dose calculation algorithm based on deep U-Net. *Phys Med Biol* 2020; 65(24):245035.
75. Fan J., Xing L., Ma M., Hu W., Yang Y. Verification of the machine delivery parameters of a treatment plan via deep learning. *Phys Med Biol* 2020; 65(19):195007.
76. Valdes G., Chan M.F., Lim S.B., Scheuermann R., Deasy J.O., Solberg T.D. IMRT QA using machine learning: A multi-institutional validation. *J Appl Clin Med Phys* 2017; 18(5):279–84.
77. Chan M., Witztum A., Valdes G. Integration of AI and Machine learning in radiotherapy QA. *Front Artif Intell* 2020; 3:26–34.
78. Ibragimov B., Toesca D.A.S., Chang D.T., et al. Deep learning for identification of critical regions associated with toxicities after liver stereotactic body radiation therapy. *Med Phys* 2020; 47(8):3721–31.
79. Ibragimov B., Toesca D., Chang D., Yuan Y., Koong A., Xing L. Development of deep neural network for individualized hepatobiliary toxicity prediction after liver SBRT. *Med Phys* 2018; 45(10):4763–74.
80. Liu C., Li Z., Hu W., Xing L., Peng H. Range and dose verification in proton therapy using proton-induced positron emitters and recurrent neural networks (RNNs). *Phys Med Biol* 2019; 64:175009.
81. Nomura Y., Wang J., Shirato H., Shimizu S., Xing L. Fast spot-scanning proton dose calculation method with uncertainty quantification using a three-dimensional convolutional neural network. *Phys Med Biol* 2020; 65(21):215007.
82. Goodfellow I., Bengio Y., Courville A. *Deep Learning*. Cambridge, MA: MIT Press, 2016.
83. Esteva A., Kuprel B., Novoa R.A., et al. Dermatologist-level classification of skin cancer with deep neural networks. *Nature* 2017; 542:115–8.
84. Gulshan V., Peng L., Coram M., et al. Development and validation of a deep learning algorithm for detection of diabetic retinopathy in retinal fundus photographs. *JAMA* 2016; 316:2402–10.
85. Chen X., Men K., Li Y., Yi J., Dai J. A feasibility study on an automated method to generate patient-specific dose distributions for radiotherapy using deep learning. *Med Phys* 2019 Jan; 46(1):56–64.
86. He K., Zhang X., Ren S., Sun J. Deep Residual Learning for Image Recognition. https://arxiv.org/abs/1512.03385; 2015.
87. Ma M., Buyyounouski M.K., Vasudevan V., Xing L., Yang Y. Dose distribution prediction in isodose feature-preserving voxelization domain using deep convolutional neural network. *Med Phys* 2019 Jul; 46(7):2978–87.
88. Liu H., Xing L. Isodose feature-preserving voxelization (IFPV) for radiation therapy treatment planning. *Med Phys* 2018 Jul; 45(7):3321–9.
89. Fan J., Wang J., Chen Z., Hu C., Zhang Z., Hu W. Automatic treatment planning based on three-dimensional dose distribution predicted from deep learning technique. *Med Phys* 2019 Jan; 46(1):370–81.
90. Liu Z., Fan J., Li M., Yan H., Hu Z., Huang P., Tian Y., Miao J., Dai J. A deep learning method for prediction of three-dimensional dose distribution of helical tomotherapy. *Med Phys* 2019 May; 46(5):1972–83.

91. Barragán-Montero A.M., Nguyen D., Lu W., Lin M.H., Norouzi-Kandalan R., Geets X., Sterpin E., Jiang S. Three-dimensional dose prediction for lung IMRT patients with deep neural networks: Robust learning from heterogeneous beam configurations. *Med Phys* 2019 Aug; 46(8):3679–91.

92. Ma M., Kovalchuk N., Buyyounouski M.K., Xing L., Yang Y. Dosimetric features-driven machine learning model for DVH prediction in VMAT treatment planning. *Med Phys* 2019; 46(2):857–67.

93. Shou Z., Yang Y., Cotrutz C., Levy D., Xing L. Quantitation of the a priori dosimetric capabilities of spatial points in inverse planning and its significant implication in defining IMRT solution space. *Phys Med Biol* 2005; 50(7):1469–82.

94. Ma L., Chen M., Gu X., Lu W. Deep learning-based inverse mapping for fluence map prediction. *Phys Med Biol* 2020. doi: 10.1088/1361-6560/abc12c.

95. Hoyeon L., Hojin K., Jungwon K., Young Seok K., Sang Wook L., Seungryong C., Byungchul C. Fluence-map generation for prostate intensity-modulated radiotherapy planning using a deep-neural-network. *Sci Rep* 2019; 9:15671.

96. Hussein M., Heijmen B.J.M., Verellen D., Nisbet A. Automation in intensity modulated radiotherapy treatment planning—a review of recent innovations. *BJR* 2018; 91(1092). doi:10.1259/bjr.20180270.

97. Zarepisheh M., Hong L., Zhou Y., et al. Automated intensity modulated treatment planning: The expedited constrained hierarchical optimization (ECHO) system. *Med Phys* 2019; 46(7):2944–54. doi:10.1002/mp.13572.

98. Huang C., Yang Y., Panjwani N., Boyd S., Xing L. Pareto Optimal Projection Search (POPS): Automated radiation therapy treatment planning by direct search of the pareto surface. *IEEE Trans Biomed Eng* 2021. doi:10.1109/TBME.2021.3055822. Published online 2021:1-1.

99. Huang C., Yang Y., Xing L. Fully Automated Noncoplanar Radiation Therapy Treatment Planning. arXiv:210400784 [physics]. Published online April 1, 2021. Accessed April 11, 2021. http://arxiv.org/abs/2104.00784.

100. Shen C., Nguyen D., Chen L., et al. Operating a treatment planning system using a deep-reinforcement learning-based virtual treatment planner for prostate cancer intensity-modulated radiation therapy treatment planning. *Med Phys* 2020; 47(6):2329–36. doi: 10.1002/mp.14114.

101. Nelms B.E., Chan M.F., Jarry G., Lemire M., Lowden J., Hampton C. and Feygelman V. Evaluating IMRT and VMAT dose accuracy: practical examples of failure to detect systematic errors when applying a commonly used metric and action levels. *Med Phys* 2013; 40:111722.

102. Stojadinovic S., Ouyang L., Gu X., Pompos A., Bao Q. and Solberg T.D. Breaking bad IMRT QA practice. *J Appl Clin Med Phys* 2015; 16:5242–54.

103. Templeton A.K., Chu J.C.H. and Turian J.V. The sensitivity of ArcCHECK-based gamma analysis to manufactured errors in helical tomotherapy radiation delivery. *J Appl Clin Med Phys* 2015; 16:4814.

104. Lam D., Zhang X., Li H., Deshan Y., Schott B., Zhao T., Zhang W., Mutic S., Sun B. Predicting gamma passing rates for portal dosimetry-based IMRT QA using machine learning. *Med Phys* 2019 Oct; 46(10):4666–75.

105. Valdes G., Scheuermann R., Hung C.Y., Olszanski A., Bellerive M., Solberg T.D. A mathematical framework for virtual IMRT QA using machine learning. *Med Phys* 2016 Jul; 43(7):4323.

106. Interian Y., Rideout V., Kearney V.P., et al. Deep nets vs expert designed features in medical physics: An IMRT QA case study. *Med Phys* 2018; 45:2672–80.

107. Tomori S., Kadoya N., Takayama Y., et al. A deep learning-based prediction model for gamma evaluation in patient-specific quality assurance. *Med Phys* 2018; 45:4055–65.
108. Zhen H., Nelms B.E. and Tome W.A. Moving from gamma passing rates to patient DVH-based QA metrics in pretreatment dose QA. *Med Phys* 2011; 38:5477–89.
109. Fan J., Xing L., Ma M., Hu W., Yang Y. Verification of the machine delivery parameters of a treatment plan via deep learning. *Phys Med Biol* 2020 Sep 30; 65(19):195007.
110. Fan J., Xing L., Yang Y. Independent verification of brachytherapy treatment plan by using deep learning inference modeling. *Phys Med Biol* 2021 Jun 16; 66(12). doi: 10.1088/1361-6560/ac067f.
111. Dong P., Xing L. Deep DoseNet: A deep neural network for accurate dosimetric transformation between different spatial resolutions and/or different dose calculation algorithms for precision radiation therapy. *Phys Med Biol* 2020 Feb 4; 65(3):035010.
112. Xing Y., Nguyen D., Lu W., Yang M., Jiang S. Technical note: A feasibility study on deep learning-based radiotherapy dose calculation. *Med Phys* 2020 Feb; 47(2):753–8.
113. Kontaxis C., Bol G.H., Lagendijk J.J.W., Raaymakers B.W. DeepDose: Towards a fast dose calculation engine for radiation therapy using deep learning. *Phys Med Biol* 2020 Apr 8; 65(7):075013.
114. Fan J., Xing L., Dong P., Wang J., Hu W., Yang Y. Data-driven dose calculation algorithm based on deep U-Net. *Phys Med Biol* 2020 Dec 22; 65(24):245035.

5

Reinforcement Learning for Radiation Therapy Planning and Image Processing

Dan Nguyen, Chenyang Shen, Xun Jia, and Steve Jiang

UT Southwestern Medical Center

CONTENTS

5.1 Introduction and Overview

Reinforcement learning (RL)[1] refers to a type of widely employed machine learning technique that trains agents, i.e., computer models, to learn the optimal policy of interacting with environments, i.e., existing systems, to accomplish certain tasks automatically. The main idea is to let the agent extensively interact with the environment, and either be rewarded or penalized for its actions. Over time, the agent learns how to take action in order to maximize its reward. More specifically, in each step of RL, the computer agent takes a state produced by the environment as input and outputs an action of how to interact with the environment. This action is then applied to interact with the environment. As a reaction, the environment produces a new state in response to the action, along with a reward. This reward is defined specifically for the task to achieve. It quantifies the quality of the action in terms of its impact on the task. With this interactive process being repeated for a number of times, the agent observes and learns from all the states, actions, and rewards generated. It gradually learns the optimal policy of taking actions to maximize the reward based on interactions between the agent and the environment. Note that the whole RL process is analogous to the natural

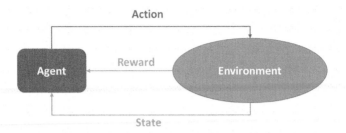

FIGURE 5.1
Illustration of the reinforcement learning process. An environment indicates an existing system that produces a state after interacting with an agent. The gain in the interaction is evaluated by a pre-defined reward function. An agent in the form of a DNN observes the state of the environment and determines an action. The overall goal of DRL is to train a deep neural network-based agent to maximize the reward automatically by interacting with the environment.

trial-and-error learning process of a human. In theory, extra training samples can always be produced by simply executing more interactions between the agent and the environment. Instead of always having the agent to decide the actions, random search strategy is sometimes applied to enhance the diversity in the state–action pairs produced during the interactions. A commonly employed random search strategy is the ϵ-greedy search, which chooses to take random actions with a probability of ϵ during the interactions. In addition, experience replay strategy is often utilized to avoid training the agent using sequentially generated samples that are highly correlated with each other. Upon the success of RL, the agent acquires the ability to accomplish the task by interacting with the environment, similar to the decision-making capability of an experienced human (Figure 5.1).

With the rapid advancement in deep learning (DL), *deep reinforcement learning* (DRL),[2] which incorporates a deep neural network (DNN) to model the agent, has become a popular form of RL. Note that DRL generally follows the same learning strategy as RL, while it incorporates the superior perception and function approximation capability of DNNs into the RL framework to improve the decision-making performance, especially for those complex environments and tasks. This leads to the tremendous success of DRL in many modern applications. For instance,[3,4] combined DRL with Q-learning[5] to achieve human level or super-human level controls in playing Atari games. Another famous example is the successful development of AlphaGo,[6,7] a DRL-based computer agent that beats top professional human players in the game of Go.

With its capability of achieving human-level decision-making capability demonstrated in many real-world applications, DRL holds a strong potential for solving clinical problems that require human inputs. In the following sections, we will first briefly go over existing applications of DRL in the regime of radiation therapy (RT) treatment planning and medical imaging. Then, the challenges and limitations of the existing DRL approaches will be discussed, followed by some future perspectives.

5.2 Status

5.2.1 DRL Application in Treatment Planning for RT

Early reinforcement learning studies, such as the study by Tseng et al.,[8] studied the feasibility of an RL agent to adapt dose fractionation protocols for non-small cell lung cancer (NSCLC) patients. They first collected 114 NSCLC patients, and, because of the limited data size, they trained a generative adversarial network (GAN) to generate synthetic data as a data augmentation technique. They then constructed an artificial environment containing the real and synthetic data and trained a deep Q-network (DQN) to interact with this environment to learn the best adaptive dose per fraction (from 1 to 5 fractions). They found that the DQN's policies were similar to those used in clinical protocols (RMSE=0.5 Gy) and were much better than a traditional temporal difference algorithm (RMSE=3.3 Gy). Such a DQN may lay the groundwork for a fully automated clinical decision support system for adaptive dose schemes. Another study by Jalalimanesh et al.[9] used an agent-based simulation of vascular tumor growth and then applied Q-learning to learn the policy for fractionation and dose per fraction. Based on their particular model, they showed the feasibility of the Q-learning algorithm to find the optimal fractionation and dose protocol. The performance of these types of algorithms heavily depends on the accuracy of the environment modeling, which may depend on the specific biology, and may be limited depending on the approximations made by the environment.

Shen et al. demonstrated the ability of a DRL agent to model a human planner's actions and behaviors in a treatment planning optimization scenario for both high-dose rate (HDR) brachytherapy for cervical cancer[10] and intensity modulated RT (IMRT) for prostate cancer.[11] The DRL agent learned how to automatically fine-tune the structure weights (in both studies) as well as fine-tune the threshold dose (for the prostate IMRT study). In these studies, it was found that the RL agent was capable of improving the quality score of the HDR brachytherapy plans by 10.7%, as compared to human planners. For the prostate cancer IMRT, the DRL agent was able to increase the planning score by an average of 70%, as compared to the initialized plan parameters, as shown in Figure 5.2. These studies demonstrated the feasibility of an RL framework to automatically learn and fine-tune hyperparameters of a treatment planning optimization process.

RL can also be used for the optimization of beam orientations for IMRT applications. Barkousaraie et al. showed that it is possible to (1) first train a neural network to learn a policy or an optimization algorithm, known as column generation (CG),[12] followed by (2) using an RL technique called Monte Carlo Tree Search (MCTS) in order to find a set of beam angles that better minimize the objective in less time than CG.[13] In the first phase, the trained neural network is capable of finding a non-inferior set of beam angles, but

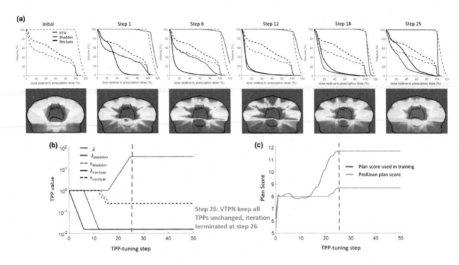

FIGURE 5.2

From Shen et al.[11] Evolution of dose–volume histograms and dose distributions (a), treatment planning parameter (TPP) values (b), and original and modified ProKnow scores (c) in the planning process of a test patient case.

under a fraction of a second as opposed to the many minutes it took for CG to solve. In addition, the neural network does not require all of the candidate dose influence matrices to be calculated like CG, saving potentially many hours of beamlet-based dose calculation. In the second step, MCTS is utilized, but to more efficiently navigate the policy search space, the neural network from part 1 is utilized to guide the search. This allowed for the ability to find a superior beam orientation set as opposed to CG, with respect to minimizing the cost function. This method can still solve the problem faster than CG, taking about one-third of the time.

Ma et al.[14] utilized DRL to develop an automatic scatter estimation for high-efficiency photon distribution estimation. Specifically, they start with a low history GPU-based Monte Carlo calculation in order to obtain a raw, sparse signal. An optimization formulation with a sparse feature penalty modeled is then solved to estimate the scatter signal following a Poisson distribution. This optimization problem is solved with a DRL-tuned over-relaxation algorithm. The DQN interacts directly with the algorithms over-relaxation parameter and fine-tune it to maximize the convergence rate of the optimization problem. They found that they are able to achieve high accuracy dose estimation, with one scatter image generation taking less than 2 seconds.

5.2.2 DRL Applications in Medical Image Processing for RT

Recently, DRL has been successfully applied to enable an intelligent reconstruction framework[15,16] in which computer agents were established to automatically adjust the regularization parameters in iterative CT reconstruction for high image quality. With the aid of the carefully designed image regularization terms, such as the total variation (TV),[17,18] tight frame (TF),[19,20] and nonlocal mean (NLM),[21,22] iterative reconstruction algorithms have been demonstrated to achieve superior reconstruction quality compared to the conventional reconstruction methods. However, selecting the optimal regularization parameters in reconstruction models is critically important for the success of the iterative reconstruction, since it greatly impacts the quality of the reconstructed image. Manual parameter tuning for the optimal reconstruction quality is tedious and time consuming, and it becomes a very challenging task when multiple regularization parameters are involved in the algorithm.

To release the manually parameter-tuning efforts and fully automate the reconstruction process, Shen et al.[15] established a DNN model via DRL to determine the optimal way of tuning regularization parameter in a similar manner as human experts. Specifically, to show the power of DNN in automatic parameter tuning, an extreme case where each pixel in a CT image has an independent regularization parameter to be adjusted was considered. Such a large number of parameters is apparently beyond the capability of a human and, therefore, manual parameter tuning is infeasible. The DNN model was established to observe an image patch extracted from a CT image and predict the direction and the magnitude of parameter adjustment for the pixel in the center. Q-learning framework with an experience replay mechanism was employed for the training of the DNN model. The reward function was designed based on the distance between the reconstructed patch and the reference patch. The results showed that the fully trained DNN was able to automatically adjust the regularization parameter for each pixel to reduce the reconstruction error. The image quality outperforms that of the CT images reconstructed using parameters manually adjusted by a human expert. In addition, the DNN-adjusted regularization parameters are similar to the optimal parameters theoretically derived based on the reference images. As the DNN takes local image patch as input, a large number of training samples can be extracted for each training image. Furthermore, the DRL generates numerous training patches reconstructed with a wide variety of regularization parameters in the training process. These together guarantee the success of DNN training using a relatively small number of training images.

One obvious drawback of the approach developed in the aforementioned study[15] is the need for a high-quality reference image for each CT in the training dataset. This is generally infeasible for most of the real applications. The key is to develop a reference image-free quality evaluation metric for CT images. To solve this problem, a quality-guided DRL framework was developed in ref. [16]. The main idea is to build a quality assessment network (QAN) model to judge the quality of a CT image patch. The training of QAN is performed in a similar way as training a discriminator network in the

GAN framework.[23] It was trained to differentiate reconstructed patches from those extracted from high-quality CT images by assigning 0 to the reconstructed patches and 1 to the high-quality patches. Note that high-quality CT scans of any patient can be used in this case without the need of being paired with the training images, and hence it eliminates the data feasibility concern. The training of QAN was integrated with the DRL in which QAN and the parameter-tuning DNN were trained alternatively: QAN serves as a reward function to evaluate the reconstruction quality and guide the training of parameter-tuning DNN, while patches reconstructed in the DRL process were employed to refine QAN. The results showed that both QANs were successfully trained in the quality-guided DRL framework. QAN was able to serve as a CT image quality evaluation metric as it predicted higher scores for patches with better image quality. The parameter-tuning DNN was able to adjust the regularization parameter to produce high-quality CT reconstruction automatically.

Furthermore, Shen et al.[24] proposed a DRL-based framework to achieve optimal quality of CT reconstruction by learning a personalized CT scan strategy. Conventional CT scan acquires projection data using evenly distributed angles and imaging dose, which might not be optimal for different patients. This study[24] aimed at to develop a patient-specific projection angle and dose selection strategy to allow optimal reconstruction quality. Specifically, with the number of projections and total CT dose fixed, DRL was implemented to train an agent that can automatically adjust the scanning angle and the corresponding dose delivered at this angle to optimize the reconstruction quality. The angles and dose of different projections were adjusted adaptively in a sequential manner. The reward used in DRL was the quality change in the images before and after adjustment, while the image quality was evaluated using the peak-to-noise ratio. The results of 2016 NIH-AAPM-Mayo Clinic Low Dose CT Grand Challenge dataset showed that the DRL-based agent was able to learn effective angle and dose adjustment policy to improve the reconstruction quality, demonstrating the potential of the proposed algorithm in personalized CT scan. Of course, this study shares the same drawback as in ref. [15] which needs paired high- and low-quality CT images.

Moreover, novel DRL-based strategies have also been developed for magnetic resonance imaging (MRI), which has attracted increasing interest in RT. For instance, Pineda et al.[25] employed DRL to optimize the data acquisition process in k-space with a goal of reducing the total number of measurements, while preserving MRI reconstruction quality. The strategy has shown to be effective in producing decent MRI with a substantially accelerated acquisition process.

Another DRL application in medical imaging closely related to RT is image segmentation. Before the era of DL, RL has already been successfully employed for medical image segmentation. For instance, in ref. [26], an RL-based model was successfully trained to adjust the local threshold and structuring element values for prostate segmentation, while in ref. [27], the authors incorporated the human intention in the RL framework to develop an agent that is able to perform accurate segmentation with reduced user interventions. With the rapid advancements in algorithm and computational power, DNN models became feasible and have immediately shown great promise in medical image segmentation. Since then, the focus of DRL in segmentation has been switched to adjusting the training strategy, e.g., learning rate and data augmentation,[28-30] and hyperparameters, e.g., network architecture,[31] of deep segmentation models to improve their performance.

DRL has also been successfully applied to solving the image registration problem, which is of interest in RT. The early studies[32,33] focused on a simpler setup of rigid registration, in which deep agents were trained via DRL to sequentially adjust the six parameters (three for translation and three for rotation) defining a rigid transformation. The registration results of the established models were shown to outperform the state-of-the-art optimization-based algorithms. Then, the DRL-based algorithm was extended to the non-rigid case, including the deformable registration. To reduce the degree of freedom in deformable registration, Krebs et al.[34] proposed the characterization of deformation statistically via the dominating modes in principle component analysis for which adjustment actions can be defined. The results showed promising registration performance achieved by the DRL-based model.

5.3 Current and Future Challenges

Despite the great success achieved in the RT field, DRL is still facing several challenges from both theoretical and practical perspectives. The first issue is the data diversity. In contrast to other DL strategies, the limited number of training samples in RT-related applications is not that much of a concern, since DRL automatically produces training samples by random exploration and intensive agent–environment interactions. However, this process does not eliminate the diversity issue in the training dataset. We expect a well-trained DRL agent to fail on a case that is distinct from the training samples and all the samples produced based on the training data during the DRL process. Fundamentally speaking, the problem of data diversity heavily depends on the degree of independence and the inherent dimension of the data.[35] A learning problem is well-defined only when the independence of the samples in a dataset is equal to the inherence dimension. Otherwise, the samples in a dataset cannot fully represent the complete characteristics of the data, therefore causing the diversity concern.

Another issue of DRL is the lack of model interpretability and robustness, which is a common issue shared with other types of DL strategies. This is due to the complex function forms of DNN models, which makes it a very challenging task to understand exactly how the models work from a theoretical point of view. With little knowledge about the working principle, it is almost impossible to ensure the robustness of a DNN model as identified in many studies.[36–40] This becomes a serious concern for RT-related applications, since the lack of model robustness may negatively influence patient safety and treatment outcome.

Furthermore, the computational time needed to execute the random exploration/agent–environment interactions in DRL-based approaches has been identified as a concern for RT-related applications. As we know, a numerous time of random exploration and agent–environment interactions is always needed to produce sufficient training samples for DRL to train the computer agent. As such, a DRL process can be very time consuming when a long execution time is needed for each exploration/interaction. This time will grow further with the size of state–action space. Using DRL for RT treatment planning as an example, one time of plan optimization needs to be conducted in each exploration/interaction, leading to a training time of more than a week for a simple treatment planning task.

5.4 Future Perspective

In this chapter, we provided an overview of major RL technologies developed for radiotherapy treatment planning and image processing. Specifically, we discussed RL in the context of dose fractionation protocols, optimization hyperparameter tuning, beam orientation selection, and high-efficiency dose distribution estimation for treatment planning. For image processing, we discussed RL for automatic regularization parameter tuning, projection angle and dose selection policies, data acquisition optimization in k-space for MRI, image segmentation with reduced user segmentation, and image registration parameter tuning. We outlined their current statuses, advantages, as well as the limitations.

To further expand the horizon of DRL in RT treatment planning and image processing, a key step would be to improve the data collection, sharing, and pre-processing to enhance the diversity of data as much as possible. As we mentioned in previous sections, the diversity of data is critically important for the success of DRL algorithms. While an effective theoretical measure of diversity is still missing so far, a practical approach that could be taken to improve the diversity of data is to expand the capacity of dataset, which can be done through more effective data collection and sharing among different institutions. In addition, pre-processing also plays an essential role, which can help to remove redundant and low-quality data, preventing the training from being deviated to undesired directions.

In addition, further investigations to improve interpretability and robustness for DRL models are highly desired for RT and other applications in healthcare. While theoretical analysis remains to be a challenging task, practical measures, such as conducting a comprehensive model evaluation study, should be taken to inspect what the model exactly does under a wide range of different situations. In addition, human experts should involve closely in monitoring the model behaviors during both model evaluation and routine application stages to minimize the risk of deploying DRL models with limited interpretability and robustness in real clinical applications.

Another important task to address is the efficiency of DRL, which can be tackled mainly from two different angles. The first is to reduce the time cost for environment to response to an action taken either by the agent or by random search. Using intelligent reconstruction as an example, one can implement GPU-based iterative reconstruction algorithms to substantially shorten the time needed to perform reconstruction, and thereby reduce the overall total computational time needed by DRL. The second angle is to develop algorithms that can reduce the total number of random explorations/agent–environment interactions needed to train the agent. One potential solution is to incorporate human experience as guidance for DRL to improve the learning efficiency of the agent, which has been shown to be effective in a preliminary study aiming at to improve the training efficiency of DRL-based agent for RT treatment planning.[41]

References

1. Sutton, R. S. & Barto, A. G. *Reinforcement Learning: An Introduction.* (Cambridge, MA: MIT Press, 2018).
2. François-Lavet, V., Henderson, P., Islam, R., Bellemare, M. G. & Pineau, J. An introduction to deep reinforcement learning. *Foundations and Trends® in Machine Learning* **11**, 219–354 (2018).
3. Mnih, V. et al. Playing atari with deep reinforcement learning. *arXiv preprint arXiv:1312.5602* (2013).
4. Mnih, V. et al. Human-level control through deep reinforcement learning. *Nature* **518**, 529–533. doi:10.1038/nature14236. https://www.nature.com/articles/nature14236#supplementary-information (2015).
5. Watkins, C. J. & Dayan, P. Q-learning. *Machine Learning* **8**, 279–292 (1992).
6. Silver, D. et al. Mastering the game of Go with deep neural networks and tree search. *Nature* **529**, 484. doi:10.1038/nature16961. https://www.nature.com/articles/nature16961#supplementary-information (2016).
7. Silver, D. et al. Mastering the game of Go without human knowledge. *Nature* **550**, 354. doi:10.1038/nature24270. https://www.nature.com/articles/nature24270#supplementary-information (2017).
8. Tseng, H. H. et al. Deep reinforcement learning for automated radiation adaptation in lung cancer. *Medical Physics* **44**, 6690–6705 (2017).

9. Jalalimanesh, A., Haghighi, H. S., Ahmadi, A. & Soltani, M. Simulation-based optimization of radiotherapy: Agent-based modeling and reinforcement learning. *Mathematics and Computers in Simulation* **133**, 235–248 (2017).

10. Shen, C. et al. Intelligent inverse treatment planning via deep reinforcement learning, a proof-of-principle study in high dose-rate Brachytherapy for cervical cancer. *Physics in Medicine & Biology* **64**, 115013 (2019).

11. Shen, C. et al. Operating a treatment planning system using a deep-reinforcement learning-based virtual treatment planner for prostate cancer intensity-modulated radiation therapy treatment planning. *Medical Physics* **47**, 2329–2336 (2020).

12. Sadeghnejad Barkousaraie, A., Ogunmolu, O., Jiang, S. & Nguyen, D. A fast deep learning approach for beam orientation optimization for prostate cancer treated with intensity-modulated radiation therapy. *Medical Physics* **47**, 880–897 (2020).

13. Sadeghnejad-Barkousaraie, A., Bohara, G., Jiang, S. & Nguyen, D. A reinforcement learning application of a guided Monte Carlo Tree Search algorithm for beam orientation selection in radiation therapy. *Machine Learning: Science and Technology* **2**, 035013 (2021).

14. Ma, J. et al. Monte Carlo simulation fused with target distribution modeling via deep reinforcement learning for automatic high-efficiency photon distribution estimation. *Photonics Research* **9**, B45–B56 (2021).

15. Shen, C., Gonzalez, Y., Chen, L., Jiang, S. & Jia, X. Intelligent parameter tuning in optimization-based iterative CT reconstruction via deep reinforcement learning. *IEEE Transactions on Medical Imaging* **37**, 1430–1439 (2018).

16. Shen, C. et al. in *15th International Meeting on Fully Three-Dimensional Image Reconstruction in Radiology and Nuclear Medicine*. 1107203 (International Society for Optics and Photonics).

17. Rudin, L. I., Osher, S. & Fatemi, E. Nonlinear total variation based noise removal algorithms. *Physica D: Nonlinear Phenomena* **60**, 259–268 (1992).

18. Jia, X., Lou, Y., Li, R., Song, W. Y. & Jiang, S. B. GPU-based fast cone beam CT reconstruction from undersampled and noisy projection data via total variation. *Medical Physics* **37**, 1757–1760. doi:10.1118/1.3371691 (2010).

19. Jia, X., Dong, B., Lou, Y. & Jiang, S. B. GPU-based iterative cone-beam CT reconstruction using tight frame regularization. *Physics in Medicine & Biology* **56**, 3787 (2011).

20. Shen, C. et al. Multi-energy element-resolved cone beam CT (MEER-CBCT) realized on a conventional CBCT platform. *Medical Physics* **45**, 4461–4470 (2018).

21. Li, B. et al. Multienergy cone-beam computed tomography reconstruction with a spatial spectral nonlocal means algorithm. *SIAM Journal on Imaging Sciences* **11**, 1205–1229 (2018).

22. Tian, Z., Jia, X., Dong, B., Lou, Y. & Jiang, S. B. Low-dose 4DCT reconstruction via temporal nonlocal means. *Medical Physics* **38**, 1359–1365 (2011).

23. Goodfellow, I. et al. in *Advances in neural information processing systems*, 2672–2680.

24. Shen, Z., Wang, Y., Wu, D., Yang, X. & Dong, B. Learning to scan: A deep reinforcement learning approach for personalized scanning in CT imaging. *arXiv preprint arXiv:2006.02420* (2020).

25. Pineda, L., Basu, S., Romero, A., Calandra, R. & Drozdzal, M. in *International Conference on Medical Image Computing and Computer-Assisted Intervention*, 23–33 (Springer).

26. Sahba, F., Tizhoosh, H. R. & Salama, M. M. in *The 2006 IEEE International Joint Conference on Neural Network Proceedings*, 511–517 (IEEE).
27. Wang, L., Lekadir, K., Lee, S.-L., Merrifield, R. & Yang, G.-Z. A general framework for context-specific image segmentation using reinforcement learning. *IEEE Transactions on Medical Imaging* **32**, 943–956 (2013).
28. Yang, D. et al. in *International Conference on Medical Image Computing and Computer-Assisted Intervention*, 3–11 (Springer).
29. Qin, T. et al. in *ICASSP 2020-2020 IEEE International Conference on Acoustics, Speech and Signal Processing (ICASSP)*, 1419–1423 (IEEE).
30. Yang, H., Shan, C. & Kolen, A. F. in *International Conference on Medical Image Computing and Computer-Assisted Intervention*, 646–655 (Springer).
31. Bae, W. et al. in *International Conference on Medical Image Computing and Computer-Assisted Intervention*, 228–236 (Springer).
32. Liao, R. et al. in *Proceedings of the AAAI Conference on Artificial Intelligence*.
33. Ma, K. et al. in *International Conference on Medical Image Computing and Computer-Assisted Intervention*, 240–248 (Springer).
34. Krebs, J. et al. in *International Conference on Medical Image Computing and Computer-Assisted Intervention*, 344–352 (Springer).
35. Shen, C. et al. An introduction to deep learning in medical physics: Advantages, potential, and challenges. *Physics in Medicine & Biology* **65**, 05TR01. doi:10.1088/1361-6560/ab6f51 (2020).
36. Papernot, N. et al. in *2016 IEEE European Symposium on Security and Privacy (EuroS&P)*, 372–387 (IEEE).
37. Kurakin, A., Goodfellow, I. & Bengio, S. Adversarial examples in the physical world. *arXiv preprint arXiv:1607.02533* (2016).
38. Yuan, X., He, P., Zhu, Q. & Li, X. Adversarial examples: Attacks and defenses for deep learning. *IEEE Transactions on Neural Networks and Learning Systems* **30**, 2805–2824 (2019).
39. Akhtar, N. & Mian, A. Threat of adversarial attacks on deep learning in computer vision: A survey. *IEEE Access* **6**, 14410–14430 (2018).
40. Shen, C. et al. On the robustness of deep learning-based lung-nodule classification for CT images with respect to image noise. *Physics in Medicine & Biology* **65**, 245037. doi:10.1088/1361-6560/abc812 (2020).
41. Shen, C., Chen, L., Gonzalez, Y. & Jia, X. Improving efficiency of training a virtual treatment planner network via knowledge-guided deep reinforcement learning for intelligent automatic treatment planning of radiotherapy. *Medical Physics* **48**, 1909–1920. doi: 10.1002/mp.14712 (2021).

6

Image Registration and Segmentation

Tomi F. Nano
University of California

Carlos Cardenas
The University of Alabama at Birmingham

Dante P. I. Capaldi
University of California

CONTENTS

DOI: 10.1201/9781003094333-6

6.1 Introduction and Background

6.1.1 Clinical Workflow in Radiation Oncology

Radiation Oncology has made significant progress since the first use of a linear accelerator in medicine almost 80 years ago.[1] One aspect that has seen the most advancement is the incorporation of medical imaging into the clinical workflow, specifically the use of three-dimensional (3D) tomographic imaging. Computed tomography (CT), as well as a whole gamut of other imaging modalities (such as magnetic resonance imaging [MRI] and positron emission tomography [PET]), is now a mainstay of the Radiation Oncology Department.[2] Advancement of imaging methods and their application in radiation oncology have led to better delineation of targets, such as highly metabolic regions in PET, the ability to change patient's treatment plan day-to-day using onboard imaging, and to follow patients post-treatment to evaluate treatment response.[3]

Figure 6.1 further emphasizes the utility of medical imaging in the clinical workflow of a patient who received radiation. In addition to the qualitative information, imaging provides quantitative metrics that can be extracted using image segmentation (commonly known as contouring). Furthermore, multiple image sessions, either at the same time using different imaging techniques or sequentially over time, can be viewed together using image fusion which relies on image registration.[9] The two image processing techniques are intimately involved in the clinic where dosimetrists, physicists, radiation oncologists, and therapists use these tools on a daily basis. Historically, methods used in the clinic heavily rely on manual input, while future work has been directed to making these processes more automated with the assistance of artificial intelligence (AI).[8]

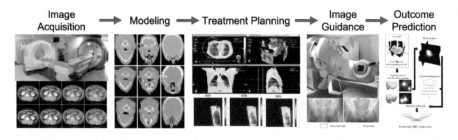

FIGURE 6.1

A general overview of the clinical workflow in Radiation Oncology. From image acquisition at simulation to outcome predictions, AI has been implemented.[4-8]

6.1.2 Image Registration and Segmentation Applications

As mentioned previously, both image segmentation and registration are integral in the radiation oncology workflow.[10] Both of these image processing techniques are commonly leveraged together to better identify (segment) tumors and organs-at-risk (OARs) by combining (registering) multiple imaging series, in an effort to help guide and optimize the delivery of radiation to patients. With the advances in radiation delivery techniques, such as intensity modulated radiation therapy (IMRT)[11,12] and volumetric modulated arc therapy (VMAT),[13] more sophisticated algorithms have been deployed to optimize radiation plans. These algorithms depend on user inputs; chiefly, the dose prescribed to the target and the limiting dose to OARs in proximity to the target.[14] Accordingly, the volumes a user wants to prescribe or limit dose to during treatment planning (to model the patient) need to be identified and easily digested by the optimization algorithm – this is performed through image segmentation (colloquially known in the Radiation Oncology community as contouring).

Image segmentation is the process of delineating target volumes and OARs on medical images, such as CT, PET, and/or MRI. In addition to contouring OARs and targets on images acquired at simulation, or before radiation treatment commences, image contouring has increasingly been performed at the time of treatment, specifically to assist in image guidance and treatment plan adaptation.[3,15,16] Adaptive radiation therapy is the process of modifying a patient's original treatment plan at simulation based on the variations in patient anatomy that occur during treatment (such as weight loss) visualized using imaging acquired at treatment.[15] Accordingly, the images acquired need to be recontoured to identify the new target as well as OARs prior to plan adaptation. As you can imagine, adaptive radiotherapy is one of the areas where high-throughput machinery, such as automated segmentation (auto-contouring), is in high demand.[17(p20)]

Image registration, commonly known as fusion or matching, is the process of aligning images based on similar features. Image registration can be relatively simple, such as the co-registering of two images from the same modality, of the same patient, in the same position, that were only acquired a few minutes apart (e.g., chest x-rays), or immensely complex, involving multiple images, of different dimensionality (e.g., 2D to 3D) that contain image contrast which was generated via different physical mechanisms. However, the overarching goal of medical image registration is to find the optional common physical space that underlies anatomical structures in images. In Radiation Oncology, image registration is used during treatment simulation and contouring targets and OARS,[5] patient setup during daily positioning,[18] motion tracking during treatment,[19–22] dose evaluation post-treatment,[23–25] adaptive radiotherapy,[16,26–28] and many others.

6.1.3 Overview of AI in Image Registration and Segmentation

In Radiation Oncology today, medical imaging plays an increasingly vital role in cancer treatment and patient treatment response. With the advent of image guidance and novel imaging techniques used to evaluate patient response, there is an increasing amount of imaging data available for clinicians to use and improve patient treatments. Imaging data is acquired at various stages of radiation therapy, which includes at diagnosis or initial findings, treatment simulation, during treatment, or post-treatment for evaluation of response. As more medical imaging data is being incorporated into the patient's clinical pathway, such as with image guidance, the need for automation in radiation oncology is clear. Automating image segmentation and registration tasks not only reduce the overall time as compared to manual processes but automation also has been shown to reduce inter- and intra-observer variability, which has been shown to be dependent on image display and acquisition settings.[17,29,30] Automation, via AI, is ultimately necessary to assist the technologically advanced delivery systems and help facilitate modern complex workflows in Radiation Oncology to provide the best quality care for all patients.

Whether it is for image segmentation or registration, there are common aspects of an AI project that utilizes imaging which should be considered for robust models. Some of the common aspects of AI studies involving imaging data include image dimensionality (e.g., 2D vs 3D), image resolution (e.g., pixel size), image matrix size, loss functions, optimizers, training methods (e.g., pre-trained models), hyper-parameter tuning, evaluation metrics, and test datasets. Furthermore, another important and similar aspect is the model architecture. Figure 6.2 shows a U-Net architecture that has been the basis of many AI models tasked with image segmentation and registration.[32] U-Net models are designed to take the input image data, through the use of multiple convolutional operations to extract features as part of a convolution neural network (CNN), and generate an output class of labels contours or generate an output of deformation vector fields that can be used for image segmentation and registration, respectively.

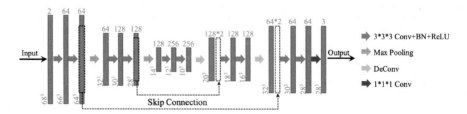

FIGURE 6.2
The architecture of a typical "U-Net" showing an encoder (left) and decoder (right) that compress the input into a set of features with reduced dimensionality and can expand the features to the desired output, respectively.[31,32]

In current state-of-the-art AI models, the optimization algorithm of choice is a flavor of gradient descent or stochastic gradient descent when searching for the best model parameters that result in the lowest loss function,[33] and hopefully the global minimum. A common deep-learning optimizer is Adam, which is a stochastic gradient descent algorithm that updates the learning rate for each network weight individually.[34] When training a model, and not only for image segmentation and registration but for all tasks, the loss function is one of the most important settings needed for making accurate predictions. The appropriate loss function depends on the task at hand, for example, image segmentation is considered a classification task and image registration is a regression task. Common classification loss functions are mean-squared error (MSE), cross-entropy or log loss, weighted cross-entropy, and Dice Score Coefficient (or 1-Dice to be more precise).[35] For image segmentation, Dice coefficient and Hausdorff distance are common metrics used to evaluate target or OAR delineation based on a ground truth mask.

Hyperparameter tuning is an important aspect when training AI models and optimizing performance for a given task and dataset. Every model has parameters, or variables, that we adjust to fit our data. For example, a common CNN architecture is composed of "neurons" or "blocks" that include a convolution kernel, pooling function, and activation function. For each CNN block, the only learnable parameters are the kernel weights, whereas pooling and activation typically do not have any learnable parameters. Whereas the hyperparameters are variables that can be adjusted during the training process and govern how the optimizer finds the model parameters that give the lowest loss. For example, common hyperparameters for CNNs are learning rate, momentum, batch size, and the number of epochs. Hyperparameters are not directly related to the training data, but rather they are configured to provide the best result during training, which is commonly done using manual grid search experiments for a given dataset.

Lastly, it should be mentioned that good AI practice includes the use of appropriate evaluation metrics for a given task and test datasets that have not been seen by the model during training and validation. Ideally, the evaluation metric should be the same as the loss function that was used during the optimization of model parameters to ensure direct generalizability between training and testing. However, that is not always possible which is commonly due to when the desired evaluation metric is not computable during training. This may be due to a lack of functionality in popular deep-learning libraries (such as PyTorch, TensorFlow, or Keras), where it is undeniable that they are extremely useful resources with many useful functional building blocks, some segmentation and registration tasks require custom loss functions that differ from the ideal evaluation metric. Performance evaluation of a deep-learning model should be completed on test data that has been separated out of the initial dataset via a fair method, such as random multiple splits to evaluate the variance of model predictions.

The goal of this chapter is to explore and discuss: (1) the applications of image registration and segmentation in Radiation Oncology; (2) the role of AI and machine learning; and (3) the current challenges limiting the implementation of these models into the clinical workflow.

6.2 Image Registration

6.2.1 Traditional Registration Methods

Traditional image registration methods that did not utilize neural networks or other AI methods include optical flow algorithms, demon deformable algorithms, advanced normalization tools, and other rigid and non-rigid tools such as Elastix.[36] Recently, many image registration methods have been published using AI methods and have been shown to achieve state-of-the-art performances in radiation oncology applications.[37] However, traditional registration methods are still the mainstay in radiation oncology commercial software.

Medical image registration is used in many radiation therapy-related applications, such as daily image guidance, motion tracking, image segmentation, dose accumulation, image reconstruction, and medical image registration is a broad topic which can be grouped from various perspectives. Registration methods can be divided into rigid, affine, and deformable methods based on their deformations. These methods can also be grouped according to anatomical sites such as head and neck, thorax, gastrointestinal, and pelvis based on the region of interest (ROI). Additionally, registration methods can be divided into 2D to 2D/2D or 3D to 2D/3D based on image dimensionality. In image registration, one image, which is called the moving image, is deformed to fit the other image, the fixed image (or reference image). In other words, registration is the problem of finding a coordinate transformation that makes the moving image spatially aligned with the fixed image.

Most intensity-based registration methodologies have the main idea to search iteratively for the geometric transformation that optimizes a similarity measure that is related to voxel intensity and is computed in the overlapped regions of the input images. The geometric transformation model used is crucial in image registration, which depends on the data and application, and can be divided into rigid (3D affine) and non-rigid classes (deformations that can be limited or free-form). The term "elastic registration" is sometimes used as a synonym for a curved or deformable registration. In flow-based registration algorithms, the registration problem is addressed as a motion problem where an image moves continually toward the reference, and flow-based registration algorithms can be divided into two further sub-classes (fluid flow and optical flow).[38] The topology of the structures represented in an image needs to be preserved during registration, which can be done by ensuring the geometric transformation, is diffeomorphism; meaning invertible and differentiable mapping. The registration methodologies that use diffeomorphic transformations are known as diffeomorphic image registration methodologies (such as affine and flow-based if not degenerated).[38]

6.2.2 Evaluation of Registration Methods

Evaluation of registration methods can be performed using similarity measures, which can be divided into two classes: intensity-based and feature-based methods. Depending on the features and ROIs used, some metrics can be included in both classes. The registration metric used for deformable image registration is usually composed of at least two terms: one related to the voxel intensity or structures similarity and the other one to the deformation field.[39] Therefore, there can be a trade-off between the "voxel intensity" and the "deformation intensity" in the cost function. This trade-off is often controlled with a constraining term (or regularization term), which can put more weight on one versus the other to penalize the loss.

Common similarity metrics are based on intensity differences, cross-correlation, or feature-based information. The sum of squared differences (SSDs) or MSE is used when one assumes that the structures in both references and moving images have identical intensities, which may not be true for multimodality imaging. When computing MSE over an ROI with "n" pixels in a 2D image, or voxels in a 3D image, the expression is given by

$$\mathrm{MSE} = \frac{1}{n}\sum_{i=1}^{n}\left(y_i - \hat{y}_i\right)^2$$

where y_i is the group truth pixel value of the ith pixel and $\hat{y}_i$ is the predicted (after the transformation map is applied post-registration). Another commonly used registration error is landmark distance, which is defined as the Euclidean distance between two points that are predetermined as a match between the registered images. There are other forms of landmark-based distances that have been analytically developed and shown to be useful, such as the use of Gaussian radial basis functions; however, they are less common and specialized for specific registration methods.

Other methods of evaluating registration accuracy involve the computation of a displacement vector (or a max/min distance between a group of points) between images or regions of interest. Target registration errors can be conceptualized as the vector between a group of landmark points relative to a centralized location. During the comparison of ROI patches, displacement vectors can be computed based on a pre-defined algorithm and used to give an overall accuracy for the given patch. The displacement vector is related to the normalized cross-correlation (NCC), which is defined by the inverse of the Fourier transform of the convolution of the Fourier transform of two images, normalized to the local sum and sigmas. This is also sometimes known as the Pearson correlation coefficient.

6.2.3 AI Registration by Anatomical Region

Image registration using AI has now been implemented across multiple imaging platforms and on many different anatomical sites.[39,40] Specifically in radiation therapy treatment planning, these categories can be further separated by segmenting either OARs or targets. Here, we will look at a variety of anatomical sites commonly treated with radiation therapy and are currently applying AI algorithms to register images.

6.2.3.1 Head and Neck

Image registration is important for head and neck patients because during the course of radiation treatment they experience a variety of changes in anatomy due to weight loss and shrinkage of parotid, tumor, and nodes. An average weight loss of approximately 5% has been reported and an estimated tumor volume reduction of an average of 70% of its initial volume at the end of treatment. These changes can be accounted for by image-guided radiation therapy, where registration plays an important role and ideally when used with deformable image registration methods.[41] Often MR-to-CT multi-modal deformable registration is used due to the different imaging mechanisms and contrast, as well as the unavoidable patient non-rigid motion between scans. This requires translating one image into the other domain, and GAN networks have been shown to be well-suited for image-to-image translation tasks. Studies have investigated GAN trained to generate head-and-neck images by taking a real CT image to generate a synthetic MR image, or a real MR image to create a synthetic CT. McKenzie et al. showed that registering synthetic CT to MR shows preservation of bulk anatomy (distinguishing bone) but misses anatomical details, whereas synthetic MR to CT shows a large discrepancy in the head pose and produces unrealistic tissue deformations.[42] They investigated landmarks in the nose, mandible, spine vertebrae, and eyes and found that synthetic images (CT or MR) resulted in one and a half times greater average registration error of landmarks when compared to CT-to-CT ground truth with an error of ~4.0 cm relative to the ~6.0 cm error with DL generated synthetic images. However, synthetic images resulted in reduced registration error when compared to multi-modality registration (CT-to-MR or MR-to-CT) which had an error of ~10.0 cm.[42] Multi-modal deformable registration is a challenging problem due to its inherent differences between material-to-material mapping; however, this inherent issue can be somewhat overcome when using synthetic images generated by DL.

One major disadvantage of conventional DIR is that the registration process is iterative and slow, in particular for multi-modality imaging. Deep learning offers a novel approach for direct transformation estimation to align the moving image to a fixed image with the generation of a synthetic image. Fu et al. investigated the use of MRI-to-CT registration with the aid of synthetic CT for head and neck patients generated with a CycleGAN architecture.[43] They found a high average NCC value of 97% between synthetic and real CTs; they showed a mean registration error of 30% lower when using synthetic CT over MRI when registering to real MRI.

Even though MR images have better soft-tissue contrast, CBCT images are still often used for daily positioning and provide patient information that may be useful for adaptive radiation therapy. Unfortunately, CBCT does not provide accurate Hounsfield Units (HUs) for dose calculations due to patient scatter, artifacts, and other issues. Thus, an adaptive radiation therapy workflow with CBCT would require accurate HU values. Liang et al. retrospectively collected 124 head and neck patients and took their CBCT images around the 20th fraction to match with their planning CT and compared registration error over 18 OARs.[18] They found that their CycleGAN method is comparable to Elastix (conventional registration) on most structures; however, it was superior for mandible, esophagus, and pharyngeal constrictor, and only inferior on the left and right brachial plexus. Although this is an impressive finding for DIR and OAR transformation, the performance of DL predictions from CBCT input data is still limited due to image artifacts.

6.2.3.2 Thorax

One of the prime regions within the body where deformable image registration has been utilized is within the thorax.[40] This is mostly due to the non-uniform transformation caused by breathing motion, resulting in individual voxels needing their own deformation field vector. As a result, deformable image registration algorithms are computationally expensive. Consequently, this limitation made them an area of interest for researchers to improve the computational speed. As it pertains to AI, 3D convolutional neural networks have been leveraged to improve accuracy and provide fast deformable registrations. For pulmonary registration, both supervised and unsupervised deep-learning models have been deployed.

Starting with supervised CNNs, Teng et al. developed a supervised model to deform both 4D-CT and 4D-CBCT images for the purpose of performing tasks needed in radiation therapy, such as contour propagation and dose accumulation, across all the different breathing phases.[44] They built a model to directly map the input moving and reference patch pairs to the corresponding deformation field vectors. Their model performed similarly to a commercially available image registration solution, with the added benefit of being faster and fully automated (without any user input). Sokoot et al. developed and implemented a fully supervised model that looked at separating the "low" and "high" frequency components to mimic large and small motion fields, respectively.[45] Their approach provided acceptable registration accuracy by integrating information at multiple scales into their proposed CNN model. Eppenhof et al. generated artificial deformable vector fields by sampling random numbers on a course-to-fine basis to assist in performing complex transformations with large displacements without any "tearing" or "folding", which have historically been minimized in traditional deformable image registration methods using the regularization term.[46] Lastly, Hering et al. looked at addressing the relatively small deformations previously generated by deep-learning models by incorporating a multi-level framework to perform large-scale lung deformable image registrations.[47] Their examples included the most extreme case when registering 3D CT lung datasets at full inspiration and expiration and demonstrated their model outperformed alternatively purposed models.

Alternative to the supervised deep-learning models, unsupervised models have the added benefit that does not require a rigorous training dataset, which can be quite time-consuming, and only require the input data, that in the case of image registration is only the moving and fixed image pairs. One such model coined "LungRegNet" was developed by Fu et al. and consisted of two subnetworks (CoarseNet and FineNet) used to assist in registering the 4D-CT lung image.[48] Additionally, they proposed to perform vessel enhancement on the CT images prior to training/testing to increase the accuracy of the registration of their network. De Vos et al. developed a course-to-fine multi-level multi-resolution model to perform both affine and deformable image registration.[39] In somewhat of a similar fashion to achieve high registration accuracies, other groups, such as Jiang et al., Lei et al., and Duan et al., have implemented this multi-scale approach coarse-to-fine strategy for 4D-CT and 4D-CBCT lung images.[49–51]

6.2.3.3 Gastrointestinal

Not just for gastrointestinal cancers, but overall, pancreatic cancer is one of the leading causes of cancer-related mortality with a poor prognosis with a 5-year survival of 9%. Stereotactic body radiation therapy has been shown to improve survival; however, it relies on image guidance with onboard CBCT for target position verification and set-up displacement correction. However, CBCT has poor soft-tissue contrast and visibility of the pancreas (or tumor) is challenging. Additionally, there are motion-induced artifacts in CBCT that further inhibit the visibility of soft-tissue anatomy. In light of the huge success of deep learning in generating synthetic images, prediction of planning CT from CBCT using deep learning has been considered to reduce artifacts, improve soft-tissue contrast, and provide accurate HU values. When it comes to synthetic image generation, CycleGAN is being developed for CBCT-to-CT predictions. Liu et al. (2020) looked at a cohort of 30 pancreatic patients that underwent SBRT and trained a modified CylceGAN architecture to perform

CBCT-to-CT transformation and evaluated registration performance for adaptive radiation therapy application.[69] The average MAE in HU between synthetic CT and CT for the patient cohort was 57 HU, compared to 81 between CBCT and CT. After performing a deformable image registration between datasets, they showed improved registration accuracy with synthetic CT compared to CBCT. Registration errors are greater near air and soft-tissue interface due to image artifacts in CBCT images.

6.2.3.4 Pelvis

Non-rigid inter-modality image registration, such as CT to MRI of prostate patients, is an active research topic in medical image analysis and radiation therapy. Accurate registration of pelvic CT and MRI is necessary to effectively fuse the information from these two modalities, which are usually acquired at different time points (diagnosis, pre-, during-, or post-treatment). Additionally, since CT and MRI are not usually scanned simultaneously, in practice there are deformations due to bladder filling or emptying and irregular rectal movement which cause large local deformations of the main pelvic organs, as illustrated in Figure 6.3. Due to these challenges, conventional image registration methods underperform, and the mainstay of clinical practice is to use manual registration. Therefore, many investigators are considering DL approaches to address this challenge.

For multi-modality imaging, a common workflow for generating synthetic images includes pre-aligning CT and MRI datasets, in which each part of CT and MRI is carefully paired. With paired data, intra-modality models can be trained directly, and metrics can be evaluated based on the aligned ground truth images. Cao et al.[31] reported on Dice metrics of the bladder, prostate, and rectum after performing registration and found synthetic MR images that were generated using DL had improved performance compared to CT images (improving Dice by as much as 10% in some OARs).

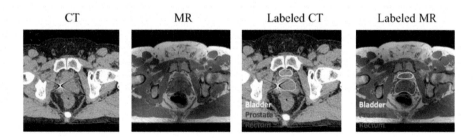

FIGURE 6.3
An example of multimodal images of pelvic CT and MR images from the same subject after affine registration. Local deformations are obvious in the bladder, prostate, and rectum.[31]
https://link.springer.com/chapter/10.1007/978-3-030-00919-9_7.

6.3 Image Segmentation

6.3.1 Traditional Segmentation Methods

Image contouring involves the process of annotating or labeling features (i.e., organs and tumors) on a pixel-wise basis of various regions in an input image. Traditionally, images were contoured manually by experts, such as radiation oncologists, dosimetrists, and/or physicists. Manual contouring suffers from being time-consuming and is susceptible to inter- and intra-user variability[17]; such variability can affect subsequent dose calculations, which ultimately has the potential for poorer patient outcomes.[30] The variability derives from multiple factors, including the image acquisition settings at the machine to the display settings at the contouring workstation. Initially, to overcome some of the issues of high variability, simple thresholding techniques were implemented.[52]

Thresholding involves defining a global threshold to partition an image $I(x)$, $x \in \Omega$ into the "background" and the "foreground" of the image based on some imaging features (i.e., signal intensities). The signal intensity threshold method assumes a difference in signal intensity between the foreground and the background. Thresholds can be either chosen based on visual inspection, automatically using methods such as Otsu's thresholding,[53] or defined based on prior physiological knowledge, such as <-950 Hounsfield units (HUs) on pulmonary CT scans representing emphysematous tissue in the lung.[54] Other historically used segmentation methods have been based on seeded region growing,[55] watershed,[56] graph-cut,[57] clustering,[58] as well as atlas deformation models[59] (as illustrated in Figure 6.4) – all of which are currently being used in the clinic to assist in contouring.

Classification algorithms, such as those employing AI, use predefined class labels and seek to apply these labels to a given sample dataset. Classification implicitly represents contouring and typically involves a training and testing phase. In the training phase of classification, different unique features and distinguishable properties are identified, while testing involves an unseen sample dataset that is recognized and assigned a predefined class label based on what the classification algorithm identified during the training phase. Some examples of classifiers include *K*-nearest neighbor,[60] maximum likelihood,[61] support vector machine,[62] and artificial neural networks.[63]

6.3.2 Evaluating Segmentation Performance

Evaluating the performance of a segmentation algorithm is not only a quantitative way for us as humans to interpret how well a model is performing but is the backbone for many loss functions used in current deep-learning models. These objective measures provide neural networks with the "goodness" of the segmentation and help in the learning process. Typically, the

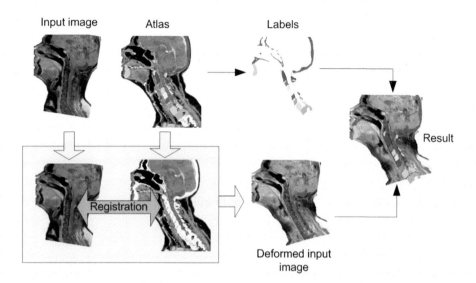

FIGURE 6.4
A demonstration of atlas deformable-based segmentation.[10] A labeled image (the atlas) is co-registered to the input image. The contours from the atlas image are then overlaid with the deformed input image. (Reproduced from https://doi.org/10.5166/jroi-4-1-19.)

segmentation accuracy is performed by comparing the produced contours from the algorithm to a ground truth, which is usually performed manually by an expert (i.e., Radiologist or Radiation Oncologist).

One of the most common methods for evaluating segmentation accuracy is the Dice similarity coefficient (DSC).[64] DSC measures the overlap of the algorithms (R_A) with the reference (R_{GT}) contour:

$$\text{DSC} = \frac{2(R_A \cap R_{GT})}{R_A + R_{GT}}$$

where DSC ranges from 0 (no overlap) to 1 (perfect overlap). Other methods for evaluating accuracy are through distance-based measurements. Distance measurements evaluate the differences between two sets of contours, either in 2D or surfaces in 3D image datasets. Root mean square error (RMSE), Hausdorff distance, mean absolute distance (MAD), and maximum absolute distance (MAXD) are all metrics that can be calculated to determine the discrepancy in distances between contours.

In addition to accuracy, another important metric to evaluate is the reproducibility (precision) of the segmentation. Inter- and intra-reproducibility is necessary to determine an algorithm's clinical utility, especially for cross-sectional, longitudinal, and multi-observer studies. One metric to evaluate reproducibility is the coefficient of variation (CoV), which is defined as

$$CoV = \frac{\sigma}{\mu}$$

where σ is the standard deviation and μ is the mean of the measurement (i.e., contour volume). Other metrics, such as the intraclass correlation coefficient (ICC), have been used to evaluate repeatability.

6.3.3 AI Segmentation by Anatomical Region

AI segmentation has now been implemented across multiple imaging platforms and on many different anatomical sites.[65] Specifically, in radiation therapy treatment planning, these categories can be further separated by segmenting either OARs or targets. Here, we will look at a variety of anatomical sites commonly treated with radiation therapy and are currently applying AI algorithms to classify and segment regions of interest.

6.3.3.1 Head & Neck

One of the earliest demonstrations of CNN for segmentation applied in radiation oncology was in head and neck cancer. Ibragimov and Xing trained a neural network to segment OARs for head and neck cancer patients on CT images.[5] Specific OARs that were detected and contoured in the model included the spinal cord, mandible, parotid glands, submandibular glands, eye globes, optic nerves, optic chiasm, larynx, and pharynx. In their demonstration, CNNs outperformed or were comparable to the state-of-the-art for structures that had recognizable boundaries, such as the spinal cord and mandible, but for objects with poorly recognizable boundaries, the model was not as effective as atlas-based segmentation. As their model was only trained and tested on CT images, they suggested that incorporating other imaging modalities, such as MRI, could improve their performance.

Another study by Zhu et al. used a publicly available dataset from the MICCAI Head and Neck Auto Segmentation Challenge 2015,[41] which included 261 head and neck CT scans, to build their model, AnatomyNet.[66] The model they implemented further expands on the initial use of the U-Net model, by incorporating new feature extraction components (i.e., squeeze-and-excitation residual blocks) and loss function to assist in tackling the segmentation of small volume structures. Furthermore, they trained their model with masked and weighted loss functions to account for and assist with the missing data problem. AnatomyNet demonstrated better performance compared to the state-of-the-art results from the MICCAI 2015 competition and produced results in a fraction of a second.

In addition to OAR segmentation, other groups have developed deep-learning models to auto-segment target volumes for head and neck cancers. Cardenas et al. investigated the use of deep auto-encoders to identify physician contouring patterns at our institution. They showed automating and standardizing the contouring of clinical target volumes (CTVs) can reduce inter-physician variability, which is one of the largest sources of uncertainty in head and neck radiation therapy.[67] The predicted volumes had a median DSC value of 0.81 and a mean surface distance of 2.8 mm compared to physician manual contours. The dosimetric effects of using auto-delineated CTVs are difficult to assess, but one can assume minimal changes owing to the high overlap between the predicted and ground-truth volumes. They found that 85% of the auto-delineated and 93% of the ground-truth volumes would be acceptable for clinical use with only minor changes.[67]

Specifically focusing on the brain, there have been multiple studies looking into auto-segmentation of targets, such as multiple brain metastasis for stereotactic radiosurgery. Dual-energy CT imaging in radiotherapy is used for its clinical relevance and accuracy in dose calculation, especially for proton therapy, and studies have investigated its use for auto-segmentation of brain tumors and OARs. Van Der Heyden et al. (2019) investigated deep-learning segmentation and assessed the clinical relevance and accuracy of automatic OAR segmentation compared to the atlas segmentation method.[68] Their 3D deep-learning approach performed better than the multi-atlas method; however, the optic nerve contours under-performed due to their relatively small volume delineated on each CT slice. Relatively small volumes on multiple axial CT slices do not necessarily form a connected 3D object and deep-learning models under-perform in these cases.[68] In addition to OAR segmentation, multiple brain lesion segmentation can be time-consuming. Deep-learning models using CNN algorithms for segmenting brain metastases on contrast-enhanced T1-weighted MRI datasets have been investigated for radiosurgery applications using the 2015 Multimodal Brain Tumor Image Segmentation (BRATS) challenge data and clinical patients' data. Liu et al. showed that DL outperforms conventional intensity-based metrics in almost all cases of brain lesions segmentation.[68] Their models were able to achieve validation results on the BRATS data yielding an average DSC of 75% in the tumor core and 80% in the enhancing tumor; however, segmentation results were lower for patient cases showing an average DSC of 65%.[68]

6.3.3.2 Thorax

In radiotherapy, success depends highly on the control of radiation exposure to OARs, such as the normal lungs, and esophagus; therefore, accurate normal tissue delineation is crucial. Non-DL segmentation techniques in the thorax utilize thresholding, generalized Hough Transform, atlas-registration-based method, or a combination of multi-atlas deformable registration. These methods result in excellent DSC of 80%–90% for airway structures (such as the trachea and lungs) and heart; however, segmentation of soft-tissue and smaller structures (such as the esophagus) was not good enough for clinical usage with DSC much below 50%.

In the 2017 AAPM Thoracic Auto-Segmentation Challenge, a dataset of 35 thoracic CT images that were delineated according to RTOG-1106 guidelines. Dong et al. developed "2.5D" patch-based GAN model and 3D GAN model and showed superior segmentation accuracy on the left lung, right lung, spinal cord, heart, and esophagus with mean DSC of 97%, 97%, 90%, 87%, and 75%, respectively.[6] They also evaluated the dosimetric impact on OARs in 20 lungs SBRT plans and showed that all of the dose metrics (D_{min}, D95, D50, D5, D_{mean}, and D_{max}) were not statistically significantly different – indicating the clinical utility of the segmentation algorithm.[6] Similar OAR segmentation results in thoracic CT images were found by Trullo et al. where multiple different CNN architectures were investigated and showed high DSC scores (>85%) for high-contrast structures (such as aorta and heart) and low DSC scores for low-contrast structures (such as esophagus).[69]

According to RTOG 0617, where radiation therapy in locally advanced non-small cell lung cancer was evaluated, the volumes in the heart receiving >5 and <30Gy were independent predictors of survival and heart dose-volume metrics are significantly associated with quality of life. Furthermore, despite QUANTEC providing whole-heart dose limits, it has been suggested that doses of sensitive cardiac substructures may lead to toxicities. Morris et al. build upon previously developed deep neural networks to create a segmentation pipeline for accurate cardiac substructure for CT and MRI pairs.[70] Looking at 32 left-sided whole-breast cancer patients, they were able to achieve DSC in approximately 90% of cardiac chambers (LA, LV, RA, RV), 70%–85% for great vessels and veins, and 50% for coronary arteries which are difficult to segment with non-DL methods having DSC <25%.[70] These results suggest that DL segmentation offers major efficiency and accuracy gains for cardiac substructure segmentation, while using only non-contrast CT and MR inputs, and has the potential to improve cardiac dose sparing during treatment planning.

For lung cancer patients, many studies have compared the segmentation accuracy of commercially available atlas-based software to DL techniques for auto-generating OARs. These studies have shown improvements in time gain for auto-segmentation; however, few studies investigate the clinical usability of these methods by comparing manual, atlas-based, and DL segmentations. Lustberg et al. performed a clinical evaluation of these different techniques on 20 patients with stage 1 NSCLC using their 4D CT scans.[71] They showed a time savings of as much as 10 minutes (50% of the total OAR contouring time) per patient when utilizing deep-learning contours. In terms of segmentation performance, there were no major differences between the auto-segmentation method for lung and mediastinum; however, significant differences were found for the esophagus, spinal cord, and heart, with deep-learning contours performing the best.[71] Evaluating time saved and contour consistency can be used to establish a protocol for auto-contouring software in clinical practice while evaluating the cost-benefit. This provides the necessary information to safely introduce contouring software into clinical practice and systematically creates a method for clinical implementation of DL methods for a treatment site and software-generated OARs.

6.3.3.3 Abdomen

An area of exciting research is focused on automated segmentation of abdominal MR to achieve similar performance as manual human contouring, particularly in complex-structure organs such as the stomach and duodenum. Previous work that utilized 2D neural networks for organ segmentation was from generic computer vision and insufficient to analyze 3D complex structures in volumetric medical images, which motivates our investigation of a multi-slice setting. Chen et al. showed that they can build on 2D Dense-UNet that is a strong model to achieve state-of-the-art performance.[72] They showed that combining multiple slices, even when a full 3D dataset is not entirely possible, can boost segmentation performance by approximately 10% for organs like the duodenum and small intestine in MR. For the pancreas, which is the most studied single, their DSC of 90% is still on par with recent state-of-the-art deep learning-based segmentation works.[72]

The main motivation of MR-Linac image-guided adaptive radiation therapy treatments is to adapt the plan to the daily patient anatomy to maximize target coverage while minimizing the toxicities to the surrounding OAR. In a clinical setting, an adaptive workflow would not be possible without help from automated segmentation due to the high resource consumption of manual segmentation. CNN-based segmentation methods have been investigated for adaptive radiation therapy to accurately segment multiple abdominal organs, such as the liver, kidneys, stomach, bowel, and duodenum, which can easily move from day-to-day treatments. Fu et al. retrospectively studied 120 patients with abdominal tumors that were treated on an MR-Linac.[73] They found that it is very challenging to automatically segment the digestive organs because of the sizes and shapes, and using traditional image segmentation methods that use hand-crafted features. Whereas CNN-based segmentation methods have shown state-of-art performance in many image processing tasks and show superior performance when segmenting OARs in the abdomen despite large variations in appearances, shapes, and sizes of stomach and bowel.

Another site where automated segmentation is a challenging task due to variations and potentially low vasculature contrast is the portal vein and liver. Conventional segmentation filter-based approaches usually fail to enhance thick vessels, such as the portal vein, and alternative enhancement does not specifically address these segmentation problems. CNNs may be well suited for this challenge as they are designed to learn consistent patterns from a training set of reference images with annotations and make predictions about previously unseen images with the hope that they learn unknown patterns which are unknown to human observers. Ibragimov et al. investigated 72 patient CT images who were treated for liver cancer and demonstrated that CNNs largely outperform alternative algorithms in the field of medical imaging segmentation.[74] Their validation of the clinical database achieved a segmentation DSC median above 80% when segmentations were restricted with ROIs over the portal vein.[74] A similar segmentation study of liver CTs used a DL algorithm to simultaneously locate and segment the initial liver surface by the liver probability map learned from 3D CNN. Lu et al. used a DL algorithm with a graph cut refinement to automatically segment the liver in CT scans.[75] The 3D CNN model detects most of the liver region and closely matches ground truth, with a mean DSC of approximately 80%, which is state-of-the-art performance.

6.3.3.4 Pelvis

Recent work aims to develop an automated segmentation method benefiting from the high soft-tissue contrast of MR images. In clinical practice, pelvic CBCT is acquired before treatment delivery and is used for treatment positions. The displacement of OARs between CBCT images and the treatment planning CT images can be measured using image registration and segmentation. The contrast of some organs, such as the prostate, is poor on CBCT images, which is further degraded by CBCT artifacts caused by scatter contamination. Lei et al. proposed a novel method to automatically segment multiple organs on pelvic CBCT for prostate cancer patients by synthesizing synthetic MRIs from CBCT images to provide superior soft-tissue contrast, and then used a deep attention network to automatically capture the significant features to differentiate the multi-organ margins in synthetic MRI.[76] They demonstrated retrospective feasibility with 100 clinical patient cases and compared their CycleGAN-based synthetic MRI generation model to deformable registration-based methods, which achieve an average DSC (range) of 0.80 (0.65–0.87) for prostate, 0.77 (0.63–0.87) for rectum, and 0.73 (0.34–0.91) for bladder. Whereas CycleGAN-based segmentation showed 6%, 14%, and 22% higher DSC for prostate, rectum, and bladder, respectively. The potential clinical impact due to such improvements in dose estimation and treatment replanning is not yet fully understood and this technique could provide real-time accurate target and organ contours for adaptive radiation therapy, which would greatly facilitate clinical workflow.

Prostate segmentation in MR images is difficult due to varying prostate boundaries across patients and varying high-dimensional shape features.[77] Multi-atlas-based and deformable-model-based methods are currently used for prostate segmentation in T2-weighted MR prostate images. But both types of these methods require careful feature engineering to identify correspondences between a new testing image and each atlas image or to discriminate features for separating the target object (e.g., the prostate) from the background. Compared with handcrafted features, deep learning has the advantage of designing effective features for a new task by trial and error, exploiting complex and abstract feature patterns, and learning features that can be optimized for a certain task, such as segmentation, thus boosting the final performance. Guo et al. showed how hierarchical feature representation from MR prostate images by deep feature learning can be integrated into a sparse patch matching framework and a deformable model is adopted to segment the prostate by combining the shape prior with the prostate likelihood map derived from sparse patch matching.[77] This method was extensively evaluated on 66 T2-weighted MR 3D prostate images that were manually contoured by a radiation oncologist. The deep-learning unsupervised proposed method outperforms the supervised method, the intensity-based deformable model, and the handcrafted-based deformable model by 10.7%, 2.1%, and 1.6%, respectively. A systematic review found similar results reviewing 28 studies and summarizing contributions, benefits, and limitations of segmentation and classification using MRI for prostate segmentation.[78] Almeida and Tavares discussed that a classic U-Net model improved DSC prostate scores by 60% for harder cases, and deep learning could achieve a mean DSC of over 90%, which was higher than conventional non-DL methods.[78]

Few investigations have focused on automatic localization and segmentation of rectal cancer using MRI diffusion-weighted imaging (DWI) or dynamic-contrast enhanced (DCE). Although MRI is gaining in popularity, and DCE-MRI tends to give a much clearer and less noisy signal compared to DWI, most auto-segmentation methods focus on FDG-PET and standardized uptake value (SUV). Deep-learning methods are being used to improve the speed and accuracy of MRI-based rectum segmentations in clinical settings.[79] Trebeschi et al. retrospectively investigated 140 patients with biopsy-proven locally advanced rectal carcinoma that had undergone multiparametric (MP) MRI, consisting of T2 weighted and DWI MRI.[79] They found a training DSC accuracy of approximately 90% for prostate segmentation, and a validation DSC accuracy of 70% between two expert readers, showing generalizability between different experts. To understand statistical analysis of the underlying relationship between the OARs' toxicity and the extracted dose-volume parameters, the key lies in the possibility of employing the dose distribution information for induced OAR toxicity prediction. A CNN model can be used to analyze rectum dose distribution and predict rectum toxicity in patient datasets by adopting a transfer learning strategy to overcome the limited patient data issue. Zhen et al. pre-trained a VGG-16 CNN on a large-scale natural image database, and then fine-tuned with the patient datasets.[80] They achieve satisfactory prediction results and demonstrated the feasibility of transferring the learned CNN knowledge from natural images to medical images, even though the substantial difference between the two applications suggests that such transfer may be impossible. Further improvement to CNN architectures has been suggested for rectal segmentation. Men et al. showed a deep-dilated CNN method outperformed the U-Net and the average DSC value can be improved by 5% for CTV, bladder, femoral head, intestine, and colon.[81] Studies have also implemented a CNN-based rectum tumor auto-segmentation on T2-weighted MR images in an 85 patient cohort, showing that the performance of this model was comparable to the interobserver difference.[82] Studies such as these show that even a simple deep-learning neural network has the potential to perform segmentation for rectum cancer comparable to a human.

6.4 Conclusion

The success of auto-segmentation and auto-registration can be measured, among others, in terms of the number and a variety of software tools available and investigators publishing novel work. In recent years, the number of commercial automated image segmentation and registration tools has been increasing across many clinics. The realization of registration and segmentation software, which some have combined into a colloquial term "Regmentation" software,[10] as a widespread clinical tool is expected to evolve and increase over the next decades. Meanwhile, automated image Regmentation remains an active topic in the research community and there are many exciting discoveries to look forward to.

Though image registration has been extensively studied in the recent past, deep learning-based medical image registration is a relatively new research area. Many novel methods could be classified into multiple categories and combine different approaches from varying fields. For example, GANs were mostly used in combination with supervised or unsupervised transformation to predict generic painting with different styles and transform horses-to-zebras and vice versa. We can expect to see new and exciting methods being transferred from outside fields into Radiation Oncology in the future. A common feature that is used in both traditional DIR and DL-based methods is multi-scale strategy across multi-modality imaging. Multi-scale registration could help the optimization avoid local maxima and allow large deformation registration.

One of the major challenges for DL-based registration methods is the lack of training datasets with known transformations. This problem could be alleviated by various data augmentation methods; however, data augmentation needs to be done in a monitored and well-understood method so as to not introduce bias or unrealistic changes. Several groups have demonstrated good generality of the trained network by applying them to datasets different from the training datasets (i.e., external datasets from other institutions). We can speculate that more research will aim to combine supervised and unsupervised methods so to improve registration performance while also expanding applications into novel areas.

In clinics today, segmentation still represents a significant burden in terms of time and human resources in Radiation Oncology. Incorporating AI into clinics could help reduce the intrinsic inter-observer variability between human experts, while also ensuring contouring quality and reducing the time required for treatment planning. The different solutions proposed in the literature as experimental approaches give promise that auto-segmentation can significantly reduce this burden. However, if we use the role of thumb that 5,000 labeled examples are required for a well-trained model, then most of the presented studies in Radiation Oncology still relatively small and require many more datasets to produce a robust and generalizable algorithm.

In conclusion, the application of AI (and DL) has great potential in Radiation Oncology when it comes to medical image registration and segmentation. However, there is still not an "off-the-shelf" solution as other machine learning techniques on tabular data. Deep-learning medical image registration and segmentation continues to be "more of an art than science" and the Radiation Oncology community needs to make bigger efforts in standardizing large datasets that are publicly available for future collaboration. This would hopefully facilitate new technologies into daily care, ultimately leading to improved outcomes for all cancer patients.

References

1. Verellen D., De Ridder M., Storme G. A (short) history of image-guided radiotherapy. *Radiother Oncol J Eur Soc Ther Radiol Oncol.* 2008; 86(1): 4–13. doi: 10.1016/j.radonc.2007.11.023.
2. Schlegel W., Bortfeld T., Grosu A., eds. *New Technologies in Radiation Oncology.* Heidelberg: Springer; 2006.
3. Mackie T.R., Kapatoes J., Ruchala K., et al. Image guidance for precise conformal radiotherapy. *Int J Radiat Oncol.* 2003; 56(1): 89–105. doi: 10.1016/S0360-3016(03)00090-7.
4. Zhao W., Lyu T., Chen Y., Xing L. Dual-energy Computed Tomography Imaging from Contrast-enhanced Single-energy Computed Tomography. *ArXiv201013253 Phys.* Published online October 25, 2020. Accessed May 12, 2022. http: //arxiv.org/abs/2010.13253.
5. Ibragimov B., Xing L. Segmentation of organs-at-risks in head and neck CT images using convolutional neural networks. *Med Phys.* 2017; 44(2): 547–557. doi: 10.1002/mp.12045.
6. Dong X., Lei Y., Wang T., et al. Automatic multiorgan segmentation in thorax CT images using U-net-GAN. *Med Phys.* 2019; 46(5): 2157–2168. doi: 10.1002/mp.13458.
7. Zhao W., Shen L., Han B., et al. Markerless pancreatic tumor target localization enabled by deep learning. *Int J Radiat Oncol Biol Phys.* 2019; 105(2): 432–439. doi: 10.1016/j.ijrobp.2019.05.071.

8. Litjens G., Kooi T., Bejnordi B.E., et al. A survey on deep learning in medical image analysis. *Med Image Anal.* 2017; 42: 60–88. doi: 10.1016/j.media.2017.07.005.

9. Hill D.L.G., Batchelor P.G., Holden M., Hawkes D.J. Medical image registration. *Phys Med Biol.* 2001; 46(3): R1–R45. doi: 10.1088/0031-9155/46/3/201.

10. Erdt M., Steger S., Sakas G. Regmentation: A new view of image segmentation and registration. *J Radiat Oncol Inform.* 2012; 4(1): 1–23. doi: 10.5166/jroi-4-1-19.

11. Mackie T.R., Holmes T., Swerdloff S., et al. Tomotherapy: A new concept for the delivery of dynamic conformal radiotherapy. *Med Phys.* 1993; 20(6): 1709–1719. doi: 10.1118/1.596958.

12. Carol M., Grant W.H., Pavord D., et al. Initial clinical experience with the Peacock intensity modulation of a 3-D conformal radiation therapy system. *Stereotact Funct Neurosurg.* 1996; 66(1–3): 30–34. doi: 10.1159/000099664.

13. Otto K. Volumetric modulated arc therapy: IMRT in a single gantry arc. *Med Phys.* 2008; 35(1): 310–317. doi: 10.1118/1.2818738.

14. Zhang P., Happersett L., Hunt M., Jackson A., Zelefsky M., Mageras G. Volumetric modulated arc therapy: Planning and evaluation for prostate cancer cases. *Int J Radiat Oncol.* 2010; 76(5): 1456–1462. doi: 10.1016/j.ijrobp.2009.03.033.

15. Morgan H.E., Sher D.J. Adaptive radiotherapy for head and neck cancer. *Cancers Head Neck.* 2020; 5(1): 1. doi: 10.1186/s41199-019-0046-z.

16. Brock K.K. Adaptive radiotherapy: Moving into the future. *Semin Radiat Oncol.* 2019; 29(3): 181–184. doi: 10.1016/j.semradonc.2019.02.011.

17. Sharp G., Fritscher K.D., Pekar V., et al. Vision 20/20: Perspectives on automated image segmentation for radiotherapy. *Med Phys.* 2014; 41(5): 050902. doi: 10.1118/1.4871620.

18. Liang X., Morgan H., Nguyen D., Jiang S. Deep learning based CT-to-CBCT deformable image registration for auto segmentation in head and neck adaptive radiation therapy. Published online January 31, 2021. doi: 10.48550/arXiv.2102.00590.

19. Taylor R.H., Stoianovici D. Medical robotic systems in computer-integrated surgery. *Probl Gen Surg.* 2003; 20(2): 1–9. doi: 10.1097/01.sgs.0000081179.89384.ba.

20. Sarrut D., Boldea V., Miguet S., Ginestet C. Simulation of four-dimensional CT images from deformable registration between inhale and exhale breath-hold CT scans. *Med Phys.* 2006; 33(3): 605–617. doi: 10.1118/1.2161409.

21. Yang H., Ye J. A calibration process for tracking upper limb motion with inertial sensors. In: *2011 IEEE International Conference on Mechatronics and Automation*; 2011: 618–623. doi: 10.1109/ICMA.2011.5985732.

22. De Silva T., Fenster A., Cool D.W., et al. 2D-3D rigid registration to compensate for prostate motion during 3D TRUS-guided biopsy. *Med Phys.* 2013; 40(2): 022904. doi: 10.1118/1.4773873.

23. Velec M., Moseley J.L., Eccles C.L., et al. Effect of breathing motion on radiotherapy dose accumulation in the abdomen using deformable registration. *Int J Radiat Oncol.* 2011; 80(1): 265–272. doi: 10.1016/j.ijrobp.2010.05.023.

24. Andersen E.S., Noe K.Ø., Sørensen T.S., et al. Simple DVH parameter addition as compared to deformable registration for bladder dose accumulation in cervix cancer brachytherapy. *Radiother Oncol.* 2013; 107(1): 52–57. doi: 10.1016/j.radonc.2013.01.013.

25. Chetty I.J., Rosu-Bubulac M. Deformable registration for dose accumulation. *Semin Radiat Oncol.* 2019; 29(3): 198–208. doi: 10.1016/j.semradonc.2019.02.002.

26. Yan D., Vicini F., Wong J., Martinez A. Adaptive radiation therapy. *Phys Med Biol.* 1997; 42(1): 123–132. doi: 10.1088/0031-9155/42/1/008.

27. Li X.A. *Adaptive Radiation Therapy*. Boca Raton, FL: CRC Press; 2011.

28. Acharya S., Fischer-Valuck B.W., Kashani R., et al. Online magnetic resonance image guided adaptive radiation therapy: First clinical applications. *Int J Radiat Oncol.* 2016; 94(2): 394–403. doi: 10.1016/j.ijrobp.2015.10.015.

29. Fu Y., Zhang H., Morris E.D., et al. Artificial intelligence in radiation therapy. *IEEE Trans Radiat Plasma Med Sci.* 2022; 6(2): 158–181. doi: 10.1109/TRPMS.2021.3107454.

30. Huynh E., Hosny A., Guthier C., et al. Artificial intelligence in radiation oncology. *Nat Rev Clin Oncol.* 2020; 17(12): 771–781. doi: 10.1038/s41571-020-0417-8.

31. Cao X., Yang J., Wang L., Xue Z., Wang Q., Shen D. Deep learning based intermodality image registration supervised by intra-modality similarity. In: Shi Y., Suk H.I., Liu M., eds. *Machine Learning in Medical Imaging*. Lecture Notes in Computer Science. Springer International Publishing; 2018: 55–63. doi: 10.1007/978-3-030-00919-9_7.

32. Ronneberger O., Fischer P., Brox T. U-Net: Convolutional Networks for Biomedical Image Segmentation. *ArXiv150504597 Cs.* Published online May 18, 2015. Accessed May 12, 2022. http: //arxiv.org/abs/1505.04597.

33. Sudre C.H., Li W., Vercauteren T., Ourselin S., Jorge Cardoso M. Generalised dice overlap as a deep learning loss function for highly unbalanced segmentations. In: Cardoso M.J., Arbel T., Carneiro G., et al., eds. *Deep Learning in Medical Image Analysis and Multimodal Learning for Clinical Decision Support*. Lecture Notes in Computer Science. Springer International Publishing; 2017: 240–248. doi: 10.1007/978-3-319-67558-9_28.

34. Zhang Z. Improved adam optimizer for deep neural networks. In: *2018 IEEE/ACM 26th International Symposium on Quality of Service (IWQoS)*; 2018: 1–2 doi: 10.1109/IWQoS.2018.8624183.

35. Jadon S. A survey of loss functions for semantic segmentation. In: *2020 IEEE Conference on Computational Intelligence in Bioinformatics and Computational Biology (CIBCB)*; 2020: 1–7 doi: 10.1109/CIBCB48159.2020.9277638.

36. Klein S., Staring M., Murphy K., Viergever M.A., Pluim J.P.W. elastix: A toolbox for intensity-based medical image registration. *IEEE Trans Med Imaging.* 2010; 29(1): 196–205. doi: 10.1109/TMI.2009.2035616.

37. Fu Y., Lei Y., Wang T., Curran W.J., Liu T., Yang X. Deep learning in medical image registration: A review. *Phys Med Ampmathsemicolon Biol.* 2020; 65(20): 20TR01. doi: 10.1088/1361-6560/ab843e.

38. Oliveira F.P.M., Tavares J.M.R.S. Medical image registration: A review. *Comput Methods Biomech Biomed Eng.* 2014; 17(2): 73–93. doi: 10.1080/10255842.2012.670855.

39. de Vos B.D., Berendsen F.F., Viergever M.A., Sokooti H., Staring M., Išgum I. A deep learning framework for unsupervised affine and deformable image registration. *Med Image Anal.* 2019; 52: 128–143. doi: 10.1016/j.media.2018.11.010.

40. Xiao H., Teng X., Liu C., et al. A review of deep learning-based three-dimensional medical image registration methods. *Quant Imaging Med Surg.* 2021; 11(12): 4895–4916. doi: 10.21037/qims-21-175.

41. Al-Mayah A., Moseley J., Hunter S., et al. Biomechanical-based image registration for head and neck radiation treatment. *Phys Med Biol.* 2010; 55(21): 6491–6500. doi: 10.1088/0031-9155/55/21/010.

42. McKenzie E.M., Santhanam A., Ruan D., O'Connor D., Cao M., Sheng K. Multimodality image registration in the head-and-neck using a deep learning-derived synthetic CT as a bridge. *Med Phys.* 2020; 47(3): 1094–1104. doi: 10.1002/mp.13976.

43. Fu Y., Lei Y., Zhou J., et al. Synthetic CT-aided MRI-CT image registration for head and neck radiotherapy. In: *Medical Imaging 2020: Biomedical Applications in Molecular, Structural, and Functional Imaging.* Vol. 11317. SPIE; 2020: 572–578. doi: 10.1117/12.2549092.

44. Teng X., Chen Y., Zhang Y., Ren L. Respiratory deformation registration in 4D-CT/cone beam CT using deep learning. *Quant Imaging Med Surg.* 2021; 11(2): 737–748. doi: 10.21037/qims-19-1058.

45. Sokooti H., de Vos B., Berendsen F., Lelieveldt B.P.F., Išgum I., Staring M. Nonrigid image registration using multi-scale 3D convolutional neural networks. In: Descoteaux M., Maier-Hein L., Franz A., Jannin P., Collins D.L., Duchesne S., eds. *Medical Image Computing and Computer Assisted Intervention – MICCAI 2017.* Lecture Notes in Computer Science. Springer International Publishing; 2017: 232–239. doi: 10.1007/978-3-319-66182-7_27.

46. Eppenhof K.A.J., Pluim J.P.W. Pulmonary CT registration through supervised learning with convolutional neural networks. *IEEE Trans Med Imaging.* 2019; 38(5): 1097–1105. doi: 10.1109/TMI.2018.2878316.

47. Hering A., van Ginneken B., Heldmann S. mlVIRNET: Multilevel variational image registration network. In: Shen D., Liu T., Peters T.M., et al., eds. *Medical Image Computing and Computer Assisted Intervention – MICCAI 2019.* Lecture Notes in Computer Science. Springer International Publishing; 2019: 257–265. doi: 10.1007/978-3-030-32226-7_29.

48. Fu Y., Lei Y., Wang T., et al. LungRegNet: An unsupervised deformable image registration method for 4D-CT lung. *Med Phys.* 2020; 47(4): 1763–1774. doi: 10.1002/mp.14065.

49. Jiang Z., Yin F.F., Ge Y., Ren L. A multi-scale framework with unsupervised joint training of convolutional neural networks for pulmonary deformable image registration. *Phys Med Biol.* 2020; 65(1): 015011. doi: 10.1088/1361-6560/ab5da0.

50. Lei Y., Fu Y., Wang T., et al. 4D-CT deformable image registration using multiscale unsupervised deep learning. *Phys Med Biol.* 2020; 65(8): 085003. doi: 10.1088/1361-6560/ab79c4.

51. Duan L., Ni X., Liu Q., et al. Unsupervised learning for deformable registration of thoracic CT and cone-beam CT based on multiscale features matching with spatially adaptive weighting. *Med Phys.* 2020; 47(11): 5632–5647. doi: 10.1002/mp.14464.

52. Sahoo P.K., Soltani S., Wong A.K.C. A survey of thresholding techniques. *Comput Vis Graph Image Process.* 1988; 41(2): 233–260. doi: 10.1016/0734-189X(88)90022-9.

53. Otsu N. A threshold selection method from gray-level histograms. *IEEE Trans Syst Man Cybern.* 1979; 9(1): 62–66. doi: 10.1109/TSMC.1979.4310076.

54. Madani A., Keyzer C., Gevenois P.A. Quantitative computed tomography assessment of lung structure and function in pulmonary emphysema. *Eur Respir J.* 2001; 18(4): 720–730.

55. Zucker S.W. Region growing: Childhood and adolescence. *Comput Graph Image Process.* 1976; 5(3): 382–399. doi: 10.1016/S0146-664X(76)80014-7.

56. Beucher S., Lantuéjoul C. Use of Watersheds in Contour Detection, Vol. 132; 1979.

57. Boykov Y.Y., Jolly M.P. Interactive graph cuts for optimal boundary & region segmentation of objects in N-D images. In: *Proceedings Eighth IEEE International Conference on Computer Vision, ICCV 2001*. Vol. 1.; 2001: 105–112. doi: 10.1109/ICCV.2001.937505.

58. Äyrämö S., Kärkkäinen T. *Introduction to Partitioning-Based Clustering Methods with a Robust Example*; 2006. doi: 10.13140/RG.2.2.32908.33927.

59. McInerney T., Terzopoulos D. Deformable models in medical image analysis: A survey. *Med Image Anal*. 1996; 1(2): 91–108. doi: 10.1016/S1361-8415(96)80007-7.

60. Geodesic Active Contours | SpringerLink. Accessed May 24, 2022. https: //link. springer.com/article/10.1023/A: 1007979827043.

61. Dempster A.P., Laird N.M., Rubin D.B. Maximum likelihood from incomplete data via the EM algorithm. *J R Stat Soc Ser B Methodol*. 1977; 39(1): 1–38.

62. Hsu C.W., Lin C.J. A comparison of methods for multiclass support vector machines. *IEEE Trans Neural Netw*. 2002; 13(2): 415–425. doi: 10.1109/72.991427.

63. Rosenblatt F. The perceptron: A probabilistic model for information storage and organization in the brain. *Psychol Rev*. 1958; 65(6): 386–408. doi: 10.1037/h0042519.

64. Dice L.R. Measures of the amount of ecologic association between species. *Ecology*. 1945; 26(3): 297–302. doi: 10.2307/1932409.

65. Sahiner B., Pezeshk A., Hadjiiski L.M., et al. Deep learning in medical imaging and radiation therapy. *Med Phys*. 2019; 46(1): e1–e36. doi: 10.1002/mp.13264.

66. Zhu W., Huang Y., Zeng L., et al. AnatomyNet: Deep learning for fast and fully automated whole-volume segmentation of head and neck anatomy. *Med Phys*. 2019; 46(2): 576–589. doi: 10.1002/mp.13300.

67. Cardenas C.E., McCarroll R.E., Court L.E., et al. Deep Learning algorithm for auto-delineation of high-risk oropharyngeal clinical target volumes with built-in dice similarity coefficient parameter optimization function. *Int J Radiat Oncol Biol Phys*. 2018; 101(2): 468–478. doi: 10.1016/j.ijrobp.2018.01.114.

68. Liu Y., Stojadinovic S., Hrycushko B., et al. A deep convolutional neural network-based automatic delineation strategy for multiple brain metastases stereotactic radiosurgery. *PloS One*. 2017; 12(10): e0185844. doi: 10.1371/journal.pone.0185844.

69. Trullo R., Petitjean C., Ruan S., Dubray B., Nie D., Shen D. Segmentation of organs at risk in thoracic CT images using a SharpMask architecture and conditional random fields. In: *2017 IEEE 14th International Symposium on Biomedical Imaging (ISBI 2017)*; 2017: 1003–1006. doi: 10.1109/ISBI.2017.7950685.

70. Morris E.D., Ghanem A.I., Dong M., Pantelic M.V., Walker E.M., Glide-Hurst C.K. Cardiac substructure segmentation with deep learning for improved cardiac sparing. *Med Phys*. 2020; 47(2): 576–586. doi: 10.1002/mp.13940.

71. Lustberg T., van Soest J., Gooding M., et al. Clinical evaluation of atlas and deep learning based automatic contouring for lung cancer. *Radiother Oncol J Eur Soc Ther Radiol Oncol*. 2018; 126(2): 312–317. doi: 10.1016/j.radonc.2017.11.012.

72. Chen Y., Ruan D., Xiao J., et al. Fully automated multi-organ segmentation in abdominal magnetic resonance imaging with deep neural networks. *Med Phys*. 2020; 47(10): 4971–4982. doi: 10.1002/mp.14429.

73. Fu Y., Mazur T.R., Wu X., et al. A novel MRI segmentation method using CNN-based correction network for MRI-guided adaptive radiotherapy. *Med Phys*. 2018; 45(11): 5129–5137. doi: https: //doi.org/10.1002/mp.13221.

74. Ibragimov B., Toesca D., Chang D., Koong A., Xing L. Combining deep learning with anatomical analysis for segmentation of the portal vein for liver SBRT planning. *Phys Med Biol*. 2017; 62(23): 8943–8958. doi: 10.1088/1361-6560/aa9262.

75. Lu F., Wu F., Hu P., Peng Z., Kong D. Automatic 3D liver location and segmentation via convolutional neural network and graph cut. *Int J Comput Assist Radiol Surg.* 2017; 12(2): 171–182. doi: 10.1007/s11548-016-1467-3.
76. Lei Y., Wang T., Tian S., et al. Male pelvic multi-organ segmentation aided by CBCT-based synthetic MRI. *Phys Med Biol.* 2020; 65(3): 035013. doi: 10.1088/1361-6560/ab63bb.
77. Guo Y., Gao Y., Shen D. Deformable MR prostate segmentation via deep feature learning and sparse patch matching. *IEEE Trans Med Imaging.* 2016; 35(4): 1077–1089. doi: 10.1109/TMI.2015.2508280.
78. Almeida G., Tavares J.M.R.S. Deep learning in radiation oncology treatment planning for prostate cancer: A systematic review. *J Med Syst.* 2020; 44(10): 179. doi: 10.1007/s10916-020-01641-3.
79. Trebeschi S., van Griethuysen J.J.M., Lambregts D.M.J., et al. Deep learning for fully-automated localization and segmentation of rectal cancer on multiparametric MR. *Sci Rep.* 2017; 7: 5301. doi: 10.1038/s41598-017-05728-9.
80. Zhen X., Chen J., Zhong Z., et al. Deep convolutional neural network with transfer learning for rectum toxicity prediction in cervical cancer radiotherapy: A feasibility study. *Phys Med Biol.* 2017; 62(21): 8246–8263. doi: 10.1088/1361-6560/aa8d09.
81. Men K., Dai J., Li Y. Automatic segmentation of the clinical target volume and organs at risk in the planning CT for rectal cancer using deep dilated convolutional neural networks. *Med Phys.* 2017; 44(12): 6377–6389. doi: 10.1002/mp.12602.
82. Wang J., Lu J., Qin G., et al. Technical note: A deep learning-based autosegmentation of rectal tumors in MR images. *Med Phys.* 2018; 45(6): 2560–2564. doi: 10.1002/mp.12918.

7

Motion Management and Image-Guided Radiation Therapy

Dante P.I. Capaldi
University of California

Paul J. Keall
The University of Sydney

Tomi F. Nano
University of California

CONTENTS

7.1 Introduction and Background

Radiation therapy provides therapeutic benefits to cancer patients by delivering an adequate amount of radiation dose to tumors while minimizing the dose to normal tissues. Increasing dose to tumors will improve the probability of tumor control and more importantly directly relates to our primary clinical goal of long-term recurrence-free survival or the absence of symptomatic disease. However, the probability of normal tissue complication also increases with dose and may limit clinical therapeutic goals if the dose is not precisely localized to the tumor target. Therefore, external beam radiation therapy machines using linear accelerators or radioactive isotope exposures are specially designed to accurately position the patient for achieving a higher therapeutic index. For static targets, such as treatments of brain lesions with radiosurgery, accurate patient positioning is often successfully achieved with rigid frames, imaging, external markers, and surface immobilization techniques such as thermoplastic masks.[1] Alternatively, for moving targets, achieving a similar therapeutic index as static targets is more challenging and requires specialized methods to account for tumor motion. To address this issue, a number of previous landmark studies have focused on the development and validation of various motion management and image guidance strategies to provide accurate and robust beam targeting while compensating for tumor motion.

Since the advent of radiotherapy, image guidance has been at the forefront where in some of the earliest systems had primitive imaging technologies,[2] such as double exposure images obtained with an x-ray and treatment beam.[3] Over the past two decades, these methods have now advanced to three-dimensional approaches, such as cone-beam computed tomography (CBCT),[4] computed tomography (CT),[5] and magnetic resonance imaging (MRI),[6] to really facilitate dose escalation and target localization during treatment. In addition to imaging, other technologies have been developed and adopted into the clinical workflow to assist in treating moving targets.[7] Motion compensation methods have been proposed as early as the 1980s to improve the therapeutic effectiveness in situations where there is intra-fractional motion due to respiration.[8] Beam gating, where the radiation beam is triggered off and on synchronously with respiratory motion, was initially proposed and further developed by Kubo et al..[9] Around the same time, an alternative solution was proposed where patients were coached to hold their breath using active breathing control, proposed by Wong et al.[10] These two concepts of coaching and monitoring patients' breathing have now been further expanded and adopted into the vast majority of motion management solutions that monitor motion using internal and external surrogates.[11]

Motion management and image guidance methods for accurate dose delivery in radiation therapy are now being advanced within the emerging field of artificial intelligence (AI) to forge novel techniques in guiding patient setup and monitoring target position during radiation dose delivery. Figure 7.1 shows how AI methods are applied to transform model inputs (motion management and imaging) to model outputs (during-treatment imaging, adaptive and real-time tracking) in radiation therapy.[12–16] The goal of this chapter is to explore and discuss (1) current clinical use of motion management and image guidance; (2) research development using AI and machine learning (ML); and (3) future direction of AI that will translate research to clinical impact.

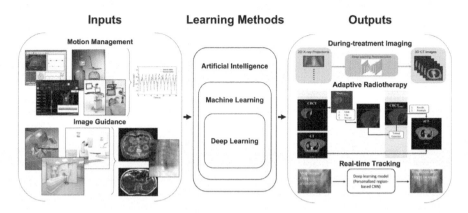

FIGURE 7.1
AI applied in motion management and image-guided radiotherapy. Information pertaining to tumor location during treatment, using imaging or motion monitoring systems, would be used as input to a model, using machine or deep learning, to predict relevant information to assist in monitoring target location and guiding radiotherapy treatments. Images were adapted from previous publications.[12–16]

7.1.1 Motion Management and Image Guidance in Radiotherapy

During the course of radiation therapy for a patient with substantial anatomical changes, position varies due to inaccurate positioning and organ motion, which consequently may result in different dose delivery than initially planned.[17,18] In radiation therapy, positional changes are classified as inter- or intra-fraction motion.[11] Inter-fraction motion refers to patient positioning differences (motion between setup positions) between each radiation therapy fraction. Intrafraction motion refers to patient positioning differences during a single fraction of radiation therapy (motion between the start and end of fraction). For deep-seated tumors where surface visual inspection is not possible, patient setup is typically performed using various imaging modalities, such as kV x-ray planar images, CBCT, and other image-guided radiation therapy (IGRT) methods. Planar kV x-ray images, radiography or fluoroscopy, are acquired with a flat panel x-ray detector and x-ray tube mounted on the treatment machine.[19] It is common to acquire CBCT images with the same x-ray imaging system used for planar kV imaging for patient setup in the treatment position.[4] As radiation dose distributions have become more conformal around tumor targets, the field of IGRT has evolved to the use of imaging from planning to positioning and dose verification.[20]

Furthermore, intra-fractional motion due to respiration affects the accuracy of targeting tumors in the thorax and near the abdomen. Previous clinical studies that have helped to form scientific task groups[21] have demonstrated and provided evidence of the need for motion management strategies when delivering radiation therapy to targets that move while breathing. Respiratory motion can be managed using free-breathing, breath-hold, or immobilization (such as with compression belts or boards). Specifically, for free-breathing techniques, radiation treatments can be gated to deliver dose only during specific breathing phases while patients perform free-breathing, as is typical with breast cancer treatments.[22,23] Breathing can also be controlled to perform a breath-hold maneuver, such as for deep inspiration breath-hold (DIBH) deliveries, which can generate reproducible motion achieved by coaching the patient as well as providing audio-visual feedback.[24–27] Lastly, abdominal compression devices can be used on patients in the treatment position if it is tolerable and does not cause discomfort.[28,29]

7.1.2 Clinically Available Solutions

There are many clinically available motion management and IGRT solutions for radiation therapy and they can be grouped based on non-transmission imaging (non-radiographic) or imaging-based systems. Non-radiographic methods that do not use radiation for motion monitoring have been previously developed; examples include infrared, optical, radio-frequency, and ultrasonic tracking.[30] Commercially available solutions include optical surface monitoring systems (OSMS) such as with AlignRT,[31] infrared surface marker monitoring such as Varian's RPM,[32] radiofrequency (RF) beacon-based tracking such as Calypso,[33] and spirometry-based methods such as ABC or Dyn'R SDX.[10,34] Imaging-based systems can be integrated into the therapy treatment machines (such as with CyberKnife[35] or MR-linacs[36–39]) or they can be used as an auxiliary system.

7.1.3 The Role of AI

As mentioned previously, AI is now touching almost all facets in medicine, including radiology and radiation oncology.[40,41] From diagnosis to treatment planning and predicting outcomes, AI is being employed as a way to automate the clinical workflow for each patient in an effort to improve efficiency as well as safety. Currently, specific applications of AI include tumor detection[42–44] and characterization and interpretation,[45,46] treatment decision-making,[47] image acquisition and reconstruction,[48,49] image analysis,[50] image guidance,[51–53] and toxicity prediction.[54–59] Although companies are starting to receive Food and Drug Administration (FDA) clearance on AI/ML-enabled medical devices (https://www.fda.gov/medical-devices/software-medical-device-samd/artificial-intelligence-and-machine-learning-aiml-enabled-medical-devices), such as Mirada Medical Ltd and Vysioneer Inc, there are no systems currently using AI for image guidance or motion management in radiation oncology.

7.2 Current AI & ML Methods

Motion management and IGRT is a growing area of interest for state-of-the-art AI and ML application development. Current AI and ML applications in this field have produced fascinating improvements in various treatment stages of radiation therapy clinical workflow, such as in (1) inter- and intra-fractional imaging, (2) adaptive radiation therapy, and (3) real-time tracking. Imaging in between treatment fractions (inter) or during the course of a given fraction (intra) has been used in AI models for generating synthetic images, 3D reconstruction methods, and enhancement of numerous tracking capabilities to improve accurate dose delivery to moving targets. Radiation treatment delivery modification methods following patient simulation, known as adaptive radiation therapy, have been further developed using AI methods for automatic image segmentation, detection of anatomical changes over the course of treatment, and creating more efficient dose computation algorithms. Real-time tumor tracking methods have been developed using AI to model breathing patterns using surrogate markers or imaging and to predict tumor motion.

7.2.1 Inter- and Intra-fractional Imaging

Imaging plays an important role in ensuring safe and effective radiation therapy. Daily patient setup accuracy, which contributes to inter-fraction motion, has been improved with technological advancements in imaging and AI applications can further improve motion management. For example, AI models can use information from kV, MV, or CBCT images and provide synthetic images that improve motion management. Additionally, intra-fractional motion of organs-at-risk (OARs) or targets in proximity to the lungs or abdomen can be better managed using AI in new treatment technologies such as MR-linac and proton therapy. As illustrated by the examples shown in Figure 7.2, AI models can facilitate improved IGRT capabilities.

Visualizing the entire target and OARs during treatment will enable the treatment team to ensure the treatment is on target, and with more advanced applications, optimally adjust the treatment beam to deliver the planned dose to the target. An AI approach to this problem from Shen et al. used a deep learning network including a representation network, transformation module, and generational network to reconstruct 3D volumes from single x-ray projections, as shown in Figure 7.2.[51] They applied this approach using CT data from upper-abdomen, lung, and head-and-neck CT patients and compared the predicted volumetric CT images, created using between one and ten projections, with the actual CT images, showing encouraging results. The finding that a 2D volume can be reconstructed from as few as one 2D projection has implications for radiation therapy image guidance systems: they postulate that simpler imaging systems could be designed than those commonly used today for image-guided procedures.

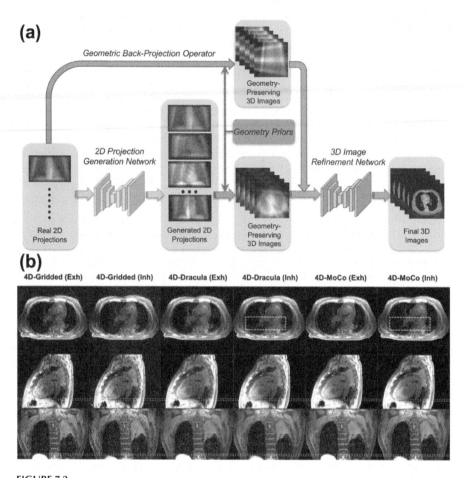

FIGURE 7.2

Images at the beginning and during the treatment session to facilitate image-guided radiotherapy can be improved with AI. Specific imaging examples that have been shown to be improved using AI are (a) using planar 2D x-ray images to generate CT volumetric images,[51] (b) improving 4MR images,[52] or (c) improving PPI quality.[53]

Currently, the vast majority of x-ray mounted imaging systems employ CBCT to acquire volumetric images of the patient to assist in image guidance. Though CBCT is helpful for patient setup, image quality is limited, as compared to planning CT and MRI. As such, Lei et al. used daily CBCT to generate synthetic MR images for providing enhanced soft-tissue contrast that may lead to more accurate OAR and target delineation between treatment fractions for prostate and head-and-neck patients.[60] They used a cycle-consistent adversarial network (CycleGAN) to map daily CBCT, acquired using the on-board imaging of a treatment machine, that was paired to a T1-weighted MRI that was acquired during treatment planning. They compared synthetic MR

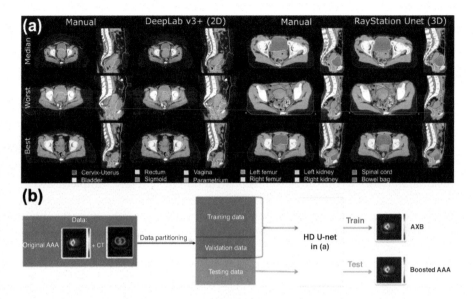

FIGURE 7.3

AI applied to adaptive radiotherapy. A common place where image guidance is used with radiotherapy treatment planning is in adaptive radiotherapy. Machine and deep learning models can be leveraged to reduce treatment times in adaptive radiotherapy, such as (a) automating treatment contouring[71] or (b) speeding-up dose calculations.[72]

images with real MR images and found low mean absolute error, high peak signal-to-noise ratio, and high normalized cross-correlation. Li et al. developed a model for generating synthetic planning CTs from daily CBCT for accurate dose calculation between fractions for nasopharyngeal carcinoma patients.[61] An encoder-decoder 2D neural network model was trained on 70 patients with paired CT/CBCT and the synthetic CT was used for planning to extract dosimetric data, such as PTV coverage. They found that synthetic CT images had more realistic HU values, reduced CBCT-image artifacts, and the average dosimetric differences were less than 1%. The impact of this study is that it can enable efficient and accurate adaptive radiation therapy by providing planning CT quality images from CBCT.

Specifically for proton radiotherapy, Charyyev et al. developed a generative adversarial network (GAN) that improved the image quality of proton portal images (PPIs), which can be used to validate tumor location in the beam's-eye-view for proton treatments albeit inherently have poor contrast and spatial resolution.[53] The model was trained using paired kV digitally reconstructed radiographs (DRRs) and PPIs (Figure 7.3), where the DRRs were used as the learning-based target for the PPIs, and showed improved spatial resolution as well as captured fine details that were missed in the PPIs. This work demonstrates how deep learning models can improve IGRT in proton therapy as well as help facilitate target localization for future "shoot-through" FLASH radiotherapy.

Moving away from x-ray-based imaging and focusing on MR-linacs, the time needed to acquire high-quality MR images as well as high field strengths to improve signal-to-noise is limited. Consequently, Chun et al. developed a deep learning model for converting low-resolution MR images that are conventionally acquired with current MR-linacs into high-resolution MRI images that can be used for target and OAR delineation.[62] The DL model includes a de-noising encoder, a down-sampling network, and an up-sampling network to increase image resolution. Similarly, Wu et al. implemented a deep residual network to optimize the reconstruction of sparsely sampled MRI to help reduce acquisition time,[63] which is needed for MR-linacs. The incorporation of *a priori* information into the deep learning model helped facilitate high acceleration factors while maintaining high image quality. These works showed how to keep MR-linac imaging times low while increasing the image quality for improved patient setup.

7.2.2 Adaptive Radiotherapy

The ability to image on the treatment machine before, during, and after treatment delivery has opened our eyes to the anatomical motion in regions of the body, such as the prostate and pancreas,[64–66] which we were not able to see without image guidance. That being said, over the recent years, adaptation of radiation treatment plans based on the inter-fractional imaging has become a reality by leveraging on-board imaging systems, such as CBCT, kV CT, and MRI systems.[2,67] One of the major challenges still facing adaptive radiotherapy is the labor-intensive workflow needed to convert the prior treatment plan using the images acquired the day of treatment, specifically re-contouring structures, re-optimizing, and performing dose calculations.[68–70] With the recent advances in AI and ML, this time-consuming workflow can be significantly simplified.

Automated segmentation of OARs and targets using AI and ML have been investigated as a way to reduce treatment replanning time and expedite the adaptive radiotherapy process. As shown in Figure 7.3, Rigaud et al. used deep learning to perform segmentation of multiple structures (cervix-uterus, vagina, parametrium, bladder, rectum, sigmoid, femoral heads, kidneys, spinal cord, and bowel bag) for adaptive radiotherapy online dose optimization in cervical cancer patients.[71] Elmahdy et al. investigated the use of transfer learning to fine-tune a baseline CNN model to a specific patient CT imaging acquired in an earlier treatment fraction to segment the prostate, seminal vesicles, bladder, and rectum for adaptive radiotherapy in prostate cancer patients.[73] Fu et al. developed a novel segmentation model using CNN-based correction network specifically to expedite the contouring process needed for MR-guided adaptive radiotherapy.[74]

In a similar vein, to reduce the time a patient needs to be on the treatment bed, AI has been applied to produce accurate dose calculation and reduce computational time for adaptive radiotherapy. Both Dong and Xing and Xing et al. used deep neural networks to transform dose distributions calculated using low-cost algorithms to ones obtained using highly accurate dose plans, shown in Figure 7.3.[72,75] Specifically, dose calculated from the anisotropic analytical algorithm (AAA, Varian Medical Systems) and the corresponding down sampled CT slice were used to train a model to predict dose, in less than 1 ms calculated, using the Acuros XB algorithm (AXB, Varian Medical Systems). These studies showed that by combining a less accurate dose calculation algorithm with AI, both high accuracy and efficient dose calculation can be achieved. Alternative models to predict dose, where predictions are based on CT and/or OAR/target contours as inputs, can also be used to improve computational efficiency during adaptive radiotherapy. Models have been trained to predict dose for head and neck,[76] prostate,[77–80] and breast cancers.[81,82] These models were trained to learn the mapping between binary masks of the contours and radiation dose distributions. Lastly, deep learning has been employed to correct CBCT images to enable dose calculation for adaptive radiotherapy.[15] Maspero et al. implemented a cycle-consistent GAN to reduce CBCT artifacts and increase similarity to the original planning CT. This enabled the ability to perform dose calculations on the synthetic CT from the cycle-GAN across a wide variety of disease sites including head and neck, lung, and breast cancers.

7.2.3 Real-time Target Position Monitoring

Knowing where the treatment target is during radiation therapy delivery is critical to maximizing the chance of treatment success and minimizing the likelihood of treatment-induced side effects. The first clinical real-time target position monitoring system with x-ray guidance was first demonstrated clinically in the late 1990s.[83] There have been multiple approaches to the real-time target position monitoring task using a variety of individual modalities and a combination of modalities. Naturally, AI applications are increasingly being investigated. The goal of real-time target position monitoring is to reduce safety margins. A reduction in geometric error leads to a reduction in both the total dose to normal tissues and the day-to-day variations in the dose. As dose is directly related to clinical outcomes, there is a clinical driver for a broader adoption of real-time target position monitoring. AI applications may provide solutions that can be broadly and easily adopted to make real-time target position monitoring more mainstream.

The real-time target position information can be used for a variety of roles depending on the treatment adaptation technology available. At the lower technology end, manual intervention to pause the beam can be performed if there is an observable shift in the target position, a large variation in the motion outside of a preset threshold (also called exception gating), or a baseline shift of the target occurs. Automated beam pause can be triggered by these events. However, an additional application of automated beam pause

TABLE 7.1

Terms and Definitions Relevant to Real-Time Target Position Monitoring

Term	Definition
Latency	The time lag between target motion and the complete execution of the system response. This time includes contributions from the position monitoring process, the computation of the temporal prediction algorithm (if used), the computation time for MLC tracking, and the execution of the MLC motion instructions. The latency can vary due to the frequencies of the position monitoring and MLC updating systems and the amount of leaf motion requested.
Position monitoring signal	The signal from the real-time target position monitoring system (defined below).
Real-time	The latency or response time of the tracking system to motion is less than the timescale of significant changes in the target position.
Real-time target position monitoring system	A device that measures the position of the target in real-time. It may be based on a variety of technologies, including optical, kV x-ray, MV x-ray, electromagnetic, MRI, and ultrasound. The target may be a single target or multiple targets, and information about the OAR positions may also be obtained.
Temporal prediction	The estimation of the target position at some time in the future, typically corresponding to the latency. Temporal prediction is used to reduce the geometric error caused by latency.

Source: Adapted from AAPM Task Group 264.[85]

is gating for the periodic components of motion, such as respiratory (and potentially cardiac) motion. At the higher technology end, automated beam-target alignment methods such as couch, gimbaled linac, multi-leaf collima-tor (MLC), or robotic systems can be used. Some terms relevant to real-time target position monitoring are defined in Table 7.1.

7.2.3.1 Spatial Prediction of Target Positions

Real-time target position monitoring requires where the target is in both space and time. Focusing on the position in space first, tools to directly mea-sure the target position during treatment are MRI and ultrasound. These technologies are not currently widely available and also have limitations. The workhorses of image guidance are the widely available gantry-mounted x-ray imaging systems integrated into most radiation therapy delivery sys-tems. The x-ray imaging systems are limited in their ability to directly detect the target position in many cases because of the small difference in x-ray attenuation between the target and surrounding tissues. The images are also two-dimensional. Due to the challenging nature of the problem, and the need for fast computation, AI applications are well suited to this task. Some of the more visible structures with x-ray imaging are the vertebral bod-ies. Spinal stereotactic ablative radiotherapy (SABR) also has a high accuracy requirement with the spinal cord often being close to or abutting the target. Roggen et al. developed a deep learning Mask R-CNN approach to vertebral landmark detection. For both phantom and clinical cases, sub-millimeter accuracy was demonstrated.[86] Similar accuracy was obtained using a deep learning patient-specific model by Zhao et al.[87]

AI has shown promise to track targets on the other extreme, where targets are more challenging to visualize with x-ray imaging. Zhao et al. developed a deep learning-based treatment target localization method to track both prostate[16] and pancreatic[88] tumors without the use of fiducial markers, which are often implanted near the target to assist in identifying soft-tissue targets using x-ray imaging. As illustrated in Figure 7.4b, the patient-specific model employed a region proposal network (RPN) and multiple deformed images generated from the labeled planning CT to create a large, labeled training dataset for deep learning.

AI was applied to x-ray tumor tracking of lung and liver tumors using a deep neural network by Hirai et al. [89] Target-labeled DRRs from 4DCT images were used for training. The network generates a target probability map. When applied to ten patients, the overall tracking accuracy was 1.6±0.7 mm with a computation time of less than 40 ms.

7.2.3.2 Temporal Prediction of Target Positions

There is a time delay between the motion of the cancer target and the ability of the target position monitoring system to detect and act on the motion. These time delays are due to the sampling rate of the monitoring system, the computation time, data transfer, and adaptive system response time (manual or automated) and comprise the system latency. If unaccounted for, the response will always lag the target position, leading to a geometric error. In some cases, for example prostate motion, the nature and timescale of the motion means that this error will be small. For faster-moving tumors, such as those in the lung and liver, the error may be significant. The best approach to reduce errors caused by latency is to reduce the latency time via improved engineering. However, there will always be residual latency. This residual latency can be measured and time-series analysis tools developed to predict ahead in time as to where the target will be at the time of the system adaptation. Key articles comparing methods of motion prediction are Sharp et al. and Krauss et al.[84,90]

AI is well suited to the motion prediction task. An early application of AI to this task was published by Riaz et al. who used multidimensional adaptive filters with support vector regression to predict patient-measured respiratory motion up to 1 second in advance with a root mean square error of less than 2 mm.[91] Fuzzy deep learning, a combination of fuzzy logic and a neural network with three or more hidden layers, has been applied to predicting inter- and intra-fraction motion from patient-measured tumor motion data, yielding reduced geometric error than observed from other algorithms investigated.[92]

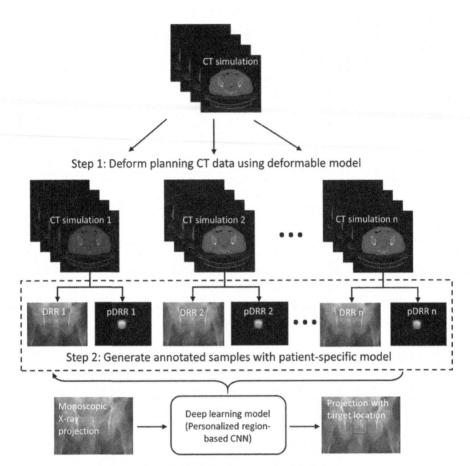

FIGURE 7.4

AI applied to real-time tracking. Motion traces acquired during treatments from either external or internal markers can be used as inputs into a model to predict target locations and reduce latency of these systems.[84] AI can also be leveraged in fluoroscopic images to identify target locations during treatment without the need of implanting fiducial markers.[16]

7.3 Future Directions and Opportunities

AI lends itself to motion management and image-guided radiation therapy as (1) large amounts of data are available from prior treatments to develop robust models; (2) prior information of the given patient is available for in-room treatment tasks, enabling patient-specific training to augment existing models; and (3) the real-time applications require information to be extracted and acted upon quickly – a general advantage of AI approaches.

This chapter has covered many existing applications of AI to motion management and image-guided radiation therapy. These applications include image reconstruction, motion prediction, target position monitoring, contour mapping, adaptive radiotherapy, and dose prediction. As the data, computational power, and AI algorithms continue to grow, expect the accuracy and robustness of these applications to continue to improve. Also expect a commensurate increase in the translation of these approaches from academic research to approved products to improve patient care with time.

Some exciting areas of IGRT are emerging where AI may play a significant role. The QUANTEC and HyTEC series of reports demonstrated that radiation dose is critically linked to patient outcomes. Using AI tools to quantify the dose delivered during treatment, optimizing the dose during treatment, and linking the dose and patient anatomy to outcomes will further improve our understanding of treatment response and guide future research directions. Adding functional information into this mix will require additional algorithmic development and computational power and hopefully achieve a commensurate increase in patient benefit. Two emerging technologies, FLASH and MRI-guided proton therapy, are ripe for AI applications. FLASH therapy[93] represents an important application for motion prediction as the delivery is so fast any errors cannot be fixed. MRI-guided proton therapy also represents a future opportunity for motion prediction.[94–97] The additional challenge for particle therapy is that the anatomy, and density, of the entire pathlength of the proton beam from the patient surface to the distal edge of the tumor needs to be accurately determined. AI approaches to MRI distortion correction[98] and electron density estimates[99,100] may be employed for this challenging task.

Looking forward, the optimal radiation therapy will have detailed knowledge at all times of the patient anatomy, patient physiology, and the capability to optimize the dose delivered to the patient in real-time on a voxel-by-voxel basis using detailed personalized radiation response models. In the absence of systems that can simultaneously image temporally changing anatomy and physiology in real-time, we will be relying on AI applications to give the best estimate of the patient state with high spatial–temporal resolution.

To improve the patient experience and resource deployment for radiation therapy, the number of treatments will be minimized and the time per treatment will be minimized. The speed of AI applications lends itself to achieving these tasks. AI applications reduce human variability and human error, encouraging safe and cost-effective deployment in low resource settings, where radiation therapy services are needed most.[101]

The future of AI in motion management and image-guided radiation therapy is exciting from a scientific perspective. More importantly, there are strong clinical drivers to harness the power of AI to improve patient outcomes, the patient experience, and the cost-effectiveness of radiation therapy. The future is bright.

Acknowledgements

PK gratefully acknowledges the assistance of Dr. Helen Ball with drafting part of this chapter.

References

1. Verhey, L. J. Immobilizing and positioning patients for radiotherapy. *Semin. Radiat. Oncol.* **5**, 100–114 (1995).
2. Verellen, D., Ridder, M. D. & Storme, G. A (short) history of image-guided radiotherapy. *Radiother. Oncol.* **86**, 4–13 (2008).
3. Weissbluth, M., Karzmark, C. J., Steele, R. E. & Selby, A. H. The Stanford medical linear accelerator. *Radiology* **72**, 242–265 (1959).
4. Jaffray, D. A., Siewerdsen, J. H., Wong, J. W. & Martinez, A. A. Flat-panel cone-beam computed tomography for image-guided radiation therapy. *Int. J. Radiat. Oncol. Biol. Phys.* **53**, 1337–1349 (2002).
5. Uematsu, M. et al. A dual computed tomography linear accelerator unit for stereotactic radiation therapy: A new approach without cranially fixated stereotactic frames. *Int. J. Radiat. Oncol.* **35**, 587–592 (1996).
6. Lagendijk, J. J. W. et al. MRI/linac integration. *Radiother. Oncol.* **86**, 25–29 (2008).
7. Korreman, S. S. Motion in radiotherapy: Photon therapy. *Phys. Med. Biol.* **57**, R161–R191 (2012).
8. Mah, K. & Henkelman, R. M. Time varying dose due to respiratory motion during radiation therapy of the thorax. in *Proceedings of the 8th International Conference on the Use of Computers in Radiation Therapy*, 294–298 (1984).
9. Kubo, H. D. & Hill, B. C. Respiration gated radiotherapy treatment: A technical study. *Phys. Med. Biol.* **41**, 83–91 (1996).
10. Wong, J. W. et al. The use of active breathing control (ABC) to reduce margin for breathing motion. *Int. J. Radiat. Oncol. Biol. Phys.* **44**, 911–919 (1999).
11. Bertholet, J. et al. Real-time intrafraction motion monitoring in external beam radiotherapy. *Phys. Med. Biol.* **64**, 15TR01 (2019).
12. Hu, Q. et al. Practical safety considerations for integration of magnetic resonance imaging in radiation therapy. *Pract. Radiat. Oncol.* **10**, 443–453 (2020).
13. Cheung, Y. & Sawant, A. An externally and internally deformable, programmable lung motion phantom. *Med. Phys.* **42**, 2585–2593 (2015).
14. Lei, Y. et al. Deep learning-based real-time volumetric imaging for lung stereotactic body radiation therapy: A proof of concept study. *Phys. Med. Biol.* **65**, 235003 (2020).
15. Maspero, M. et al. A single neural network for cone-beam computed tomography-based radiotherapy of head-and-neck, lung and breast cancer. *Phys. Imaging Radiat. Oncol.* **14**, 24–31 (2020).
16. Zhao, W. et al. Incorporating imaging information from deep neural network layers into image guided radiation therapy (IGRT). *Radiother. Oncol.* **140**, 167–174 (2019).

17. Langen, K. M. & Jones, D. T. Organ motion and its management. *Int. J. Radiat. Oncol. Biol. Phys.* **50**, 265–278 (2001).
18. Hodapp, N. The ICRU Report 83: Prescribing, recording and reporting photon-beam intensity-modulated radiation therapy (IMRT). *Strahlenther. Onkol. Organ Dtsch. Rontgengesellschaft Al* **188**, 97–99 (2012).
19. Holloway, A. F. A localising device for a rotating cobalt therapy unit. *Br. J. Radiol.* **31**, 227 (1958).
20. Mackie, T. R. et al. Image guidance for precise conformal radiotherapy. *Int. J. Radiat. Oncol. Biol. Phys.* **56**, 89–105 (2003).
21. Keall, P. J. et al. The management of respiratory motion in radiation oncology report of AAPM Task Group 76. *Med. Phys.* **33**, 3874–3900 (2006).
22. Korreman, S. S., Pedersen, A. N., Nøttrup, T. J., Specht, L. & Nyström, H. Breathing adapted radiotherapy for breast cancer: Comparison of free breathing gating with the breath-hold technique. *Radiother. Oncol. J. Eur. Soc. Ther. Radiol. Oncol.* **76**, 311–318 (2005).
23. Kini, V. R. et al. Patient training in respiratory-gated radiotherapy. *Med. Dosim. Off. J. Am. Assoc. Med. Dosim.* **28**, 7–11 (2003).
24. Hanley, J. et al. Deep inspiration breath-hold technique for lung tumors: The potential value of target immobilization and reduced lung density in dose escalation. *Int. J. Radiat. Oncol. Biol. Phys.* **45**, 603–611 (1999).
25. Barnes, E. A. et al. Dosimetric evaluation of lung tumor immobilization using breath hold at deep inspiration. *Int. J. Radiat. Oncol. Biol. Phys.* **50**, 1091–1098 (2001).
26. Balter, J. M., Lam, K. L., McGinn, C. J., Lawrence, T. S. & Ten Haken, R. K. Improvement of CT-based treatment-planning models of abdominal targets using static exhale imaging. *Int. J. Radiat. Oncol. Biol. Phys.* **41**, 939–943 (1998).
27. Rosenzweig, K. E. et al. The deep inspiration breath-hold technique in the treatment of inoperable non-small-cell lung cancer. *Int. J. Radiat. Oncol. Biol. Phys.* **48**, 81–87 (2000).
28. Negoro, Y. et al. The effectiveness of an immobilization device in conformal radiotherapy for lung tumor: Reduction of respiratory tumor movement and evaluation of the daily setup accuracy. *Int. J. Radiat. Oncol. Biol. Phys.* **50**, 889–898 (2001).
29. Bouilhol, G. et al. Is abdominal compression useful in lung stereotactic body radiation therapy? A 4DCT and dosimetric lobe-dependent study. *Phys. Medica PM Int. J. Devoted Appl. Phys. Med. Biol. Off. J. Ital. Assoc. Biomed. Phys. AIFB* **29**, 333–340 (2013).
30. Willoughby, T. et al. Quality assurance for nonradiographic radiotherapy localization and positioning systems: Report of Task Group 147. *Med. Phys.* **39**, 1728–1747 (2012).
31. Li, G. et al. Motion monitoring for cranial frameless stereotactic radiosurgery using video-based three-dimensional optical surface imaging. *Med. Phys.* **38**, 3981–3994 (2011).
32. Vedam, S. S., Keall, P. J., Kini, V. R. & Mohan, R. Determining parameters for respiration-gated radiotherapy. *Med. Phys.* **28**, 2139–2146 (2001).
33. Balter, J. M. et al. Accuracy of a wireless localization system for radiotherapy. *Int. J. Radiat. Oncol. Biol. Phys.* **61**, 933–937 (2005).
34. Simon, L., Giraud, P., Servois, V. & Rosenwald, J.-C. Lung volume assessment for a cross-comparison of two breathing-adapted techniques in radiotherapy. *Int. J. Radiat. Oncol. Biol. Phys.* **63**, 602–609 (2005).

35. Ozhasoglu, C. et al. Synchrony--cyberknife respiratory compensation technology. *Med. Dosim. Off. J. Am. Assoc. Med. Dosim.* **33**, 117–123 (2008).
36. Fallone, B. G. The rotating biplanar linac-magnetic resonance imaging system. *Semin. Radiat. Oncol.* **24**, 200–202 (2014).
37. Keall, P. J., Barton, M. & Crozier, S. The Australian magnetic resonance imaging–linac program. *Semin. Radiat. Oncol.* **24**, 203–206 (2014).
38. Raaijmakers, A. J. E., Raaymakers, B. W. & Lagendijk, J. J. W. Integrating a MRI scanner with a 6 MV radiotherapy accelerator: Dose increase at tissue-air interfaces in a lateral magnetic field due to returning electrons. *Phys. Med. Biol.* **50**, 1363–1376 (2005).
39. Dempsey, J. F. et al. A device for realtime 3D image-guided IMRT. *Int. J. Radiat. Oncol. Biol. Phys.* **63**, S202 (2005).
40. Hosny, A., Parmar, C., Quackenbush, J., Schwartz, L. H. & Aerts, H. J. W. L. Artificial intelligence in radiology. *Nat. Rev. Cancer* **18**, 500–510 (2018).
41. Huynh, E. et al. Artificial intelligence in radiation oncology. *Nat. Rev. Clin. Oncol.* **17**, 771–781 (2020).
42. Stoitsis, J. et al. Computer aided diagnosis based on medical image processing and artificial intelligence methods. *Nucl. Instrum. Methods Phys. Res. Sect. Accel. Spectrometers Detect. Assoc. Equip.* **569**, 591–595 (2006).
43. Vyborny, C. J. & Giger, M. L. Computer vision and artificial intelligence in mammography. *Am. J. Roentgenol.* **162**, 699–708 (1994).
44. Artificial Intelligence for Mammography and Digital Breast Tomosynthesis: Current Concepts and Future Perspectives | Radiology. https://pubs.rsna.org/doi/full/10.1148/radiol.2019182627.
45. Sheth, D. & Giger, M. L. Artificial intelligence in the interpretation of breast cancer on MRI. *J. Magn. Reson. Imaging* **51**, 1310–1324 (2020).
46. Codari, M., Schiaffino, S., Sardanelli, F. & Trimboli, R. M. Artificial intelligence for breast MRI in 2008–2018: A systematic mapping review. *Am. J. Roentgenol.* **212**, 280–292 (2019).
47. Feng, M., Valdes, G., Dixit, N. & Solberg, T. D. Machine learning in radiation oncology: Opportunities, requirements, and needs. *Front. Oncol.* **8**, 110 (2018).
48. The evolution of image reconstruction for CT—from filtered back projection to artificial intelligence | SpringerLink. doi: 10.1007/s00330-018-5810-7.
49. Wang, G., Ye, J. C., Mueller, K. & Fessler, J. A. Image reconstruction is a new frontier of machine learning. *IEEE Trans. Med. Imaging* **37**, 1289–1296 (2018).
50. Litjens, G. et al. A survey on deep learning in medical image analysis. *Med. Image Anal.* **42**, 60–88 (2017).
51. Shen, L., Zhao, W. & Xing, L. Patient-specific reconstruction of volumetric computed tomography images from a single projection view via deep learning. *Nat. Biomed. Eng.* **3**, 880–888 (2019).
52. Freedman, J. N. et al. Rapid 4D-MRI reconstruction using a deep radial convolutional neural network: Dracula. *Radiother. Oncol.* **159**, 209–217 (2021).
53. Charyyev, S. et al. High quality proton portal imaging using deep learning for proton radiation therapy: A phantom study. *Biomed. Phys. Eng. Express* **6**, 035029 (2020).
54. Dean, J. et al. Incorporating spatial dose metrics in machine learning-based normal tissue complication probability (NTCP) models of severe acute dysphagia resulting from head and neck radiotherapy. *Clin. Transl. Radiat. Oncol.* **8**, 27–39 (2018).

55. Gabryś, H. S., Buettner, F., Sterzing, F., Hauswald, H. & Bangert, M. Design and selection of machine learning methods using radiomics and dosiomics for normal tissue complication probability modeling of xerostomia. *Front. Oncol.* **8**, 35 (2018).

56. Dean, J. A. et al. Normal tissue complication probability (NTCP) modelling using spatial dose metrics and machine learning methods for severe acute oral mucositis resulting from head and neck radiotherapy. *Radiother. Oncol. J. Eur. Soc. Ther. Radiol. Oncol.* **120**, 21–27 (2016).

57. Moran, A., Daly, M. E., Yip, S. S. F. & Yamamoto, T. Radiomics-based assessment of radiation-induced lung injury after stereotactic body radiotherapy. *Clin. Lung Cancer* **18**, e425–e431 (2017).

58. Zhen, X. et al. Deep convolutional neural network with transfer learning for rectum toxicity prediction in cervical cancer radiotherapy: A feasibility study. *Phys. Med. Biol.* **62**, 8246–8263 (2017).

59. Luna, J. M. et al. Novel use of machine learning for predicting radiation esophagitis in locally advanced stage II-IIi non–small cell lung cancer. *Int. J. Radiat. Oncol. Biol. Phys.* **99**, E476–E477 (2017).

60. Lei, Y. et al. CBCT-based synthetic MRI generation for CBCT-guided adaptive radiotherapy. In: *Artificial Intelligence in Radiation Therapy* (eds. Nguyen, D., Xing, L. & Jiang, S.) 154–161 (Springer International Publishing, 2019). doi: 10.1007/978-3-030-32486-5_19.

61. Li, Y. et al. A preliminary study of using a deep convolution neural network to generate synthesized CT images based on CBCT for adaptive radiotherapy of nasopharyngeal carcinoma. *Phys. Med. Biol.* **64**, 145010 (2019).

62. Chun, J. et al. MRI super-resolution reconstruction for MRI-guided adaptive radiotherapy using cascaded deep learning: In the presence of limited training data and unknown translation model. *Med. Phys.* **46**, 4148–4164 (2019).

63. Wu, Y. et al. Incorporating prior knowledge via volumetric deep residual network to optimize the reconstruction of sparsely sampled MRI. *Magn. Reson. Imaging* **66**, 93–103 (2020).

64. Hegde, J. V. et al. Magnetic resonance imaging guidance mitigates the effects of intrafraction prostate motion during stereotactic body radiotherapy for prostate cancer. *Cureus* **10**, e2442 (2018).

65. Mostafaei, F. et al. Variations of MRI-assessed peristaltic motions during radiation therapy. *PLoS ONE* **13**, e0205917 (2018).

66. Corradini, S. et al. MR-guidance in clinical reality: Current treatment challenges and future perspectives. *Radiat. Oncol.* **14**, 92 (2019).

67. Dawson, L. A. & Jaffray, D. A. Advances in image-guided radiation therapy. *J. Clin. Oncol. Off. J. Am. Soc. Clin. Oncol.* **25**, 938–946 (2007).

68. Sonke, J.-J., Aznar, M. & Rasch, C. Adaptive radiotherapy for anatomical changes. *Semin. Radiat. Oncol.* **29**, 245–257 (2019).

69. Keall, P., Poulsen, P. & Booth, J. T. See, Think, and act: Real-time adaptive radiotherapy. *Semin. Radiat. Oncol.* **29**, 228–235 (2019).

70. Thorwarth, D. & Low, D. A. Technical challenges of real-time adaptive MR-guided radiotherapy. *Front. Oncol.* **11**, 332 (2021).

71. Rigaud, B. et al. Automatic segmentation using deep learning to enable online dose optimization during adaptive radiation therapy of cervical cancer. *Int. J. Radiat. Oncol. Biol. Phys.* **109**, 1096–1110 (2020).

72. Dong, P. & Xing, L. Deep DoseNet: A deep neural network for accurate dosimetric transformation between different spatial resolutions and/or different dose calculation algorithms for precision radiation therapy. *Phys. Med. Biol.* **65**, 035010 (2020).

73. Elmahdy, M. S., Ahuja, T., Heide, U. A. van der & Staring, M. Patient-specific finetuning of deep learning models for adaptive radiotherapy in prostate CT. In: *2020 IEEE 17th International Symposium on Biomedical Imaging (ISBI)*, 577–580 (2020). doi:10.1109/ISBI45749.2020.9098702.

74. Fu, Y. et al. A novel MRI segmentation method using CNN-based correction network for MRI-guided adaptive radiotherapy. *Med. Phys.* **45**, 5129–5137 (2018).

75. Xing, Y. et al. Boosting radiotherapy dose calculation accuracy with deep learning. *J. Appl. Clin. Med. Phys.* **21**, 149–159 (2020).

76. Gronberg, M. P. et al. Technical note: Dose prediction for head and neck radiotherapy using a three-dimensional dense dilated U-net architecture. *Med. Phys.* **48**, 5567–5573 (2021).

77. Jensen, P. J., Zhang, J., Koontz, B. F. & Wu, Q. J. A novel machine learning model for dose prediction in prostate volumetric modulated arc therapy using output initialization and optimization priorities. *Front. Artif. Intell.* **4**, 41 (2021).

78. Nguyen, D. et al. A feasibility study for predicting optimal radiation therapy dose distributions of prostate cancer patients from patient anatomy using deep learning. *Sci. Rep.* **9**, 1076 (2019).

79. Murakami, Y. et al. Fully automated dose prediction using generative adversarial networks in prostate cancer patients. *PLOS ONE* **15**, e0232697 (2020).

80. Kandalan, R. N. et al. Dose prediction with deep learning for prostate cancer radiation therapy: Model adaptation to different treatment planning practices. *Radiother. Oncol.* **153**, 228–235 (2020).

81. Ahn, S. H. et al. Deep learning method for prediction of patient-specific dose distribution in breast cancer. *Radiat. Oncol.* **16**, 154 (2021).

82. Hedden, N. & Xu, H. Radiation therapy dose prediction for left-sided breast cancers using two-dimensional and three-dimensional deep learning models. *Phys. Medica Eur. J. Med. Phys.* **83**, 101–107 (2021).

83. Shirato, H., Shimizu, S., Shimizu, T., Nishioka, T. & Miyasaka, K. Real-time tumour-tracking radiotherapy. *Lancet Lond. Engl.* **353**, 1331–1332 (1999).

84. Sharp, G. C., Jiang, S. B., Shimizu, S. & Shirato, H. Prediction of respiratory tumour motion for real-time image-guided radiotherapy. *Phys. Med. Biol.* **49**, 425–440 (2004).

85. Keall, P. J. et al. AAPM Task Group 264: The safe clinical implementation of MLC tracking in radiotherapy. *Med. Phys.* **48**, e44–e64 (2021).

86. Roggen, T., Bobic, M., Givehchi, N. & Scheib, S. G. Deep learning model for markerless tracking in spinal SBRT. *Phys. Med.* **74**, 66–73 (2020).

87. Zhao, W., Capaldi, D. P., Chuang, C. & Xing, L. Fiducial-free image-guided spinal stereotactic radiosurgery enabled via deep learning. *Int. J. Radiat. Oncol. Biol. Phys.* **108**, e357 (2020).

88. Zhao, W. et al. Markerless pancreatic tumor target localization enabled by deep learning. *Int. J. Radiat. Oncol.* **105**, 432–439 (2019).

89. Hirai, R., Sakata, Y., Tanizawa, A. & Mori, S. Real-time tumor tracking using fluoroscopic imaging with deep neural network analysis. *Phys. Med.* **59**, 22–29 (2019).

90. Krauss, A., Nill, S. & Oelfke, U. The comparative performance of four respiratory motion predictors for real-time tumour tracking. *Phys. Med. Biol.* **56**, 5303–5317 (2011).

91. Riaz, N. et al. Predicting respiratory tumor motion with multi-dimensional adaptive filters and support vector regression. *Phys. Med. Biol.* **54**, 5735–5748 (2009).

92. Park, S., Lee, S. J., Weiss, E. & Motai, Y. Intra- and inter-fractional variation prediction of lung tumors using fuzzy deep learning. *IEEE J. Transl. Eng. Health Med.* **4**, 1–12 (2016).

93. Favaudon, V. et al. Ultrahigh dose-rate FLASH irradiation increases the differential response between normal and tumor tissue in mice. *Sci. Transl. Med.* **6**, 245ra93 (2014).

94. Van Der Kraaij, E. et al. MRI-guided-PT: Integrating an MRI in a proton therapy system. *22nd International Conference on Cyclotrons and their Applications*, Cyclotrons2019, 4 pages, 1.156 MB (2020).

95. Hoffmann, A. et al. MR-guided proton therapy: A review and a preview. *Radiat. Oncol. Lond. Engl.* **15**, 129 (2020).

96. Oborn, B. M. et al. Future of medical physics: Real-time MRI-guided proton therapy. *Med. Phys.* **44**, e77–e90 (2017).

97. Schellhammer, S. M. & Hoffmann, A. L. Prediction and compensation of magnetic beam deflection in MR-integrated proton therapy: A method optimized regarding accuracy, versatility and speed. *Phys. Med. Biol.* **62**, 1548–1564 (2017).

98. Shan, S. et al. ReUINet: A fast GNL distortion correction approach on a 1.0 T MRI-Linac scanner. *Med. Phys.* **48**, 2991–3002 (2021).

99. Han, X. MR-based synthetic CT generation using a deep convolutional neural network method. *Med. Phys.* **44**, 1408–1419 (2017).

100. Kazemifar, S. et al. MRI-only brain radiotherapy: Assessing the dosimetric accuracy of synthetic CT images generated using a deep learning approach. *Radiother. Oncol.* **136**, 56–63 (2019).

101. Atun, R. et al. Expanding global access to radiotherapy. *Lancet Oncol.* **16**, 1153–1186 (2015).

8

Outlook of AI in Medical Physics and Radiation Oncology

Daniel X. Yang

University of Texas Southwestern Medical Center

Arman Avesta, Rachel Choi, and Sanjay Aneja

Yale University School of Medicine

CONTENTS

8.1 Introduction

Artificial intelligence (AI) holds substantial promise to transform the practice of radiation oncology. The recent increase in the availability of high-dimensional medical data, along with advances in computing capacity, has enabled the application of AI across multiple aspects of healthcare. Given the imaging-based and data-intensive nature of clinical radiation oncology and medical physics, these fields are well poised to harness advancements in AI technology. In recent years, there has been an exponential increase in research and early clinical implementation of AI systems across many complex facets of radiation oncology practice.[1,2]

Early AI systems were rules-based, meaning computers applied a defined set of logical rules programmed by human operators. These systems relied extensively on human expertise. However, over the past decade, there have been fundamental shifts in AI technology toward increased application of machine learning (and specifically, deep learning) methods, with corresponding movement away from rules-based to model-based AI. Particularly, the use of artificial neural networks to model complex clinical processes has gained significant traction and is being investigated in multiple medical settings. There has been tremendous progress in the application of neural networks in imaging-based tasks ranging from diagnosis to treatment planning.[3] Given that radiation oncology treatment is based on imaging, there has been increased interest in how to clinically apply such technologies to augment many of the tasks within the radiation oncology workflow and to ultimately improve cancer patient care.

Partly driving this shift in AI technology is also the explosion of the availability of large datasets. Clinical radiation oncology and medical physics are also well poised in this regard.[4] There are large national efforts to aggregate oncology-specific imaging datasets such as The Cancer Imaging Archive (TCIA), which enables the training of imaging-based AI algorithms.[5] The widespread implementation of common medical imaging communication standards such as Digital Imaging and Communications in Medicine (DICOM), with specific extensions for radiation therapy (DICOM-RT), have enabled imaging data to be shared and processed across different institutions.[6] In addition, the widespread adoption of electronic health records has also generated a rich source of structured and unstructured data, which can potentially be integrated with imaging data to develop more accurate AI platforms. This potential has yet to be fully realized partly due to interoperability issues and the lack of widely accepted common data models. Regardless, significant collaborative efforts between organizations and at the national level are underway to develop interoperable data structures specific to oncology. Within radiation oncology, treatment planning systems also capture large amounts of data including target and organ segmentation, dosimetry, image alignment, and setup information, among others, which provides additional dimensions for analysis within AI platforms.

In this book chapter, we review the outlook of AI in all aspects of the clinical workflow for radiation oncology and medical physics, as divided into subsections of (1) clinical assessment, (2) simulation and image acquisition, (3) treatment planning and quality assurance, and (4) treatment delivery. Finally, we conclude by describing the current outlook on integrating AI into routine radiation oncology practice, including limitations such as interpretability and the need for external validation within modern AI systems.

8.2 Clinical Assessment

The radiation oncology clinical workflow begins with initial patient evaluation during consultation by the radiation oncologist. The radiation oncologist meets with the patient and performs a physical examination as well as reviews multiple aspects of the patient's medical record, eventually coming to a treatment decision on whether radiation may be indicated and what type of radiation treatments will be recommended. Since the amount of information available to clinicians has increased significantly—often beyond what can be humanly synthesized during a single clinical encounter—AI tools can help identify the most salient clinical features to assist in truly personalized clinical decision making. Therefore, the applications of AI in clinical assessment are potentially broad and can impact multiple aspects of clinical care including diagnosis, generating personalized radiation treatment recommendations, and individualized prognostication beyond currently available clinical decision-making tools.

The incorporation of AI tools in cancer diagnosis is an active area of ongoing research and clinical implementation. For example, computer-aided systems for breast cancer detection on mammograms have been in clinical use for many years, with a recent rise in research of deep learning methods.[7] With over 40 million mammograms conducted in the U.S. annually, interpretation is time and effort-intensive and may be affected by false-positive and false-negative findings. Machine learning models such as those using convolutional neural networks (CNNs) have been developed for automated breast cancer diagnosis from mammograms. After training on a dataset of mammograms from 1,249 patients, a CNN model published in 2019 achieved an area under the curve (AUC) of 0.88 on an independent test set.[8] Another CNN that was trained on both mammograms and health records of 9611 women achieved an AUC of 0.91 in breast cancer prediction when tested on an independent set.[9] A recent large international effort demonstrated an AI system using a deep learning model was able to significantly reduce false-positive and false-negative rates when generalized across datasets from two different countries. Moreover, the model outperformed six independent human radiologists.[10] In the future, implementation of such AI systems may increase earlier detection and subsequent diagnosis of breast cancer and, therefore, lead to shifts in radiation oncology practice patterns in terms of the types of breast cancer cases and recommended treatment courses.[11] Implementation of AI systems could also potentially improve diagnostic accuracy in prostate cancer. For example, detecting prostate cancer by multiparametric magnetic resonance imaging (MRI) using AI is an active area of research. In 2003, Chan et al. developed a machine learning model that used prostate MRI sequences as input channels (including T2-weighted images, quantitative T2 mapping, and diffusion MR images) and generated a statistical map of prostate tumor probability.[12] More recently, a CNN-based pipeline for detecting prostate cancer from diffusion MRI was able to achieve an AUC of 0.84.[13]

AI tools can also potentially be used to predict treatment outcomes for individual patients, enabling further tailoring of precision treatments within radiation oncology (Figure 8.1). Radiation prescription doses and dose constraints for organs at risk are currently determined based on accepted practice guidelines, published clinical experience, and institutional and provider-specific practices. AI tools may be able to further individualize radiation prescription doses and normal tissue dose constraints, taking into account the unique clinical and tumor characteristics of each patient. For example,

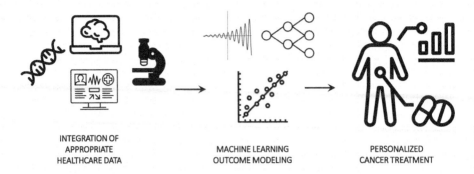

INTEGRATION OF
APPROPRIATE
HEALTHCARE DATA

MACHINE LEARNING
OUTCOME MODELING

PERSONALIZED
CANCER TREATMENT

FIGURE 8.1
Paradigm for integration of artificial intelligence for personalized outcome prediction in oncology.

a 2019 study of 944 lung cancer patients evaluated the ability of deep learning to approximate radiomic features and predict treatment outcomes given pre-therapy lung computed tomography (CT) images.[14] The authors combined the output of a deep neural network with clinical variables to derive an individualized dose per patient that would correlate with a treatment failure probability below 5%. The dose range suggested by the model was wide, suggesting that there may exist subpopulations that have a differential response to radiotherapy.[14] There are also a number of research efforts in predicting radiation treatment-related toxicities using AI. This includes predicting dermatitis in breast cancer patients undergoing radiation therapy, as well as unplanned hospitalizations in head and neck cancer patients receiving radiation.[15,16] For example, the head and neck study considered a large dataset of 2121 patients. After collecting over 700 clinical and treatment variables from electronic health records (spanning demographic, tumor characteristic, treatment, and RT data), the authors trained random forest, gradient-boosted decision trees, and logistic regression models to predict unplanned hospitalizations, feeding tube placement, and significant weight loss.

Cancer prognostication has traditionally relied on staging systems or clinician judgment incorporating a limited number of clinical and pathologic factors. More recently, prognostic biomarkers incorporating genomic information, such as commercially available multigene tests including Oncotype DX and MammaPrint in breast cancer or Decipher in prostate cancer, have also increasingly entered routine clinical practice. AI-driven biomarkers incorporating such heterogeneous clinical information is an area of active research. For example, a deep neural network-based model incorporating multi-dimensional data (clinical variables and gene expression profile data) was able to achieve better performance at predicting breast cancer patient survival than models incorporating single-dimensional data.[17] Another prospective study involving 241 patients with invasive breast cancer showed that machine learning approaches were able to identify features on CT scans that correlated with known clinical and molecular prognostic features.[18] For localized prostate cancer, an AI-based biomarker incorporating histopathology images and clinical variables from several large phase III clinical trials demonstrated superior prognostic performance compared to standard clinical and pathologic variables.[19]

8.3 Simulation and Imaging

AI solutions can improve treatment simulation by improving image acquisition and image processing for treatment planning.[4] In order to accurately delineate treatment targets and nearby organs at risk, multiple modalities of advanced imaging may be used, including CT, positron emission tomography (PET), and MRI. The treatment simulation images are acquired in the treatment position, while the patient's previous diagnostic images may have been acquired in a different position. This creates challenges and uncertainties when aligning these images for treatment planning. AI can help in image registration (i.e., aligning and overlaying the diagnostic images on top of the treatment simulation images).[20] In addition, treatment simulation images might be acquired using modalities such as MRI, while dose calculation for radiotherapy needs CT images. In such scenarios, AI can generate synthetic CT images from MR images (Figure 8.2).[21,22] AI can also improve image acquisition itself by reducing the imaging time, improving the image quality, and reducing image artifacts.[23–25]

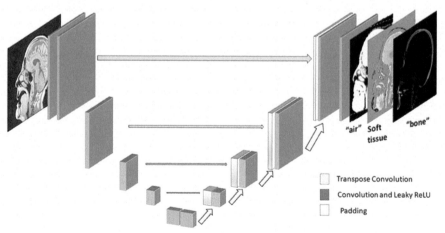

Gupta D, Kim M, Vineberg KA and Balter JM (2019). Front. Oncol.

FIGURE 8.2
Generation of synthetic CT images from MRI imaging using deep learning approaches.

Machine learning can help in image registration from MRI to CT by improving the accuracy of image registration or by accelerating the registration process.[26,27] Conventional methods for registering MR to CT images can introduce registration errors, given that the tissues appear differently on MRI and CT. Registration errors can be larger if images are not acquired in the same patient position, because of complex changes in the shapes of the organs from one position to another.[26,27] AI can provide solutions for such complex image registration tasks. A recent study used CNNs to register brain CTs to MRIs with high accuracy.[28] Another study used a deep learning model to register 4D CT images of the lungs in different phases of inspiration and expiration.[29] Registering 4D CT images of the lungs is challenging because of the complex motion of the lungs during breathing. In addition, the lung airspaces appear differently in inspiration and expiration since airspaces are denser during expiration. Therefore, lung CT images in different phases of breathing cannot be registered based on aligning similar densities. To overcome these challenges, a deep learning registration model was developed that separately predicts coarse-scale motions of the lungs as well fine-scale motions of airspaces. This model showed registration errors of less than 1 mm over 10 validation sets from the same institution, and registration errors of less than 1.6 mm over 10 validation sets from other institutions.[29]

AI can also provide solutions for MRI-only treatment planning. In MRI-only treatment planning, MRI is used instead of CT for treatment simulation. This poses a challenge since MRI signal intensity correlates with proton density rather than the electron density that is needed to calculate treatment dosing.[30,31] Thus, the generation of synthetic CT images from MR images is an active area of research. Conventional methods for synthesizing CT images center around Gaussian mixture models or atlas-based solutions.[32,33] AI has recently provided better methods for synthesizing CT images, by using CNNs, adversarial networks, and random forests.[22,34–37] For instance, a study used a CNN model to synthesize head CT from MRI.[22] The model was validated on 13 test patients by comparing synthesized CT images with actual CT images acquired from the same patients. The model generated synthetic CT images with tissue densities (in terms of Hounsfield units) similar to tissue densities in the actual acquired CT images. Other studies have used random forests to synthesize CT images from brain and prostate MRI images, showing that the synthesized CT images are similar to acquired CT images (in terms of tissue densities) and that the calculated doses derived from these synthetic CT images are close to the ones derived from actual acquired CT images.[34,38] In addition, the planning target volumes and organs at risk were similar when synthetic CT images were used as compared to acquired CT images.[34]

AI can also improve image acquisition itself, with solutions for decreasing the imaging time in MRI,[39,40] reducing the radiation dose in CT and PET,[41,42] reducing motion artifacts in MRI and PET,[24,25,43–45] and reducing metal artifacts in CT.[46–49] In modalities such as CT, MRI, and PET, deep learning can reconstruct images from the acquired signal more efficiently. This allows for compressed sensing, which constitutes acquiring less signal in shorter times in MRI, and reducing the radiation dose in CT and PET. Given that deep learning is more efficient compared to traditional methods in reconstructing images from sparse signal, this can decrease MR imaging times and reduce CT and PET radiation doses.[23,50,51] MR fingerprinting is an example of such methods, in which magnetic signals of the tissues are quantitatively measured during MR acquisition. Then, deep learning is used to generate MR images (such as T1, T2, and other image types) from the measured MR signals.[52–55] Using MR fingerprinting, imaging of the brain can be done in 6 minutes as opposed to conventional brain MR imaging which requires more than 30 minutes.[56,57] Reduced MR imaging time is especially important for children and inconsolable patients, because these individuals often cannot hold still in the MRI machine for the time needed for conventional image acquisition.[58–61] Deep learning can also reduce motion artifacts on MR and PET images, further helping the imaging of children and inconsolable patients who move during image acquisition.[24,43–45] Metal artifacts from dental fillings, cardiac pacers, and orthopedic hardware can significantly degrade image quality and pose a challenge in treatment planning. A study used generative adversarial networks to reduce metal artifacts caused by dental fillings on CT images.[46] The artifact-reduced images, derived from the generative adversarial network model, led to dose calculations similar to doses derived from the water density override method.[46] Additional studies have shown the utility of deep learning in reducing metal artifacts on PET and CT images.[47,48]

Because radiation oncology planning and treatment is imaging-based, methods to improve image acquisition, image registration, and image synthesis will be able to improve treatment accuracy and eventually patient outcomes. Advances such as reducing imaging time and synthesizing CT images to expedite and reduce the cost of treatment planning will be particularly important. Research in this area has made considerable strides in the past few years.

8.4 Treatment Planning

Once simulation images are loaded into the treatment planning system, segmentation of the tumor, planning target volumes, and organs at risk are still manually performed by the radiation oncologist in most practices. Accurate segmentation of target volumes is necessary for accurate dose delivery to the tumor, and careful delineation of organs at risk is necessary to ensure doses delivered are within acceptable limits. While time-consuming, these tasks are a crucial part of treatment planning, as incorrectly-delineated targets can lead to significant over- or under-dosing of the tumor, and incorrect delineation of organs at risk may result in excess radiation to normal tissues. While there are guidelines for segmenting tumors and organs at risk, segmentation is individualized to the patient's anatomy. In addition, segmentation is prone to inter- and intra-observer variability, even among expert radiation oncologists.[62] AI can help automate the segmentation of radiotherapy targets and organs at risk, leading to improved treatment planning.[20,63–65] While auto-segmentation methods have shown promising results, implementation of fully-automated segmentation into routine clinical practice still faces substantial challenges. Commercially available auto-segmentation tools often use knowledge-based contouring, which relies on atlases of expert-delineated images.[63,64] In brain image segmentation, for instance, software packages such as FreeSurfer use manually-segmented brain images to construct atlases for brain anatomy segmentation.[66] However, given the limited numbers of manually-segmented images used to construct atlases, it is challenging to represent the wide range of brain tumors and the anatomical distortions caused by tumors. As a result, such software packages may fail to accurately segment the brain anatomy, including the organs at risk, when a tumor distorts the anatomy.[67,68]

Deep learning has provided solutions for auto-segmentation, but challenges remain in improving the reliability of deep learning auto-segmentation methods for routine radiation oncology practice.[69] Generalizability is a major challenge for auto-segmentation algorithms. The training data cannot represent all possible anatomical variations in individual patients and all possible anatomical distortions caused by tumors. Recent research has focused on developing auto-segmentation models that can generalize to patients with novel anatomical features that are not represented in the training data.[70] Another study demonstrated that a deep learning algorithm could segment clinical target volumes for patients undergoing head and neck radiotherapy, yielding a Dice similarity coefficient of 0.81 when compared to manual segmentation. Importantly, 85% of auto-segmented structures were acceptable for clinical use, only needing minor changes.[71] In another study, deep learning was used to segment 12 cardiac substructures on MR images, including great vessels, cardiac chambers, and coronary arteries. Deep learning could achieve high segmentation accuracy for cardiac chambers and great vessels with Dice scores of 0.88 and 0.85, respectively. Segmentation of coronary arteries, however, was suboptimal, yielding a Dice score of 0.50. Nevertheless, the segmentation time per patient was 14 seconds, suggesting significant potential for improved clinical efficiency.[72] Using AI for segmentation is exemplified through a recent online competition. Within a short 10-week period, the competition garnered multiple crowd-sourced AI algorithms for lung tumor segmentation. Moreover, an ensemble composed of the top five algorithms could achieve a Dice score of 0.79.[73] While we highlight only a few studies here, there are a large number of recent advancements across all anatomic sites including the brain, head and neck, thorax, abdomen, and pelvis.[65] With further refinements and prospective

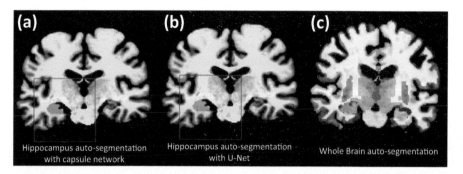

FIGURE 8.3
Auto-segmentation of brain anatomy using deep learning. The right hippocampus is auto-segmented using two different deep learning models: capsule network (A) and U-Net (B). Auto-segmentation of the whole brain anatomy (C) including organs at risk such as hippocampi and optic nerves can ease radiation therapy planning.

validations, clinical implementation of auto-segmentation tools is within reach, with the potential to reduce the time that radiation oncologists should spend on time-consuming segmentation tasks as well as to improve segmentation accuracy (Figure 8.3).[65] However, current auto-segmentation methods still require substantial input from the radiation oncologist and often require manual edits of the contoured targets or organs.[74]

After segmenting the target and organs at risk, the medical dosimetrist generates an optimized treatment plan based on dose prescription and constraints. This is done using either forward planning or inverse planning, the latter of which uses statistical methods to optimize dose distributions based on clinical treatment parameters.[75] However, this is a resource- and labor-intensive process that often requires iterative input from the dosimetrist and the radiation oncologist. AI tools are being explored to optimize dose distributions with the goal of expediting treatment plan generation. For example, a recent study showed the feasibility of AI in predicting radiation dose from planning target volumes and organs at risk for prostate cancer radiation therapy. The radiation dose predicted by this AI solution was close to the prescribed dose, with a mean absolute difference of under 5% of the prescription dose.[76] Another recent study used a modified U-Net model to generate dose distributions for prostate radiation therapy. This method showed high accuracy in dose calculation in a small sample of eight test patients while generating radiotherapy plans in approximately 1 second.[77] Recent research has also focused on generating radiation treatment plans using deep learning methods that do not require feature selection. One such efforts incorporated knowledge-based planning using generative adversarial networks for dose prediction. This method could generate treatment plans that satisfied 77% of clinical criteria, as compared to conventional plans that could satisfy 67% of clinical criteria.[78] In upcoming years, AI tools will increase the efficiency of dose prediction and optimal treatment plan generation, with the possibility of automating the radiation planning process.

Once the radiation treatment plan is generated and approved by the radiation oncologist, medical physicists play a crucial role in ensuring the quality and accurate delivery of the treatment plan. This quality assurance (QA) process also stands to benefit from AI tools. Patient-specific verification of radiation dose is an important part of radiation delivery and can also be a time- and resource-intensive process, especially for complex treatment plans such as those using intensity-modulated radiation therapy.[79] While only a small minority of plans fail to pass patient-specific QA, there are a large number of QA assessments including checking the accuracy of treatment parameters and verifying the treatment plan dose with the delivered dose. A recent multi-institutional study implemented an AI tool to accurately predict gamma passing rates.[80,81] Various efforts are also underway to evaluate applications of AI in machine QA, where the accuracy of medical accelerators or radiation treatment machines may require daily, weekly, monthly, or annual checks.[82] For example, a recent study showed the feasibility of using support vector data description clustering to identify deviations in radiation field measurement.[83] With the plethora of data availability from dosimetry and beam data, as well as delivery log files, multiple AI-driven approaches are being explored to most efficiently allocate QA resources and efforts of medical physicists in the QA as well as the overall radiation treatment process.[84–86]

8.5 Treatment Delivery

The radiation treatment delivery process involves patient setup in the same position during each treatment session. During each dose of radiation, the patient's position must be reproduced with high precision in order to ensure accurate delivery of radiation to the tumor while minimizing unnecessary doses to the nearby organs. Reducing day-to-day setup differences (interfraction motion) and target or organ motion during each treatment (intrafraction motion) are crucial for increasing the precision and efficacy of radiation treatment. AI tools can be leveraged to account for and adapt to inter- and intrafraction motion. For example, a recent study used a neural network to predict acceptable increases in mean heart dose due to changes in heart position during deep inspirational breath hold for breast cancer treatment. The study concludes that the trained neural network can potentially assist clinicians in identifying an action level tolerance for the treating staff, thereby identifying scenarios where position shifts are acceptable and scenarios where additional action may be required prior to proceeding with treatment.[87] On-treatment imaging, such as x-rays or cone-beam CTs, is also frequently used to confirm patient positioning and enable precise tumor targeting. AI tools can also be used to analyze these images to identify the treatment target. A recent study showed that a neural network can localize pancreatic tumor target on on-treatment x-ray images with high accuracy. Given high dose per fraction treatments for pancreatic cancer often rely on the placement and localization of fiducials within the tumor for accurate localization, this approach may potentially allow for fiducial-less pancreatic cancer radiation treatments in the future.[88] Another recent example in prostate cancer showed that a deep learning model could identify the prostate position on on-treatment x-ray images. Moreover, among patients with fiducials implanted in their prostate, the locations predicted using deep learning were highly consistent with locations derived from the implanted fiducials.[89]

The use of adaptive radiation treatment is becoming more widely available and is another area of treatment delivery that will likely benefit substantially from AI tools in the years to come. Adaptive treatment refers to treatment re-planning occurring during the radiation treatment course, which may be prompted by changes in the patient's anatomy and setup positioning due to tumor or organ changes, or other patient-specific factors such as significant weight loss. The adaptation of the irradiated volume to account for such changes has been postulated to lead to benefits in toxicity and tumor control.[90,91] However, the treatment re-planning process is labor- and resource-intensive and often takes days to complete. AI technology has the potential to predict which patients might require adaptive radiation treatments and at which point re-planning should occur. For example, in a retrospective analysis of head and neck cancer patients, a machine learning classifier was used to identify and suggest patients who might benefit from re-planning.[92] Another recent study in pancreatic cancer showed an online plan re-optimization system using an artificial neural network was able to rapidly re-generate treatment plans, requiring clinician review only for organs at risk within 3 cm from the planning target volume.[93] There are also emerging commercial vendor offerings incorporating AI into adaptive radiotherapy platforms to enable rapid plan re-optimization, and there will likely be increased implementation of such tools into routine clinical practice in the near future.[90]

8.6 Integrating AI into Radiation Oncology Practice

As AI technologies mature, they will continue to impact all aspects of medical physics and clinical radiation oncology (Figure 8.4). In this chapter, we have discussed a few applications and the outlook of AI within different aspects of the radiation oncology workflow, ranging from patient assessment to treatment planning and quality assurance to treatment delivery. While we are optimistic about AI technology, there are limitations to current AI systems, and the remaining barriers must be addressed prior to their safe and effective integration into routine clinical practice.

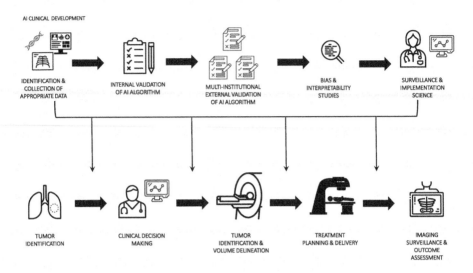

FIGURE 8.4
Opportunities for integration of artificial intelligence within clinical radiation oncology workflow.

One major limitation to the application of AI in radiation oncology is the unavailability of large, well-organized datasets needed to develop and validate algorithms. This is a particular barrier for treatment planning, which currently lacks large standardized multi-institutional radiotherapy datasets to train and test machine learning models. Another dataset-related issue is the need for imaging data to be labeled with clinical and outcome variables, so that supervised learning methods can be applied. Proposed solutions to these problems include standardization and pooling of pan-omics radiation oncology patient data.[94] These efforts will require buy-in from multiple stakeholders and support from professional societies and at the national level. External and prospective validation of AI tools will also be needed. To date, there have only been a few instances of external and prospective validation of radiation oncology-specific machine learning models.[3,95]

In addition, explainable and interpretable models are needed to garner greater patient and clinician trust in AI technology. There is evidence suggesting discordant views between patients and clinicians regarding the use of AI in healthcare overall.[96] Interpretable AI models are necessary to maintain clinical context and to allow clinicians to accurately interpret model predictions. A well-cited example is a study using a neural network model suggesting that patients with asthma and pneumonia were at lower risk for death from pneumonia. In this case, the researchers were able to identify the cause of the discrepancy between the algorithm and the clinical context. At the study hospital, patients with pneumonia and asthma tended to be admitted to the ICU directly, with the goal of preventing complications. This led the algorithm to interpret *the presence of asthma* as a protective variable.[97] This issue becomes more alarming given that many deep learning algorithms are considered black box models since the multilayer, non-linear mappings between their inputs and outputs are difficult to interpret. Within oncology, there is increasing recognition of the need to include interpretability in AI models.[98] For example, a recent study demonstrated the use of Shapley values to visualize non-linear interactions in the prediction of overall survival in patients with prostate cancer.[99]

While AI will likely never completely replace the roles of the radiation oncology team in the care of cancer patients, we conclude that it will likely supplement the current processes in medical physics and radiation oncology to further personalize and improve patient care. At the time of this writing, the FDA has published action plans for regulating machine learning and AI-based software as medical devices. However, for AI tools to keep pace with advancements in radiation oncology care, there needs to be continuous evaluation of existing and novel algorithms, as well as emerging ethical and regulatory challenges.[100] To optimize the potential of AI in radiation oncology, in addition to model development and novel clinical applications, future research efforts should include developing standardized pooled data resources, rigorous validation including vigilance for bias, and maintaining the interpretability of AI models for both clinicians and patients.

References

1. Kann B.H., Thompson R., Thomas C.R., Dicker A., Aneja S. Artificial intelligence in oncology: Current applications and future directions. *Oncol Williston Park N.* 2019; 33(2):46–53.
2. Kotecha R., Aneja S. Opportunities for integration of artificial intelligence into stereotactic radiosurgery practice. *Neuro-Oncol.* 2021; 23(10):1629–1630. doi:10.1093/neuonc/noab169.
3. Kann B.H., Hicks D.F., Payabvash S., et al. Multi-institutional validation of deep learning for pretreatment identification of extranodal extension in head and neck squamous cell carcinoma. *J Clin Oncol Off J Am Soc Clin Oncol.* 2020; 38(12):1304–1311. doi:10.1200/JCO.19.02031.
4. Thompson R.F., Valdes G., Fuller C.D., et al. The future of artificial intelligence in radiation oncology. *Int J Radiat Oncol Biol Phys.* 2018; 102(2):247–248. doi:10.1016/j.ijrobp.2018.05.072.
5. Clark K., Vendt B., Smith K., et al. The Cancer Imaging Archive (TCIA): Maintaining and operating a public information repository. *J Digit Imaging.* 2013; 26(6):1045–1057. doi:10.1007/s10278-013-9622-7.
6. Law M.Y.Y., Liu B. Informatics in radiology: DICOM-RT and its utilization in radiation therapy. *Radiogr Rev Publ Radiol Soc N Am Inc.* 2009; 29(3):655–667. doi:10.1148/rg.293075172.

7. Joel M.Z., Umrao S., Chang E., et al. Using adversarial images to assess the robustness of deep learning models trained on diagnostic images in oncology. *JCO Clin Cancer Inform.* 2022; 6:e2100170. doi:10.1200/CCI.21.00170.

8. Shen L., Margolies L.R., Rothstein J.H., Fluder E., McBride R., Sieh W. Deep learning to improve breast cancer detection on screening mammography. *Sci Rep.* 2019; 9(1):12495. doi:10.1038/s41598-019-48995-4.

9. Akselrod-Ballin A., Chorev M., Shoshan Y., et al. Predicting breast cancer by applying deep learning to linked health records and mammograms. *Radiology.* 2019; 292(2):331–342. doi:10.1148/radiol.2019182622.

10. McKinney S.M., Sieniek M., Godbole V., et al. International evaluation of an AI system for breast cancer screening. *Nature.* 2020; 577(7788):89–94. doi:10.1038/s41586-019-1799-6.

11. Dembrower K., Wåhlin E., Liu Y., et al. Effect of artificial intelligence-based triaging of breast cancer screening mammograms on cancer detection and radiologist workload: A retrospective simulation study. *Lancet Digit Health.* 2020; 2(9):e468–e474. doi:10.1016/S2589-7500(20)30185-0.

12. Chan I., Wells W., Mulkern R.V., et al. Detection of prostate cancer by integration of line-scan diffusion, T2-mapping and T2-weighted magnetic resonance imaging; a multichannel statistical classifier. *Med Phys.* 2003; 30(9):2390–2398. doi:10.1118/1.1593633.

13. Yoo S., Gujrathi I., Haider M.A., Khalvati F. Prostate cancer detection using deep convolutional neural networks. *Sci Rep.* 2019; 9(1):19518. doi:10.1038/s41598-019-55972-4.

14. Lou B., Doken S., Zhuang T., et al. An image-based deep learning framework for individualising radiotherapy dose: A retrospective analysis of outcome prediction. *Lancet Digit Health.* 2019; 1(3):e136–e147. doi:10.1016/S2589-7500(19)30058-5.

15. Saednia K., Tabbarah S., Lagree A., et al. Quantitative thermal imaging biomarkers to detect acute skin toxicity from breast radiation therapy using supervised machine learning. *Int J Radiat Oncol Biol Phys.* 2020; 106(5):1071–1083. doi:10.1016/j.ijrobp.2019.12.032.

16. Reddy J.P., Lindsay W.D., Berlind C.G., et al. Applying a machine learning approach to predict acute radiation toxicities for head and neck cancer patients. *Int J Radiat Oncol Biol Phys.* 2019; 105(1):S69. doi:10.1016/j.ijrobp.2019.06.520.

17. Sun D., Wang M., Li A. A multimodal deep neural network for human breast cancer prognosis prediction by integrating multi-dimensional data. *IEEE/ACM Trans Comput Biol Bioinform.* Published online February 15, 2018. doi:10.1109/TCBB.2018.2806438.

18. Park E.K., Lee K.S., Seo B.K., et al. Machine learning approaches to radiogenomics of breast cancer using low-dose perfusion computed tomography: Predicting prognostic biomarkers and molecular subtypes. *Sci Rep.* 2019; 9(1):17847. doi:10.1038/s41598-019-54371-z.

19. Development and validation of a prognostic AI biomarker using multi-modal deep learning with digital histopathology in localized prostate cancer on NRG Oncology phase III clinical trials. | *Journal of Clinical Oncology.* Accessed March 27, 2022. https://ascopubs.org/doi/abs/10.1200/JCO.2022.40.6_suppl.222.

20. Estienne T., Lerousseau M., Vakalopoulou M., et al. Deep learning-based concurrent brain registration and tumor segmentation. *Front Comput Neurosci.* 2020; 14. Accessed January 18, 2022. https://www.frontiersin.org/article/10.3389/fncom.2020.00017.

21. Chen S., Qin A., Zhou D., Yan D. Technical note: U-net-generated synthetic CT images for magnetic resonance imaging-only prostate intensity-modulated radiation therapy treatment planning. *Med Phys*. 2018; 45(12):5659–5665. doi:10.1002/mp.13247.

22. Gupta D., Kim M., Vineberg K.A., Balter J.M. Generation of synthetic CT images from MRI for treatment planning and patient positioning using a 3-Channel U-Net trained on sagittal images. *Front Oncol*. 2019; 9. doi:10.3389/fonc.2019.00964.

23. Zhu B., Liu J.Z., Cauley S.F., Rosen B.R., Rosen M.S. Image reconstruction by domain-transform manifold learning. *Nature*. 2018; 555(7697):487–492. doi:10.1038/nature25988.

24. Küstner T., Armanious K., Yang J., Yang B., Schick F., Gatidis S. Retrospective correction of motion-affected MR images using deep learning frameworks. *Magn Reson Med*. 2019; 82(4):1527–1540. doi:10.1002/mrm.27783.

25. Li T., Zhang M., Qi W., Asma E., Qi J. Motion correction of respiratory-gated PET images using deep learning based image registration framework. *Phys Med Biol*. 2020; 65(15):155003. doi:10.1088/1361-6560/ab8688.

26. Ulin K., Urie M.M., Cherlow J.M. Results of a multi-institutional benchmark test for cranial CT/MR image registration. *Int J Radiat Oncol Biol Phys*. 2010; 77(5):1584–1589. doi:10.1016/j.ijrobp.2009.10.017.

27. van Herk M., Kooy H.M. Automatic three-dimensional correlation of CT-CT, CT-MRI, and CT-SPECT using chamfer matching. *Med Phys*. 1994; 21(7):1163–1178. doi:10.1118/1.597344.

28. Islam K.T., Wijewickrema S., O'Leary S. A deep learning based framework for the registration of three dimensional multi-modal medical images of the head. *Sci Rep*. 2021; 11(1):1860. doi:10.1038/s41598-021-81044-7.

29. Fu Y., Lei Y., Wang T., et al. LungRegNet: An unsupervised deformable image registration method for 4D-CT lung. *Med Phys*. 2020; 47(4):1763–1774. doi:https://doi.org/10.1002/mp.14065.

30. Nyholm T., Nyberg M., Karlsson M.G., Karlsson M. Systematisation of spatial uncertainties for comparison between a MR and a CT-based radiotherapy workflow for prostate treatments. *Radiat Oncol Lond Engl*. 2009; 4:54. doi:10.1186/1748-717X-4-54.

31. Jonsson J.H., Karlsson M.G., Karlsson M., Nyholm T. Treatment planning using MRI data: An analysis of the dose calculation accuracy for different treatment regions. *Radiat Oncol Lond Engl*. 2010; 5:62. doi:10.1186/1748-717X-5-62.

32. Koivula L., Kapanen M., Seppälä T., et al. Intensity-based dual model method for generation of synthetic CT images from standard T2-weighted MR images - Generalized technique for four different MR scanners. *Radiother Oncol J Eur Soc Ther Radiol Oncol*. 2017; 125(3):411–419. doi:10.1016/j.radonc.2017.10.011.

33. Price R.G., Kim J.P., Zheng W., Chetty I.J., Glide-Hurst C. Image guided radiation therapy using synthetic computed tomography images in brain cancer. *Int J Radiat Oncol Biol Phys*. 2016; 95(4):1281–1289. doi:10.1016/j.ijrobp.2016.03.002.

34. Shafai-Erfani G., Wang T., Lei Y., et al. Dose evaluation of MRI-based synthetic CT generated using a machine learning method for prostate cancer radiotherapy. *Med Dosim Off J Am Assoc Med Dosim*. 2019; 44(4):e64–e70. doi:10.1016/j.meddos.2019.01.002.

35. Wang Y., Liu C., Zhang X., Deng W. Synthetic CT generation based on T2 weighted MRI of nasopharyngeal carcinoma (NPC) using a deep convolutional neural network (DCNN). *Front Oncol*. 2019; 9. doi:10.3389/fonc.2019.01333.

36. Lei Y., Harms J., Wang T., et al. MRI-only based synthetic CT generation using dense cycle consistent generative adversarial networks. *Med Phys*. 2019; 46(8):3565–3581. doi:10.1002/mp.13617.

37. Lei Y., Harms J., Wang T., et al. MRI-based synthetic CT generation using semantic random forest with iterative refinement. *Phys Med Biol*. 2019; 64(8):085001. doi:10.1088/1361-6560/ab0b66.

38. Yang X., Lei Y., Shu H.K., et al. Pseudo CT estimation from MRI using patch-based random forest. In: *Medical Imaging 2017: Image Processing*. Vol. 10133. SPIE; 2017:775–782 doi:10.1117/12.2253936.

39. Ueda T., Ohno Y., Yamamoto K., et al. Compressed sensing and deep learning reconstruction for women's pelvic MRI denoising: Utility for improving image quality and examination time in routine clinical practice. *Eur J Radiol*. 2021; 134:109430. doi:10.1016/j.ejrad.2020.109430.

40. Dai Y., Zhuang P. Compressed sensing MRI via a multi-scale dilated residual convolution network. *Magn Reson Imaging*. 2019; 63:93–104. doi:10.1016/j.mri.2019.07.014.

41. Theruvath A.J., Siedek F., Yerneni K., et al. Validation of deep learning-based augmentation for reduced 18F-FDG Dose for PET/MRI in children and young adults with lymphoma. *Radiol Artif Intell*. 2021; 3(6):e200232. doi:10.1148/ryai.2021200232.

42. Liu J., Malekzadeh M., Mirian N., Song T.A., Liu C., Dutta J. Artificial intelligence-based image enhancement in PET imaging: Noise reduction and resolution enhancement. *PET Clin*. 2021; 16(4):553–576. doi:10.1016/j.cpet.2021.06.005.

43. Pawar K., Chen Z., Seah J., Law M., Close T., Egan G. Clinical utility of deep learning motion correction for T1 weighted MPRAGE MR images. *Eur J Radiol*. 2020; 133:109384. doi:10.1016/j.ejrad.2020.109384.

44. Duffy B.A., Zhao L., Sepehrband F., et al. Retrospective motion artifact correction of structural MRI images using deep learning improves the quality of cortical surface reconstructions. *NeuroImage*. 2021; 230:117756. doi:10.1016/j.neuroimage.2021.117756.

45. Lee J., Kim B., Park H. MC2-Net: Motion correction network for multi-contrast brain MRI. *Magn Reson Med*. 2021; 86(2):1077–1092. doi:10.1002/mrm.28719.

46. Koike Y., Anetai Y., Takegawa H., Ohira S., Nakamura S., Tanigawa N. Deep learning-based metal artifact reduction using cycle-consistent adversarial network for intensity-modulated head and neck radiation therapy treatment planning. *Phys Medica PM Int J Devoted Appl Phys Med Biol Off J Ital Assoc Biomed Phys AIFB*. 2020; 78:8–14. doi:10.1016/j.ejmp.2020.08.018.

47. Arabi H., Zaidi H. Deep learning-based metal artefact reduction in PET/CT imaging. *Eur Radiol*. 2021; 31(8):6384–6396. doi:10.1007/s00330-021-07709-z.

48. Huang X., Wang J., Tang F., Zhong T., Zhang Y. Metal artifact reduction on cervical CT images by deep residual learning. *Biomed Eng Online*. 2018; 17(1):175. doi:10.1186/s12938-018-0609-y.

49. Liang K., Zhang L., Yang H., Yang Y., Chen Z., Xing Y. Metal artifact reduction for practical dental computed tomography by improving interpolation-based reconstruction with deep learning. *Med Phys*. 2019; 46(12):e823–e834. doi:10.1002/mp.13644.

50. Kang E., Min J., Ye J.C. A deep convolutional neural network using directional wavelets for low-dose X-ray CT reconstruction. *Med Phys*. 2017; 44(10):e360–e375. doi:10.1002/mp.12344.

51. Higaki T., Nakamura Y., Tatsugami F., Nakaura T., Awai K. Improvement of image quality at CT and MRI using deep learning. *Jpn J Radiol.* 2019; 37(1):73–80. doi:10.1007/s11604-018-0796-2.

52. Fang Z., Chen Y., Hung S.C., Zhang X., Lin W., Shen D. Submillimeter MR fingerprinting using deep learning-based tissue quantification. *Magn Reson Med.* 2020; 84(2):579–591. doi:10.1002/mrm.28136.

53. Panda A., Mehta B.B., Coppo S., et al. Magnetic resonance fingerprinting-an overview. *Curr Opin Biomed Eng.* 2017; 3:56–66. doi:10.1016/j.cobme.2017.11.001.

54. Chen Y., Panda A., Pahwa S., et al. Three-dimensional MR fingerprinting for quantitative breast imaging. *Radiology.* 2019; 290(1):33–40. doi:10.1148/radiol.2018180836.

55. Panda A., Obmann V.C., Lo W.C., et al. MR fingerprinting and ADC mapping for characterization of lesions in the transition zone of the prostate gland. *Radiology.* 2019; 292(3):685–694. doi:10.1148/radiol.2019181705.

56. Fujita S., Hagiwara A., Aoki S., Abe O. Synthetic MRI and MR fingerprinting in routine neuroimaging protocol: What's the next step? *J Neuroradiol J Neuroradiol.* 2020; 47(2):134–135. doi:10.1016/j.neurad.2020.02.001.

57. Warntjes J.B.M., Leinhard O.D., West J., Lundberg P. Rapid magnetic resonance quantification on the brain: Optimization for clinical usage. *Magn Reson Med.* 2008; 60(2):320–329. doi:10.1002/mrm.21635.

58. Lindberg D.M., Stence N.V., Grubenhoff J.A., et al. Feasibility and accuracy of fast MRI versus CT for traumatic brain injury in young children. *Pediatrics.* 2019; 144(4):e20190419. doi:10.1542/peds.2019-0419.

59. Ahmad R., Hu H.H., Krishnamurthy R., Krishnamurthy R. Reducing sedation for pediatric body MRI using accelerated and abbreviated imaging protocols. *Pediatr Radiol.* 2018; 48(1):37–49. doi:10.1007/s00247-017-3987-6.

60. Kozak B.M., Jaimes C., Kirsch J., Gee M.S. MRI techniques to decrease imaging times in children. *Radiogr Rev Publ Radiol Soc N Am Inc.* 2020; 40(2):485–502. doi:10.1148/rg.2020190112.

61. Andica C., Hagiwara A., Hori M., et al. Review of synthetic MRI in pediatric brains: Basic principle of MR quantification, its features, clinical applications, and limitations. *J Neuroradiol.* 2019; 46(4):268–275. doi:10.1016/j.neurad.2019.02.005.

62. Vinod S.K., Min M., Jameson M.G., Holloway L.C. A review of interventions to reduce inter-observer variability in volume delineation in radiation oncology. *J Med Imaging Radiat Oncol.* 2016; 60(3):393–406. doi:10.1111/1754-9485.12462.

63. Delpon G., Escande A., Ruef T., et al. Comparison of automated atlas-based segmentation software for postoperative prostate cancer radiotherapy. *Front Oncol.* 2016; 6. doi:10.3389/fonc.2016.00178.

64. Lee H., Lee E., Kim N., et al. Clinical evaluation of commercial atlas-based autosegmentation in the head and neck region. *Front Oncol.* 2019; 9. doi:10.3389/fonc.2019.00239.

65. Cardenas C.E., Yang J., Anderson B.M., Court L.E., Brock K.B. Advances in auto-segmentation. *Semin Radiat Oncol.* 2019; 29(3):185–197. doi:10.1016/j.semradonc.2019.02.001.

66. Ochs A.L., Ross D.E., Zannoni M.D., Abildskov T.J., Bigler E.D., Alzheimer's Disease Neuroimaging Initiative. Comparison of automated brain volume measures obtained with NeuroQuant and FreeSurfer. *J Neuroimaging Off J Am Soc Neuroimaging.* 2015; 25(5):721–727. doi:10.1111/jon.12229.

67. Selvaganesan K., Whitehead E., DeAlwis P.M., et al. Robust, atlas-free, automatic segmentation of brain MRI in health and disease. *Heliyon.* 2019; 5(2):e01226. doi:10.1016/j.heliyon.2019.e01226.
68. Yaakub S.N., Heckemann R.A., Keller S.S., McGinnity C.J., Weber B., Hammers A. On brain atlas choice and automatic segmentation methods: A comparison of MAPER & FreeSurfer using three atlas databases. *Sci Rep.* 2020; 10(1):2837. doi:10.1038/s41598-020-57951-6.
69. Despotović I., Goossens B., Philips W. MRI segmentation of the human brain: Challenges, methods, and applications. *Comput Math Methods Med.* 2015; 2015:e450341. doi:10.1155/2015/450341.
70. Avesta A., Hui Y., Krumholz H., Aneja S. 3D Capsule Networks for Brain MRI Segmentation. Published online March 16, 2022:2022.01.18.22269482. doi:10.1101/2022.01.18.22269482.
71. Cardenas C.E., McCarroll R.E., Court L.E., et al. Deep learning algorithm for auto-delineation of high-risk oropharyngeal clinical target volumes with built-in dice similarity coefficient parameter optimization function. *Int J Radiat Oncol.* 2018; 101(2):468–478. doi:10.1016/j.ijrobp.2018.01.114.
72. Morris E.D., Ghanem A.I., Dong M., Pantelic M.V., Walker E.M., Glide-Hurst C.K. Cardiac substructure segmentation with deep learning for improved cardiac sparing. *Med Phys.* 2020; 47(2):576–586. doi:10.1002/mp.13940.
73. Mak R.H., Endres M.G., Paik J.H., et al. Use of crowd innovation to develop an artificial intelligence-based solution for radiation therapy targeting. *JAMA Oncol.* 2019; 5(5):654–661. doi:10.1001/jamaoncol.2019.0159.
74. Ahn S.H., Yeo A.U., Kim K.H., et al. Comparative clinical evaluation of atlas and deep-learning-based auto-segmentation of organ structures in liver cancer. *Radiat Oncol.* 2019; 14(1):213. doi:10.1186/s13014-019-1392-z.
75. Chui C.S., Spirou S.V. Inverse planning algorithms for external beam radiation therapy. *Med Dosim Off J Am Assoc Med Dosim.* 2001; 26(2):189–197. doi:10.1016/s0958-3947(01)00069-3.
76. Nguyen D., Long T., Jia X., et al. A feasibility study for predicting optimal radiation therapy dose distributions of prostate cancer patients from patient anatomy using deep learning. *Sci Rep.* 2019; 9(1):1076. doi:10.1038/s41598-018-37741-x.
77. Xing Y., Nguyen D., Lu W., Yang M., Jiang S. Technical note: A feasibility study on deep learning-based radiotherapy dose calculation. *Med Phys.* 2020; 47(2):753–758. doi:10.1002/mp.13953.
78. Babier A., Mahmood R., McNiven A.L., Diamant A., Chan T.C.Y. Knowledge-based automated planning with three-dimensional generative adversarial networks. *Med Phys.* 2020; 47(2):297–306. doi:10.1002/mp.13896.
79. Agazaryan N., Solberg T.D., DeMarco J.J. Patient specific quality assurance for the delivery of intensity modulated radiotherapy. *J Appl Clin Med Phys.* 2003; 4(1):40–50. doi:10.1120/jacmp.v4i1.2540.
80. Valdes G., Scheuermann R., Hung C.Y., Olszanski A., Bellerive M., Solberg T.D. A mathematical framework for virtual IMRT QA using machine learning. *Med Phys.* 2016; 43(7):4323. doi:10.1118/1.4953835.
81. Valdes G., Chan M.F., Lim S.B., Scheuermann R., Deasy J.O., Solberg T.D. IMRT QA using machine learning: A multi-institutional validation. *J Appl Clin Med Phys.* 2017; 18(5):279–284. doi:10.1002/acm2.12161.
82. Klein E.E., Hanley J., Bayouth J., et al. Task Group 142 report: Quality assurance of medical accelerators. *Med Phys.* 2009; 36(9):4197–4212. doi:10.1118/1.3190392.

83. El Naqa I., Irrer J., Ritter T.A., et al. Machine learning for automated quality assurance in radiotherapy: A proof of principle using EPID data description. *Med Phys.* 2019; 46(4):1914–1921. doi:10.1002/mp.13433.

84. Chan M.F., Witztum A., Valdes G. Integration of AI and machine learning in radiotherapy QA. *Front Artif Intell.* 2020; 3. doi:10.3389/frai.2020.577620.

85. Zhao W., Patil I., Han B., Yang Y., Xing L., Schüler E. Beam data modeling of linear accelerators (linacs) through machine learning and its potential applications in fast and robust linac commissioning and quality assurance. *Radiother Oncol.* 2020; 153. doi:10.1016/j.radonc.2020.09.057.

86. Atwood T.F., Brown D.W., Murphy J.D., Moore K.L., Mundt A.J., Pawlicki T. Establishing a new clinical role for medical physicists: A prospective phase ii trial. *Int J Radiat Oncol.* 2018; 102(3):635–641. doi:10.1016/j.ijrobp.2018.06.040.

87. Malone C., Fennell L., Folliard T., Kelly C. Using a neural network to predict deviations in mean heart dose during the treatment of left-sided deep inspiration breath hold patients. *Phys Medica PM Int J Devoted Appl Phys Med Biol Off J Ital Assoc Biomed Phys AIFB.* 2019; 65:137–142. doi:10.1016/j.ejmp.2019.08.014.

88. Zhao W., Shen L., Han B., et al. Markerless pancreatic tumor target localization enabled by deep learning. *Int J Radiat Oncol Biol Phys.* 2019; 105(2):432–439. doi:10.1016/j.ijrobp.2019.05.071.

89. Zhao W., Han B., Yang Y., et al. Incorporating imaging information from deep neural network layers into image guided radiation therapy (IGRT). *Radiother Oncol.* 2019; 140:167–174. doi:10.1016/j.radonc.2019.06.027.

90. Glide-Hurst C.K., Lee P., Yock A.D., et al. Adaptive radiation therapy (ART) strategies and technical considerations: A state of the ART review from NRG Oncology. *Int J Radiat Oncol.* Published online October 24, 2020. doi:10.1016/j.ijrobp.2020.10.021.

91. Hall W.A., Paulson E., Li X.A., et al. Magnetic resonance linear accelerator technology and adaptive radiation therapy: An overview for clinicians. *CA Cancer J Clin.* 2022; 72(1):34–56. doi:10.3322/caac.21707.

92. Guidi G., Maffei N., Meduri B., et al. A machine learning tool for re-planning and adaptive RT: A multicenter cohort investigation. *Phys Medica PM Int J Devoted Appl Phys Med Biol Off J Ital Assoc Biomed Phys AIFB.* 2016; 32(12):1659–1666. doi:10.1016/j.ejmp.2016.10.005.

93. Bohoudi O., Bruynzeel A.M.E., Senan S., et al. Fast and robust online adaptive planning in stereotactic MR-guided adaptive radiation therapy (SMART) for pancreatic cancer. *Radiother Oncol J Eur Soc Ther Radiol Oncol.* 2017; 125(3):439–444. doi:10.1016/j.radonc.2017.07.028.

94. Mayo C.S., Moran J.M., Bosch W., et al. American association of physicists in medicine task group 263: Standardizing nomenclatures in radiation oncology. *Int J Radiat Oncol Biol Phys.* 2018; 100(4):1057–1066. doi:10.1016/j.ijrobp.2017.12.013.

95. Hong J.C., Eclov N.C.W., Dalal N.H., et al. System for high-intensity evaluation during radiation therapy (SHIELD-RT): A prospective randomized study of machine learning-directed clinical evaluations during radiation and chemoradiation. *J Clin Oncol Off J Am Soc Clin Oncol.* Published online September 4, 2020. doi:10.1200/JCO.20.01688.

96. Khullar D., Casalino L.P., Qian Y., Lu Y., Chang E., Aneja S. Public vs physician views of liability for artificial intelligence in health care. *J Am Med Inform Assoc JAMIA.* 2021; 28(7):1574–1577. doi:10.1093/jamia/ocab055.

97. Cabitza F., Rasoini R., Gensini G.F. Unintended consequences of machine learning in medicine. *JAMA*. 2017; 318(6):517. doi:10.1001/jama.2017.7797.
98. Trister A.D. The tipping point for deep learning in oncology. *JAMA Oncol*. 2019; 5(10):1429–1430. doi:10.1001/jamaoncol.2019.1799.
99. Li R., Shinde A., Liu A., et al. Machine learning-based interpretation and visualization of nonlinear interactions in prostate cancer survival. *JCO Clin Cancer Inform*. 2020; 4:637–646. doi:10.1200/CCI.20.00002.
100. Lehman C.D., Wu S. Stargazing through the lens of AI in clinical oncology. *Nat Cancer*. 2021; 2(12):1265–1267. doi:10.1038/s43018-021-00307-4.

Index

Note: **Bold** page numbers refer to tables; *italic* page numbers refer to figures.